MW00635141

Write from the Heart

A Resource Guide to Engage Writers

Veldorah J. Rice

www.WriteFromTheHeart.org

Copyright page

Write from the Heart: A Resource Guide to Engage Writers by Veldorah J. Rice Published by Write from the Heart PO Box 1451 Indiana, Pa 15701

www.WriteFromTheHeart.org

For information about special discounts available for bulk purchases, sales promotions, fund-raising and educational needs, contact Write from the Heart at inquiry@writefromtheheart.org.

Cover by Carrie Scrufari.

All student examples used by permission.

Printed in the United States of America

First Edition

ISBN: 978-1-7353465-0-2 (paperback)

ISBN: 978-1-7353465-1-9 (ebook)

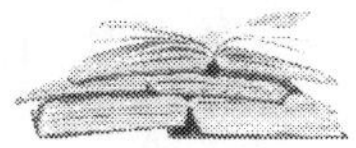

About Write from the Heart

Write from the Heart is an online writing and literature program designed for middle and high school students. We believe that every student should not only be able to read and write but should be able to do both in a way that displays their uniqueness. No student is the same, and each one has a distinct perspective on the world. However, expressing that perspective in written form can sometimes be difficult—for some students, there is a disconnect between what is in their heads and what ends up on the page. We desire to bridge that gap and give every writer the tools to more closely connect voice, ideas, and writing.

Write from the Heart offers full credit composition and literature classes for homeschooled middle and high school students, including an accredited AP® English course. We also offer four-week skills workshops for students in any learning environment, as well as individualized coaching for students through college.

Founded in 2005, Write from the Heart has served families all over the world. Our students are recognized in publications and contests every year, and several have won college scholarships for works they completed through our classes.

Our offerings can be found at **www.writefromtheheart.org**.

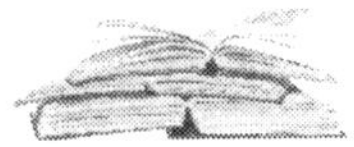

How to Use This Book

This Resource Guide moves you through the writing process, from planning to drafting to revising. It has a special section devoted to adding voice to writing, and it goes into detail about the main styles of writing, with in depth instructions about how to create each one.

This guide was written directly to middle and high school students, offering real-life examples from their peers. It can be used as a homeschool curriculum by working through the activities at the end of every section, or it can be used as a resource for a co-op or writing workshop. It would also serve well as a resource manual in both public and private schools.

Every section includes instruction, writing tips, and ideas for applying the techniques. Activities are flexible and could be completed more than once with different subject matter to obtain mastery of the concepts. All students in Write from the Heart online classes use this resource guide throughout their courses.

Please note: throughout this work, we use real student examples. These students are in 6th-10th grade and turned in these papers as assignments through the Write from the Heart online program. They are excellent examples and represent the appropriate skills expected for middle school students. I made the decision to leave them mostly unedited to preserve both the authenticity as well as help others see the reality of what writing at this age looks like. Some grammatical changes were made for clarity or ease of instruction.

A companion Grammar Workbook is available separately.

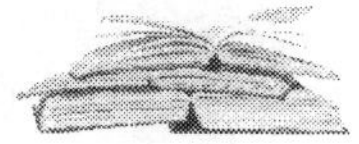

Acknowledgements

This Resource Guide is the book I never knew I had started. I have been working with students for almost fifteen years at Write from the Heart and have used dozens of writing guides written by other people. They all had something to offer, but I felt like I was always creating handouts and additional explanations to supplement their instruction. During a routine update of all of my documents, I looked at all of the things I had created and realized I had inadvertently created my own resource guide, and that it was the one I wished someone would have written a long time ago.

The problem with a lot of those other guides is that they focus on the mechanics of writing, which is important, but isn't the whole story. Writing is a way to express who you are through the written word. You and your unique voice should never get buried in structure or grammar. Instead, those tools should be utilized to support the perspective you have to share with the world. That is the focus of this Resource Guide. We don't want to just teach the mechanics of writing. We want to help create writers.

I would like to acknowledge several others who have helped create this work. Stephanie Constantino spent countless hours of her own time working on grammar guides, being a sounding board for my ideas, and investing in bringing this book about. I would not be at this point without her encouragement and selflessness. This book has her fingerprints all over it. The backbone of many of these resources was built by Denise Botsford many years ago—there aren't words for how her vision changed my life. I am grateful every day for her initiative to create the original program, and her belief in me to carry it into the future. This would not exist without the spark she set to flame in me. I would also like to thank Jodi Tahsler and Kaitlin Wingert who stepped in and took a mess of documents and helped me edit them into the work you now have in your hands. I could not have done it without them.

All the coaches who have worked with our program over the last fifteen years have lent their expertise in helping to find the gaps in resources and have passionately engaged our students in ways that went far beyond their required duties. Thanks to Jodi Tahsler, Abigail Kurtz, Katie Wolfe, Diana Paisley, Dana Mattini, Jenny Cowan, Nicola Vitiello, Hannah Kimmel, Linda Quinlisk, Jen Calano, Stephanie Constantino, Courtney Swafford, Barb O'Neill, Tammy

Kester, Jayme Doerfler, Sarah McGrath, and Kaitlin Wingert for their investment in our students and teaching with me over the years. They have all made a huge difference in countless students' lives, and their companionship in this journey has been invaluable.

I would also like to thank my family for their sacrifice and encouragement over the years. My husband, Michael Perry, has been unwavering in his faith in my abilities, and his willingness to answer "just one more question" over and over reminds me of how much he loves me. I am the luckiest. My son, Izaak, has grown from my little buddy into a fabulously confident companion, and he makes me grateful I chose this life every day. My daughter, Lorelei, is the most contented baby and I loved having that little dream playing next to me while I was working on this one. And finally, my parents, Jim & Heather Rice, the readers of my stories and encouragers of my dreams since before I had memory. Their support enabled this leap into entrepreneurship and a nontraditional career and they have faithfully given of themselves so that I could learn and grow and become. Thank you.

And thanks most of all to my students, who have wholeheartedly embraced learning with me day in and day out. It is their questions and ideas and revisions and beautiful pieces that have inspired this work. I have always wanted to be a writer. Along the way, I found my community at Write from the Heart and I have spent the last fifteen years pouring my words out to them in countless discussions and revisions. I have built relationships and grown as a teacher. Being able to collect all those words together into this book feels like a dream come true. Thank you for inspiring me and keeping me writing every day.

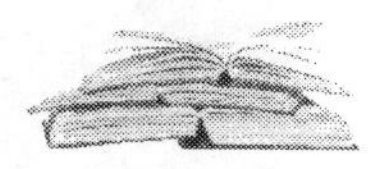

Contents

Introduction: The Writing Process

Many people think of writing as a one-time event: you sit down at a computer or with a cute journal, you record your thoughts, and you're done! Sure, maybe you need to check your spelling and grammar, but somehow your work has come out from your mind to the paper pretty much complete.

All lies.

It's this wrong idea that leads to the writing all-nighter, where a student tries to complete a paper the night before it's due, and they end up stressed, frustrated, and with a sub-par piece of work to turn in. They get their paper back with red marks all over it and a C- at the top.

Many students fall into this pattern, which leads them to believe that they are bad writers. They see writing as a chore, or perhaps even a special type of torture, where a blank screen taunts them and they feel like they are failing before they even begin.

But they are not actually bad writers. They are victims of the lie that writing is a one-time event. But it's not—writing is a process.

Let me say that again: writing is a process.

No one, not even the most talented of writers, ever sits down to a blank piece of paper and creates a masterpiece, any more than Michelangelo could have free-handed the Sistine Chapel in an afternoon. That feat took him four years—the planning stage alone lasted three months. He had four assistants helping him as well. Writing is very similar—you need a plan, you need time to work, and you need assistance in order to create a masterpiece.

Writing Tip:
During the process, your work is called a draft, not a paper. Drafts are in process. A paper is a draft that has been through the complete writing process.

If you utilize this process with each piece of writing you are assigned, you will find that your final product is far better than anything you could do in one night or one draft. But notice that this process takes time! When you are assigned a writing project, make sure that you start early and take your time through each step.

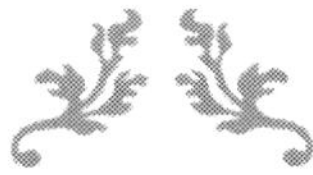

The Four Steps of Writing

The writing process consists of four steps, all of which is covered in this book.

1) Planning Your Writing—you find a topic, then create a plan for what you want to say about it to your audience.

2) Creating a Draft—you write a draft based on your plan and following the style requirements for the assignment, making sure to include your voice throughout.

3) Revising Your Draft—this is where you need assistants! Have several people look at the *content* of your draft, transforming your work in between each person.

4) Edit Your Revised Draft—once your content has been revised and is in its best form, check it for grammar errors.

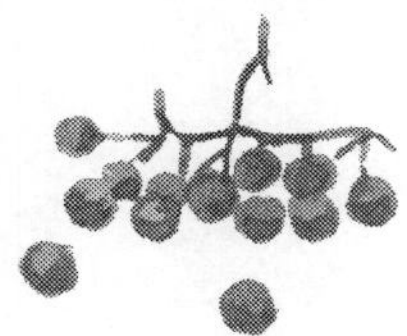

Section 1: Planning Your Writing

The first step of the writing process is creating a plan for your paper. You don't want to rush this. Preparing to write is one of the most difficult parts of the writing process. Many students struggle to gather their ideas. Sometimes, students have too many ideas, and they don't know how to sort through their ideas and determine which idea will work the best. Other times, students struggle to come up with any ideas. This section will help both types of writers.

Chapter 1: Finding and Narrowing a Topic

A topic is who or what you are writing about. You can find topics in many different places: your own interests and hobbies, your personal experience, in a subject you studied in school, or an article you read. A good topic needs to interest you—the writing process can be long, so don't ever choose something that you think will impress someone else, or because you think it will be "easy." You will end up frustrated and hate sitting down to write! Make sure you *want* to write about your topic. It also needs to be a topic that you can say something about. Don't pick a topic that is above your expert level—a seventh grader is not going to be able to easily write a paper that discusses the technical aspects of brain surgery at the level of a medical student! But a seventh grader could certainly do some research and write a paper about what a brain surgeon does and why that career might be an interesting one to pursue.

You also want to pick a topic that is narrow enough for the assignment. If you are asked to write a research paper, don't choose whole swaths of history or large subjects to try to cover in one paper. You won't be able to do it! But you can talk about a *part* of a larger subject. For example, you couldn't write an eight-page paper on the entire second World War; but you could write a paper on one battle, or one historical figure during that time. The same holds true in other types of writing: a persuasive paper on "gun control" isn't going to go well because there is so much to cover. But discussing whether a certain law should be passed, or how an incident should be handled would be an excellent choice. When writing a fictional short story, you don't want to plan a sweeping epic that rivals *Lord of the Rings*—you can't possibly do justice to your ideas! But you can write a piece of a longer story: perhaps an incident

that happens to a character or a simple side adventure that happens in the same world. Save the novel for later.

Remember, writing isn't a one-time event. You don't have to say all the things in one paper! Art pieces are called "pieces" for a reason: they are a part of a larger selection of works that add up to an artist's "vision." The same is true in writing. Each piece of writing is simply a part of what you think and understand about the world. It's okay to not say it all at one time. You'll have a chance to write other pieces! Pick one part and write it well.

You might have a great idea for one paper, and then be completely stumped on another. Or perhaps you know the general topic you want to write about but can't figure out how to narrow it down. That's okay! There are lots of strategies for finding a topic. All the strategies in this chapter can be used for both finding and narrowing a topic.

Brainstorming

Brainstorming is simply the gathering of ideas. When picking a topic, it's a good to gather as many ideas as you can. There's a saying: "In brainstorming, there are no bad ideas" and it's true. Sometimes even the craziest idea can become the best paper.

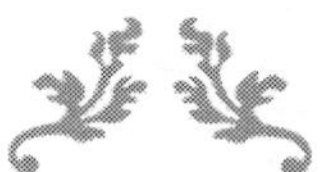

A good topic should:

- Interest you
- Be something you can talk about
- Be narrow enough for the assignment

The most basic form of brainstorming is to talk about your assignment and topic ideas with a friend or family member. Ask the other person if they would be willing to listen to you talk out loud about your ideas and ask you questions about your ideas. A fifteen-minute conversation with another person can help you to realize how many great ideas you have as well as which ideas will work the best for the particular piece you are writing. The key to a successful brainstorming conversation is to take notes during and after the conversation about the ideas that you and your conversation partner generate.

Clustering

There are lots of different ways to brainstorm, but one very effective method is using **clustering**, which is sometimes called a "bubble map" or "mind map."

It is a visual way for you to come up with lots of different ideas for your writing.

Begin with a blank piece of paper. Draw a circle in the center of the paper and inside the circle write down the basic question you are answering. For example, if you were asked to write about a holiday that is important to you, you would write "Holidays that are important to me" in the center bubble.

Then, draw a line reaching away from the center bubble and draw a circle there. Inside that bubble you would write down one of your ideas for an essay. You might write "Christmas" inside that bubble. You would repeat this for as many different ideas for essay topics as you can think of.

Then, you want to develop some of those ideas. You'd add more lines to your idea bubbles, and further develop them. For example, you would add reasons to the Christmas bubble that Christmas is important to you. One bubble might say "getting to see extended family." Another might say "attending Christmas Eve service." Do this for a few of your topic ideas. When you are done, you will see which ones stand out as being your strongest ideas to write about.

This is an excellent brainstorming technique if you are a visual person. Some people like lists and can come up with ideas to write down very easily. If that's not you, try clustering!

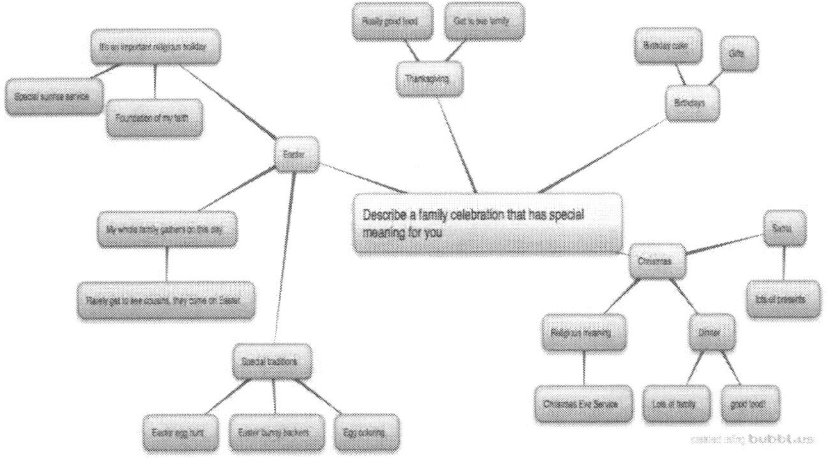

Journaling

Journaling—also sometimes called freewriting in academic circles—is a great option when you just aren't sure where to begin. Unlike clustering, which requires you to come up with your central topic before you use the brainstorming technique, you can start journaling before you have any ideas.

Get a blank sheet of paper and a pen (or open a blank document on your computer, if you prefer to type). Make sure you are in a quiet space, and, if you are on a device, turn off the notifications so that you aren't distracted. Set a timer for ten minutes. Start writing about the general assignment, and don't stop until the timer goes off! Your mind may seem blank but be willing to write "My mind is blank." Then start writing *why* it is blank, or any other idea that comes to mind. Eventually, as you write, you will likely come up with an idea...or two or three, even! You will be surprised how helpful a targeted focus and time goal could be for your writing.

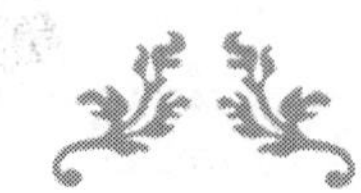

Brainstorming tip:
Keep all your ideas somewhere special. You can always come back to them for a different assignment!

As tempted as you might be to judge your ideas, cross out an idea, pick apart your grammar or spelling, or conclude that an idea that is not good enough while you are journaling, <u>don't do it!</u> Instead, wait until the timer goes off to reread your writing and decide which ideas might be worth keeping, and which ideas likely won't make it into your piece.

Once you come up with a main idea, take a brief break. Then, go ahead and journal about your main topic. Continue journaling about key connected ideas, thesis points, organizational structures, and voice techniques you might use in your piece of writing.

Asking Questions

Asking questions is a great brainstorming technique for writers who don't quite know where to begin. With this strategy, the writer comes up with as many *who, what, where, when, why*, and *how* questions as possible and then answers those questions. In essence, the writer pretends that they are preparing for an interview on the topic.

For example, if I am planning to write an expository essay about playing the violin, I would take five minutes to create the following list of questions for myself:

1. *Who* can play the violin?
2. *When* do most people start playing violin?
3. *Why* is playing the violin enjoyable?
4. *What* is the first step to learning to play the violin?

5. *Where* does someone find a violin?
6. *How* does someone find a violin teacher?
7. *What* are the greatest obstacles to learning to play the violin?

There are certainly many other questions that you could ask of yourself during the brainstorming questions. Once you have your list of questions, start responding to the questions, one at a time, with as much detail as you can. By the end of the process, you will be surprised about how much information you've already written and can incorporate into your outline and essay!

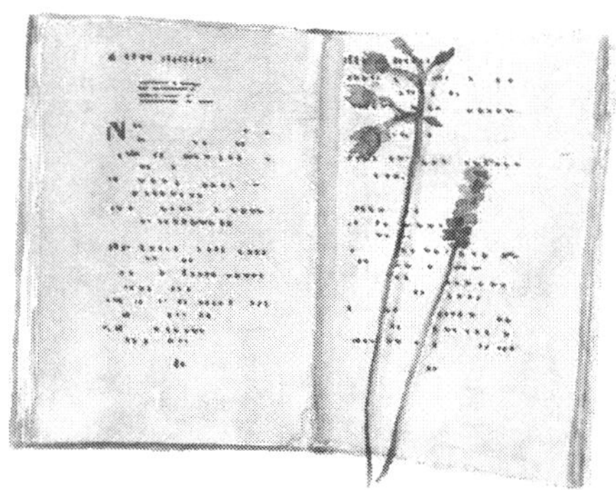

Activities

Key Terms

Define the following key terms: topic, narrowed topic, brainstorming, clustering, journaling, asking questions

Comprehension

1) How do you know you have a good topic?
2) What are some ways you can find a topic?

Practice

1) Create a cluster map on one of the following topics: activities for a rainy day, best places for a vacation, ideas for a birthday party.
2) Look through your social media feed (or a parent/friend's). Believe it or not, your social media is a type of diary or journal, a recording of important events and articles of interest. Create a list of topics that you could further research based on the posts you find.
3) Pick a career you might be interested in. Write a list of questions you could ask if you wanted to investigate that topic.
4) Choose an issue that people are arguing about right now (in the news, on social media, etc.). Imagine you can only write a two-page essay about this topic. Come up with three narrowed topics that are related to this larger issue that you could write for that length. Remember, you are not trying to cover every aspect of the issue! Then pick one of those topics and write a two-page essay.

Application

1) Write a paragraph about your favorite hobby—only pick one. Use the techniques listed here to brainstorm.
2) Write an essay on one of the topics you found in the Practice section.

More activities and student examples available at **www.writefromtheheart.org/resourceguide**.

Chapter 2: Audience

Writing is an art form. And there's one thing that every piece of art has: someone looking at it. A painter paints partly so that someone to purchase the piece and hang it in their living room, museum, or office. We talk about how a particular painting "speaks" to us, and what we think it means.

The same thing happens with writing. When we write, we are always writing FOR someone. The people we are writing for are called our **audience**. An audience could be one person, like a teacher, or it could be a group of people, like a novel written for young adults. Even something private, like a diary or a journal, has an audience: you. Isn't the point to go back and remember what happened to you on a certain day or at a particular time in your life? The older version of you is your audience.

The audience for our work matters. It affects what we say, how we say it, and what language and reasoning we use. We have to consider the audience every time we write.

Let me give you an example. Imagine you really dislike a girl named Susan. Maybe you have a diary and wrote: "I saw that dumb Susan today. She just thinks she's soooo cool. But she always makes fun of me!! Today, she made fun of my shoes and called me a clown. I can't stand her! Ugh. Stupid Susan. I HATE HER!!!"

This is private, just for you. You would be embarrassed if Susan saw it, right? Maybe you would also be embarrassed if your mom saw it. But your mom probably already knows that you and Susan don't get along. So how would you talk about the same incident with your mom?

Maybe you would say, "Susan made fun of me again today. She said my shoes were ugly and made me look like a clown. I can't stand being around her, Mom! She always makes me feel so bad about myself. Do I have to go back tomorrow? I can't stand her!"

See how you changed the story just slightly? You didn't use words like dumb, stupid, and hate, because your mom might talk to you about being nice and you know she doesn't like those words...and you know that it's a mean way to talk. Even though you feel that way, you find a more polite way to say it.

What about if you saw Susan's mom somewhere? If it came up, would you share all your angry feelings? Probably not. You might say something like, "Yeah, Susan and I don't really have a lot in common..." You aren't going to outright lie, but you are definitely going to choose your words differently!

The same thing happens in our writing. We need to consider our audience in what we write. You already know how to do this. When we text someone, it's okay to use abbreviations like "U here?" but we would never write like that in an English paper! Different audiences require different ways to communicate.

When you think about your audience, you need to consider the following things:

- What does the audience know or not know?
- What is the perspective or opinion of the audience on this subject?
- What word choice and style will help my audience take me seriously?

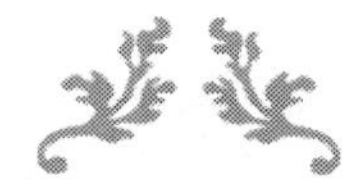

When thinking of an audience, remember:

- Word choice
- Definitions
- Reasoning

As you consider these things, your audience should affect your language choices, your evidence, and the way you explain things. For example, if you are writing a paper about video games, your teacher might not know how certain games are played—you will have to explain that in your paper! Or if you are writing a letter to a senator to ask for a law to be changed, you will want to use examples about how the change would help people and make things better, and not just say that you think it's a bad law—you need to convince with reasons that a senator would care about! Thinking about your audience might mean you leave some things out and add other things in. There is nothing wrong with that—you want to make sure your points are understandable to your audience.

But what if there is more than one audience? Perhaps you are writing a paper for class about video games—your classmates might understand the references, but your teacher won't. We always want to write to the **main audience**, the people we are trying to reach. In this case, it's the teacher. Your classmates won't mind if you explain the video game in your paper even if they already know what it is.

There are also times when people you weren't expecting to read your work will look at it. This is called an **unintended audience**. There's nothing that you can do about this, but you should be aware of it. A medical journal is intended for doctors, but we might read an article now and then. We aren't the intended audience, so we will need to go look up some of the words, but we should still be able to get something out of it. It happens to novelists all the time—we are still reading Shakespeare, Charles Dickens, and Jane Austen. There are words we might not know, or customs we don't understand, so we need to discuss it with others or read an explanation about the specific custom or holiday. But it doesn't mean we stop reading. We simply understand that they talked and wrote differently then but can still enjoy the novel. The same thing can be true when we read novels that don't have the same worldview that we do, or we read a political article from a perspective other than ours. There can be value in reading something from a different perspective—maybe it can help us think differently!

So as we write, we do need to consider our language and reasoning is not just for the intended audience, but to possibly help an unintended audience, too. That's why we want to avoid what is called **incendiary language** (words that would "inflame" someone else). We want to be honest, but we also want to avoid certain wording, like calling politicians we don't like "stupid"—someone who reads that would be turned off and never get to your actual reasoning!

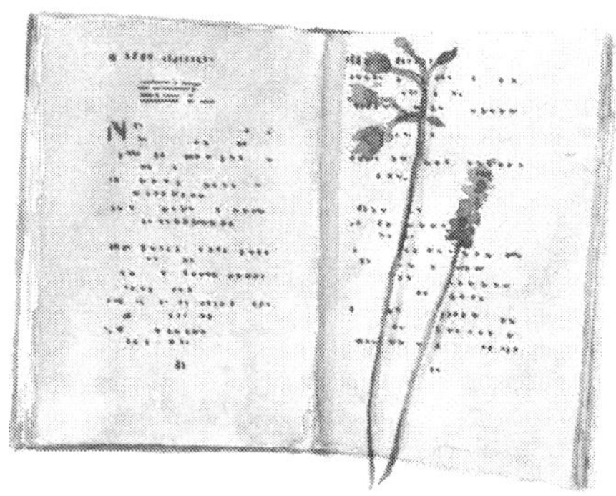

Activities

Key Terms

Define the following key terms: audience, main audience, unintended audience, incendiary language

Comprehension

1) Why do we need to consider our audience?
2) What are some things that we should change when our audience changes?

Practice

1) Find an article in a newspaper or magazine or online. Explain who the main audience is and what they believe.
2) Look at that same article and explain what an unintended audience might not understand or react to.

Application

1) Imagine you got lost at an amusement park. Write a dialogue you would have with a security guard. Then write a dialogue you would have with your best friend when you get home describing the incident.
2) Choose a hobby you have and write an essay explaining what it is and why you enjoy it with an audience of people in a nursing home.

More activities and student examples available at **www.writefromtheheart.org/resourceguide**.

Chapter 3: Outlining

An **outline** is a way to organize your thoughts in a logical format so that, when you write your essay, you know which order makes sense for sharing your ideas clearly. One way to organize your ideas before writing your essay is by creating an outline.

Even if you end up departing from the structure you create with the outline, making an outline will be helpful to your writing process. Outlines also help you to think of your work in sections or "chunks." Breaking down a piece of writing into smaller sections makes it easier to write without feeling overwhelmed. Outlines, as well as thesis statements (**see Chapter 4**), can and should be revised as you write. Your ideas will become sharper and more refined throughout the writing process.

An outline is an organized list of information that will allow you to think through some of the specific details of your essay and will allow you to plan the logical organization of your thoughts.

There are two main types of outlines: the topic outline and the sentence outline.

A **topic outline** lists the main ideas that you will talk about in your essay in short phrases. This is especially useful for shorter essays, such as standardized testing essays.

A **sentence outline** also talks about your main ideas, but it uses complete sentences and thoughts. Generally, a sentence outline will include more details and is helpful when you are writing a longer paper.

Sometimes people combine these and write sentences for the main parts of the outline, and topics for the supporting details. You should experiment and see what works best for you!

Most outlines follow this format using roman numerals and letters:

I. Main idea #1
  a. Supporting detail
    i. Supporting fact or statistic
    ii. Supporting fact or statistic
  b. Another supporting detail
II. Main idea #2
  a. Supporting detail
  b. Supporting detail

When planning an essay, how you format the outline is not as important as having a clear visual—what some might call a "roadmap"—of how you want to organize all your ideas and information. The most important part of creating an outline is clearly expressing your general ideas and how they are supported by specific details. If you have taken the time during your brainstorming session to come up with some clear supporting ideas for your topic, you will already have a head start on your outline.

Student Example 1: Topic Outline

1. Introduction
   a. Descriptive sentences of my sister asking me to go to Europe
   b. Daydreaming of activities
   c. Thesis—Although there are significant traveling expenses to England, London holds quaint attractions and famous landmarks that are worth traveling to.
2. Expenses
   a. Airline tickets
   b. Car rentals
   c. Food costs
3. Restaurants and surrounding countryside
   a. Best Tea Rooms in London
   b. Balthazar Restaurant and others
   c. York, England
4. Famous Landmarks
   a. Kensington and Buckingham Palace
   b. Palace of Westminster and Westminster Abbey
5. Conclusion
   a. Other countries that are accessible
   b. Re-state thesis

You can see from this outline that the author plans to have five paragraphs. The first paragraph will be an introduction. She lists the details of what will comprise the introduction in the points below the heading. She'll include a descriptive sentence, a scene of daydreaming, and her thesis (**see Chapter 4**).

After that, she will go on to discuss expenses. She gets more specific about what expenses she will specifically cover in the paper under the heading "expenses." Each section corresponds to a paragraph or paragraphs in her paper. By looking through her outline, you can see both the general ideas she will discuss, as well as the supporting details that her paragraphs will go into detail about.

Student Example 2: Sentence Outline

Introduction

Describe what it feels like to bike on a dangerous street.

Thesis: Shipley Road should have a bike/running path because it would make it safer for bikers and runners, it would connect bike paths, and it would create a healthier environment.

Safety

A bike path makes it safer for bikers to bike on the side of the road and safer for runners

Families can safely get to parks

Connecting paths

Putting a bike path along Shipley road between Washington Street Extension and Wilson Road would connect bike and running paths that already exist

There would be more options for bikers and runners.

Healthy Environment

If there were a bike path, less people would drive a short distance when they can safely bike/walk.

There would be less pollutants

People would get more exercise

Conclusion

Restate the thesis: Creating a bike path along Shipley Road would help improve safety, the options for bikers, and the health of our community.

Describe what the neighborhood would feel like with the path in place.

Everyone should write to the counsel in support of the path, or come to the meeting next Thursday to show your support.

This outline shows the author's plans for a persuasive essay. The outline clearly shows the main ideas that the author will use to support her position: Safety, Connecting Paths, and Healthy Environment. Under each of those headings, the author lists the sp\ecific facts and details that she will use to support her main ideas.

Student Examples

Look at these two essays. They were both written to answer the question, "What are the qualities of a good parent?" The first essay was written without an outline. The second essay utilized an outline before the student began writing.

Essay 1

As I walk up my stairs to our kitchen a heaven like smell hits me faster than I could blink. It was my Mom's delicious and great smelling cooking. As I walk through the kitchen and take a big smell of the delicious food my mom is preparing, I walk into the garage my and see my Dad hard at work in the garage. To me these are the qualifications of a good parent. One of my qualifications for my Mom is that she can cook and believe me she can.

The qualification for my Dad would have to be that he's a hard worker. I like it when I see my Dad working hard cause it makes me work hard too.

The last and biggest qualification for both my parents is that they're loving and caring parents that are always there for me.

In conclusion these are the qualifications for my parents and these are what I love to see in parents.

Essay 2

My family gathers around the table for a delicious meal. The smell of chicken wafts from the covered dishes and my mom begins to pass the food. As we serve ourselves, my dad asks each of us what the best part of our day was. They are great parents. There are many qualifications to be a good parent. The most important are that the parents listen to their children attentively, teach them the basic issues about safety, and discipline them when they do something inappropriate.

The point that is most important for a great parent is to listen to their child attentively. That means that they should sit down and give all the attention to the kid. Parents should take time with each of their children to find out about their interests and what they like.

A second point is that a good parent teaches safety. If the child feels safe at home or with their parents, he/she will stay safe and learn to follow the rules. For example, one easy rule to teach a child is when you cross the street. First, you look right and left before you cross. There are many other safety rules that you may learn while watching your parents or be told by your parents.

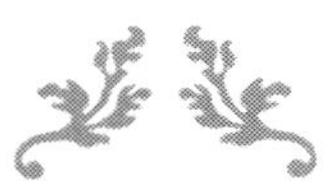

Questions as you read:
What is the main idea for each essay?
What are the supporting points?
In what ways is the first essay underdeveloped?

The third point I want to discuss is discipline. It's hard for parents to discipline their kids, but they do it for their child's own good. There are different types of discipline and the parents have to be sensitive to use the right one and at the right time. If they don't discipline their child, the child will never learn what is right or wrong. Also, he/she will have trouble later in life dealing with it.

I could talk about so many other points that make for good parents, but these three are the most important. Great parents are present and are involved in the kids' lives. They watch out for safety and they do the right things in correcting their kids.

Activities

Key Terms

Define the following key terms: topic outline, sentence outline

Comprehension

1) What function does an outline serve?
2) What is the difference between a topic outline and a sentence outline?

Practice

1) Answer the questions listed with the student examples.
2) Create a topic outline for the second essay in the Student Example section.
3) Create a sentence outline for the second essay in the Student Example section.

Application

1) Choose from the following topics and create an outline for an essay you might write: ways to get exercise, reasons to adopt a pet, activities to do in the summer.
2) Write an essay answering the following question (include an outline!): If you could create a new national holiday, what would it be and why should we celebrate it?

More activities and student examples available at **www.writefromtheheart.org/resourceguide**.

Section 2: Parts of a Draft

Once you have chosen your essay topic and organized your ideas into an outline, you can write your draft. Easy, right? Not always.

This is where a lot of writers get stuck. But a lot of times it's because they don't understand the next step and simply end up staring at a blank screen. This section will give you the tools you need to feel confident moving from planning to drafting. We will be covering all the pieces you need to create a solid draft that clearly explains your ideas.

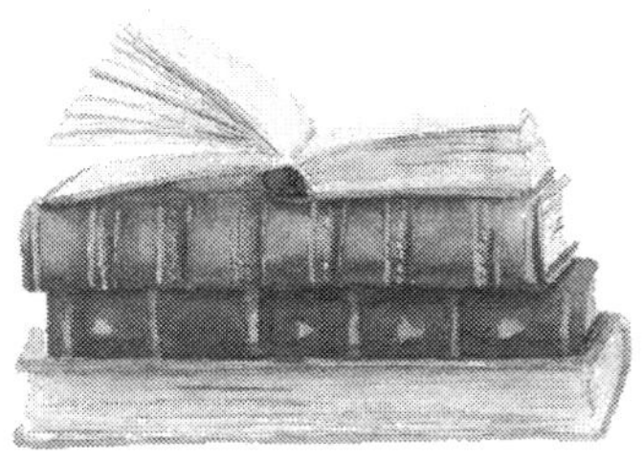

Chapter 4: Thesis Statements

One of the most important parts of writing an essay - whether it's expository, comparative, persuasive, analytical, or a research paper - is a clear thesis statement.

Although the phrase "thesis statement" might sound complicated, it is actually a very simple idea. The purpose of a thesis statement is to tell your reader exactly what to expect when they read your paper. A **thesis statement** is the central idea or the main point of your essay. It should be no longer than one or two sentences. It should be concise, meaning that you won't be able to fit every detail of your paper into it, but it should also be specific enough that it reflects all the main arguments that you present in your paper.

Thesis = topic + what you will show or prove about topic

Typically, your thesis statement should appear in your introduction. By putting your thesis in either the first or second paragraph of an essay, you tell your reader right away what you plan to discuss and help give a sense of direction for your paper.

A second version of your thesis statement should also appear at the end of a paper, in the conclusion. In the final paragraph of your essay, you will do what we call "restating" your thesis. Summarizing your argument and reminding your audience what they just learned is a perfect way to end the paper. When you restate your thesis, you do not use the exact same words that you used in your original thesis statement that was in the introduction, but the *idea* that you communicate remains exactly the same. However, having your thesis statement in the last paragraph of your paper is *not* enough. You need to have your thesis statement in the beginning of your paper, too!

Elements of a Thesis

At its simplest, a thesis explains your topic and what the paper will be showing or proving about the topic. But there are three elements to consider in making sure that you are doing this well.

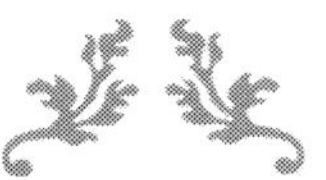

Writing tip:

If you have narrowed your topic correctly in the planning stages, you should already have a specific thesis.

First, **a good thesis should be specific.** A thesis statement narrows your topic down to a manageable subject. In a history research paper, you're not going to try to talk about the entire Civil War but might cover just one battle or one figure. In a paper about a book for English class, you're not going to try to look at a whole novel but should focus on just one character or one theme. A specific thesis statement can be proven with 3-4 points.

BAD THESIS: There are many reasons that boats sink.

This statement is very general and doesn't tell us much about your paper. It's too vague to tell your reader what you plan to talk about. All we know is that your paper will be about sinking boats.

GOOD THESIS: The sinking of the Titanic was caused by several major human errors that could have been prevented.

This thesis tells us in detail exactly what you plan to talk about in your paper. It specifically tells me which boat you are talking about and what you will be proving in your paper: human errors caused the sinking of the ship. That information makes me want to read your paper and hear what you have to say!

Second, **a good thesis should tell what you are going to show or prove about the subject**. A thesis statement does more than just announce a subject. Instead, it tells your reader the conclusion that you have reached on that subject.

BAD THESIS: Captain Cook was a very successful Captain.

This statement announces the topic you plan to write about, but it doesn't tell me why he was so successful. It leaves me unsure of what you plan to show or

prove in the paper. This thesis doesn't tell me about any conclusions you made about Captain Cook.

✔ **GOOD THESIS**: Captain Cook was one of the most successful captains the world has ever known because of the curiosity, bravery, and leadership he displayed on his three main voyages.

This is a good thesis because it tells me that you have looked at all of the information about Captain Cook and have come to the conclusion that his success was due to curiosity, bravery, and leadership. Now I know that your paper will focus on showing me how he showed these qualities on his three voyages.

Lastly, **a good thesis statement should be clear and concise.** It should not be too wordy or include long lists of details. You don't have to write your whole paper in one sentence!

🚫 **BAD THESIS**: The Great Depression had a lot of elements that were involved such as the stock market crash when stocks lost their value, the dust bowl which involved a lot of crops dying, and the banks that failed due to not being insured, as well as a lot of other elements like America's Europe policy, and people spending less money in the market too.

Although this thesis is very specific, it is not clear and concise. It is a long list of information that is confusing to read. A thesis shouldn't be explaining the arguments but giving an overview of them.

✔ **GOOD THESIS**: The main reasons for the Great Depression were the Wall Street crash of 1929, the failing of the banks, and the Dust Bowl.

This thesis picks out what the author believes are the three most important causes of the Great Depression and clearly states what will be discussed in the paper in a concise way.

Relationship between the Thesis Statement and Supporting Paragraphs

Once you have come up with a thesis statement, the next step in writing an effective essay is clearly organizing your information within the essay. You might have a specific, clear, thought-provoking thesis statement, but if your essay doesn't clearly support it, or goes off topic, then your essay won't be very effective.

A good thesis statement should provide you with a clear structure of organization for your essay! Look at these student examples of thesis statements and see if you can guess what their supporting paragraphs might be.

Student Examples

- While the path of an emergency physician is challenging and the profession is difficult, helping people in crisis and saving lives is a valuable and worthy calling.
- It is important for the United States of America to have a strong military to protect and defend its people and borders.
- Amelia Mary Earhart was a famous female aviationist who inspired many women with her adventurous spirit, bravery, and bold speeches.
- Anne Sullivan had a hard childhood, but with her eager heart to learn she succeeded and became a great teacher.
- Both Claude Frollo and Romeo Montague have similar goals, to acquire unattainable love, but the way they proceed in getting that love is where they differ.

At the outline stage, a thesis is usually called a **preliminary thesis statement**. This means that you are saying that the thesis statement is the one that you THINK you are going to prove. Sometimes, in the course of writing, you find that your thesis statement no longer accurately describes exactly what the paper is arguing. It is perfectly fine to adapt your thesis statement accordingly Most professional writers adjust their thesis statement based on their final product.

Avoiding "I think..." and "In this paper..."

A thesis statement is a sentence that tells your audience what you plan to show or prove about your topic. But for a lot of students, it is really tempting to tell the audience what they *think* about the topic.

Example: *I think that the best way to lose weight is to exercise and eat healthy.*

This is not a good way to formulate a thesis statement for a few reasons. First, your name is at the top of the paper, so adding in the words "I think" isn't necessary—it doesn't keep your thesis clear and concise. Secondly, your thesis should confidently state what you are going to show or prove, and when you say "I think" it makes it sound like you aren't sure if you are right. It's like saying "I think the answer to that math problem is 57??" Putting "I think" is a

way of checking with another person because you aren't sure. But you did the research, and you have supporting evidence, so you should feel confident that your paper is going to prove your point! Don't downplay your hard work by saying "I think..."

The same thing goes for the statement "In this paper, I am going to..." What this amounts to is wordiness. We already know it's your paper. We already know that you are going to try to show us or convince us of something. Just tell us what it is. For example, suppose you are going to answer the essay question "Explain how to lose weight." Which sounds better?

"In this paper, I am going to tell you how to lose weight."

"The best way to lose weight is to exercise and eat healthy."

The second one, right?

The other problem with the "In this paper..." format is that it really isn't a thesis statement. Look at the first sentence again. Does that sentence include the second piece of a thesis statement, what you are going to show or prove? No. It just repeats the original essay question, and that's not a thesis statement.

If you have either of these phrases in a thesis statement, you need to eliminate them.

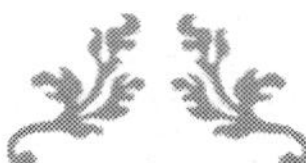

Other phrases that mean the same as "I think":

- I believe
- I wonder
- I am going to tell you

Check Your Thesis

To ensure that your thesis statement has all the elements it needs, ask these questions:

- Does my thesis answer a "how" or a "why" question? (if it doesn't, then you did not include the show or prove portion of a thesis)
- Have I written something that I need to explain or prove? (If you don't, then you are probably just making a statement)
- Do I use generic words like "good" or "successful"? Was I specific about what makes something good or successful? (If you weren't, your thesis isn't specific enough)
- Did I use "I think" or "In this paper"? (If you did, eliminate them!)

Activities

Key Terms

Define the following key terms: thesis statement, preliminary thesis statement

Comprehension

1) What are the elements of a good thesis statement?
2) Why should you avoid "I think" or "In this paper"?

Practice

1) Change the following bad thesis statements into good thesis statements:
   a. People use many lawn chemicals.
   b. The North and South fought the Civil War for many reasons, some of which were the same and some different.
   c. The American steel industry has many problems.
   d. I think sales calls are terrible.
   e. George Washington was America's first president.
   f. In this paper, I will tell you about the art of glassblowing.
2) Look at the section entitled "Relationship Between the Thesis Statement and Supporting Paragraphs." Choose two of the student examples and state what their supporting paragraphs probably were.

Application

1) Write a thesis statement for the following questions:
   a. Should parents monitor children's internet use? Why?
   b. How can bullying be eliminated?
   c. What is the greatest challenge that teenagers face today?
2) Write an essay based on one of the above questions. Don't forget to outline!

More activities and student examples available at **www.writefromtheheart.org/resourceguide**.

Chapter 5: Paragraphs

A **paragraph** is a combination of sentences all focused on a single idea. They come together in a specific structure to create one main point. Perhaps the entire piece of writing consists of a single paragraph, or maybe several paragraphs work together to form an essay. The paragraph breaks are clear indicators of where the supporting ideas of your essay begin and end. No matter what you're writing, though, a paragraph always has the following three elements:

- Topic Sentence
- Supporting Sentences
- Concluding Sentence

Using a variety of techniques and strategies, you can create a well-structured, engaging paragraph on just about any topic.

Topic Sentences

A **topic sentence** is the main idea of a paragraph. It sets the tone. Even more, it tells the reader exactly what information they should expect to find. A good topic sentence will cover what is in the paragraph, without referencing something that either appears in another paragraph, or worse, something not in the essay at all.

A topic sentence can appear anywhere in a paragraph—it does not need to be the first sentence. Sometimes, putting it at the end makes more sense. Other times, it can go somewhere in the middle. As you advance in paragraph writing, you can also try an **implied topic sentence**, where the sentence doesn't appear anywhere, but the reader understands what it would be just by reading the paragraph—this is most often used in narrative and descriptive writing.

For example, let's take a look at the following student examples:

> **One advantage that comes from being on a youth soccer team is learning to work with and depend on others.** Learning to be part of a team is useful in many areas of life. Children can learn how to build friendships, how to strengthen teamwork, and how to listen to someone in charge. Children also need to be able to offer help to others. When children grow up, they will get a job and will need to be able to work with others. Also, there will be times they need to depend on others for help. The ability to work with others will be helpful throughout their whole lives —Sarah F., 11

What does the topic sentence say? It tells the reader that "One advantage that comes from being on a youth soccer team is learning to work with and depend on others." This is a good topic sentence because it explains exactly what the reader should expect to find within the details of the paragraph: all the ways being on a team will help them learn to help and depend on others.

Notice that the topic sentence was specific; it doesn't just say "learning." It clearly explains that the paragraph will include how to "work with and depend on others." This is definitely an effective topic sentence.

Let's look at another example:

> Bluetooth has benefited us in many ways. One way people have been benefited by it is by being able to wirelessly connect devices without any cost. For instance, a phone can be wirelessly connected to a car so that hands-free can be used. This enables people to talk on the phone without even having to get their phone out, which makes driving safer because they are not distracted by holding their phone. An iPad can also be connected to a keyboard by using Bluetooth, so that people can type on a keyboard instead of using the keyboard that pops up on the screen. This makes it easier and faster to type, and it is also less strenuous on their hands. **The benefits Bluetooth has given people has made their lives much easier than it would have been without Bluetooth.**
> —Misa S., 12

In this case, the topic sentence is at the end of the paragraph, with a general introduction sentence at the beginning.

Supporting Sentences

The **supporting sentences**, also sometimes called the detail sentences, are the meat of the paragraph. They are what the main idea is all about. Supporting sentences offer explanations, definitions, examples, and all other forms of development.

As you write the supporting sentences of your paragraph, ask yourself:

- Do these details all relate to the topic?
- Do these details help the reader better understand the topic?
- Do these details define everything that was covered in the topic?

For example, let's think back to the example paragraph about Bluetooth benefits. That paragraph should *not* include sentences that discuss types of Bluetooth devices. That wouldn't fit within the scope of the topic sentence.

Additionally, supporting sentences can be broken into two categories: major and minor details. A **major detail** is a main point that supports the paragraph's topic sentence, while a **minor detail** is a sentence that expands on a major detail. For instance, we can look at the sentences in the following paragraph about using calm breathing to manage stage fright:

It sounds obvious, but calm breathing is very important. Not only does it help keep us alive, but strategic breathing can calm overexcited nerves. Deep, relaxing breathes are scientifically proven to calm the body and mind and lower the heart rate. We breathe deeply while sleeping, and if we mimic this while awake it helps relax us. Many people who experience stage fright tend to hyperventilate. Hyperventilating is very bad both for your body and for acting. While hyperventilating, the brain goes into panic mode and starts sending more endorphins to make you feel even more anxious. It is also hard to sing and act when you are breathing that fast. **So, it is important to be mindful of your breathing and try to stay relaxed.** —Sarah S., 16

Major Detail 1: Deep, relaxing breathes are scientifically proven to calm the body and mind and lower the heart rate.

Minor Detail 1: We breathe deeply while sleeping, and if we mimic this while awake it helps relax us.

Major Detail 2: Hyperventilating is very bad both for your body and for acting.

Minor Detail 2: While hyperventilating, the brain goes into panic mode and starts sending more endorphins to make you feel even more anxious.

Notice how each minor detail further explains the idea introduced in the major detail. They work together to fully explain the topic sentence of the paragraph.

Concluding Sentences

The **concluding sentence** is the final sentence of a paragraph. Its goal is to wrap up the main idea in a meaningful way.

Sometimes, the concluding sentence is also the topic sentence. But when it's not, it's very important to avoid crafting a conclusion sentence that restates the topic sentence with similar wording. This can be very repetitive for the reader. Instead, aim to answer the question, "So what?" What do you want the reader to take away from the paragraph? Why should they care?" Answer those questions to craft the conclusion sentence of your paragraph.

Or, if the paragraph is a part of an essay (and not the entire essay on its own), a great strategy for crafting your conclusion sentence is to relate the main idea of the paragraph back to the thesis. How does the information in the paragraph prove that the thesis is true? The answer to that question can help you write your paragraph's final sentence.

Focus

Just like a camera lens taking a picture needs to be in focus to capture everything in the scene, a paragraph needs to help the reader focus on what the paragraph is saying. Essentially, **focus** means that the paragraph explains only the details that support the main idea of the topic sentence and uses proper grammar and transitions.

First, be sure that you stay consistent in your point of view and verb tense. For instance, if you're writing a paragraph talking about an issue from a first person point of view (using "I" and "me"), it can be confusing to a reader if you switch to second person (saying "you") in the middle of the paragraph. Additionally, pay close attention to verb tense. If you switch from past to present tense, your reader will feel that jump, which is a bit of a distraction. See **Section 3** for information about person and point of view. See **Section 9** for information about grammar.

Another strategy is to use transition words within your paragraph, not just between them. For instance, you can connect sentences with words like "also" and "additionally." Using those kinds of words can help the reader see how

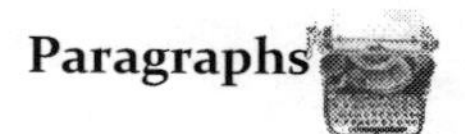

the ideas within a paragraph are related, which improves the overall focus of the main idea. **Chapter 6** will give you more information about transitions.

Overall, the best strategy to ensure focus is to separate the elements of your paragraph. Read each supporting sentence in turn to make sure that it is included in the main idea of the topic sentence. Then, read the topic sentence and make sure it doesn't promise more information than what appears in the paragraph.

With all these steps, your paragraph will remain focused and well-structured.

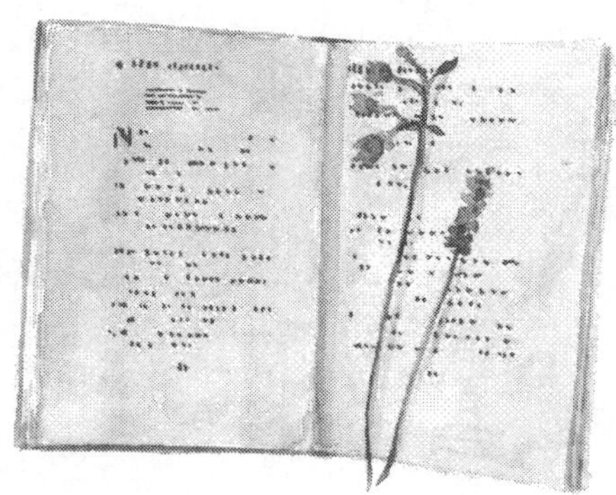

Activities

Key Terms

Define the following key terms: paragraph, topic sentence, implied topic sentence, supporting sentences, major detail, minor detail, concluding sentence, focus

Comprehension

1) Why is it important to have a topic sentence?
2) What is the relationship between major and minor details?

Practice

Write a topic sentence for the following paragraphs:

1) There are many genres of this art form, a few of which are ballet, jazz, hip-hop, and contemporary. The art of dance has been enjoyed for centuries in many different countries. Throughout history, people have participated in tribal dances around campfires, waltzes in ballrooms, and tap dancing in old black and white movies.
2) One reason that a book is written is for entertainment. Some of these books are really written well so that when you pick it up you can't put it down until you finished it. Others make you think that you are in the book, and you feel the way people in the book do. For example, if the main character is lonesome and sad, the one who is reading the book should feel that way too. Another reason books are written is to teach a lesson. For instance, there might be a book where a character does bad things and learns at the end that he has done wrong when he gets into trouble. That might help you know when you are doing wrong so you can fix it quickly. Characters in the book might be doing the bad habits or things you do, and you can learn from them.

Application

1) Write a paragraph about a hobby you have and put the topic sentence at the beginning and include three supporting details.
2) Write a paragraph about your favorite season and put your topic sentence at the end.
3) Write a paragraph about a time you went on an outing and have an implied topic sentence.

More activities and student examples available at **www.writefromtheheart.org/resourceguide**.

Chapter 6: Transitions

The one burning question that young writers ask more often than pretty much anything else is this: "Does my writing flow?"

What we mean when we say *flow* is difficult for many of us to describe. Most of us can tell whether someone else's writing does or does not flow smoothly, but it's hard to know when we read our own work. Why? It's easiest to follow our own writing, because our thought process makes sense to us while we are writing. With someone else's work, however, we need to read carefully in order to follow the train of thought. Without careful organization, ordering, and transitions, we struggle to understand what someone else is saying—no matter how brilliant their ideas might be.

Look at this student paragraph:

Here in America we take baking for granted. Instead of putting something in your microwave, bake something! It is much more nutritious, so you will be getting a lot more vitamins and nutrients. It will most likely be more delicious. You will have the accomplished feeling that you made your dinner! Baking is a rewarding learning experience for anyone.

When we read this, we can understand it, but it sounds rather choppy—the supporting sentences don't flow.

Now look at the same paragraph with transitions:

Here in America we take baking for granted. Instead of putting something in your microwave, bake something! First of all, it is much more nutritious, so you will be getting a lot more vitamins and nutrients. Secondly, it will most likely be more delicious. And third, you will have the accomplished feeling that you made your dinner! Baking is a rewarding learning experience for anyone. —Julia R., 11

This sounds much better, doesn't it?

Think of **transitions** as sign-posts that guide your reader along the path of your ideas: "Up next: brilliant idea," one sign-post might say. "Not so fast...I have more to say," another might instruct. Still another sign might tell the reader, "Wait! You thought I had made a decision, but I'm about to change my mind!"

Transitions can be very simple phrases that a writer uses within or between paragraphs to direct the reader from one idea to another. In addition to creating flow, good writers strategically order their sentences and make sure that those sentences follow a clear progression that is easy to follow. As writers mature, transitions still often contain keywords, but they become slightly longer and more specific to each piece of writing.

Word Choice: Transition Phrases

There are several often-used **transition phrases** that every writer should know. These are a word or words that you add to help you slide from one sentence to the next, or one paragraph to the next. When you are ready to revise your writing (**see Section 6**), it is extremely helpful to keep a list of transition phrases in front of you so that you can pick exactly the right phrase to add to your writing. When deciding between transition phrases, always ask yourself: What purpose should this transition phrase serve?

There are several common categories of transition phrases:

- *Introducing* a new idea or providing order to your ideas
- *Adding* onto ideas
- *Giving* examples to support or demonstrate ideas
- *Comparing* a similar idea
- Providing a *contrasting* idea (in other words: a different or opposite idea)
- *Emphasizing* an idea
- *Describing* the effect of an idea
- Providing a *concession* to a different opinion
- *Concluding* your discussion of an idea

Introduce/ Provide Order	Add onto ideas	Give Examples	Compare a similar idea	Introduce a contrasting idea	Emphasize an idea	Describe an effect	Provide a concession	Conclude
First, Second, Third	Additionally	For example	Similarly	In contrast	In particular,	As a result	Although	In conclusion
First and foremost	Also	Such as	Likewise	On the other hand	Most importantly,	Consequently	While	Ultimately
Initially	In addition	Namely	In the same way	However	Indeed	Thus	Admittedly	In the end
Subsequently	Moreover	For instance	Also	Nonetheless	Undoubtedly	Therefore	It is true that	In sum
Next	Further	In fact	In a similar manner	Conversely	While	Evidently	Certainly	Above all
Finally	What's more	As an example		Yet	Certainly	Accordingly	Even though	Overall
Lastly	Not only... but also				Of course	Hence		In short

Word Order: Known-New Contract

When you write, your sentences must have their words in the correct order, right? If not, your writing won't make any sense. Between sentences, the ideas need to be clear, and the progression from one sentence to the next needs to be easy for the reader to follow. How does a writer do that? They follow what we call the **known-new contract**.

The known-new contract states that you ALWAYS want your transition sentences to start with *known* information (information from the previous sentence or paragraph) and then end with *new* information (information that you haven't shared yet with your audience).

Example: This example is incorrect because the sentences are out of order.

> My family recently traveled to New York City. In the city, we went to the Statue of Liberty, the 9/11 Memorial, and the Empire State Building. Unlike the New York City crowds, the peace and quiet of North Carolina's beaches really appeals to me. At the Empire State Building, we had to wait in line for hours, and the whole city was crowded.

Did you notice that the third sentence doesn't begin with *known* information? The known information would relate to the locations where the author traveled - the Statue of Liberty, the 9/11 Memorial, and the Empire State Building. We can find that kind of reference to the known information at the beginning of the fourth sentence ("At the Empire State Building,...").

Notice what happens when we switch the third and fourth sentences:

> My family recently traveled to New York City. In the city, we went to the Statue of Liberty, the 9/11 Memorial, and the Empire State Building. At the Empire State Building, we had to wait in line for hours, and the whole city was crowded. Unlike the New York City crowds, the peace and quiet of North Carolina's beaches really appeals to me.

Much better, right? Now, what would you expect the next sentence to be about, if the author continues to follow the known-new contract? (If you said North Carolina beaches, then you are correct!)

The known-new contract means that, instead of using a transitional phrase, the writer is repeating and rewording earlier information *to function as* a transitional phrase. As you develop as a writer, your ideas will become more and more complicated. In order to guide your reader along in your thought process, you will need more and more sophisticated transitions. This is particularly helpful when moving from paragraph to paragraph in an essay, when a simple transition word isn't strong enough.

When NOT to use the Known-New Contract:

- Step-by-step instructions
- Description paragraphs

What does that look like, exactly? In order to understand the difference between basic transitions and sophisticated transitions, read this excerpt of a student's essay about John Steinbeck's *The Pearl*:

The Pearl focuses on a native man named Kino; his wife, Juana; and their infant son, Coyotito. Kino is a pearl diver who one day finds the priceless pearl. He idolizes this pearl, and he realizes that he simply must have it. Even when people try to rob him of it and his wife encourages him to get rid of it, he hangs on. Kino becomes selfishly attached to the pearl. It entangles him and enslaves him to his own desires for success, and this obsession has consequences on Kino—most obviously, the consequence of his son's death. These consequences are a result of Kino's selfish nature, a nature that is evidenced in our modern culture as well.

One example of human selfishness in the culture is in the area of money. America is the wealthiest and freest country in the world, but so often, Americans take that for granted. There is a nationwide, or in some cases worldwide, preoccupation with material things. Some have called this preoccupation "affluenza." On the back of the book *Affluenza* by John de Graaf, David Wann, and Thomas H. Naylor, affluenza is defined as "a painful, contagious, socially transmitted condition of overload, debt, anxiety, and waste resulting from the dogged pursuit of more." That's

exactly what's happening all over America today—the dogged pursuit of more. Affluenza is a direct result of humanity's selfish nature that craves whatever happens to be wanted or even idolized at the time. Sadly, this craving manifests itself in drastic ways in our society: the total amount of credit card debt in America as of November 2009 was 2,464.6 billion dollars ("Consumer Credit"). **This epidemic of desire for material things parallels quite closely with Kino's obsession over his pearl.** He was so attached to it that he couldn't let go, just as some Americans can't stop spending money and wanting more (and therefore, falling deeper and deeper into debt). Another similarity between Kino's experience and the current consumerist state of America is that both Kino and Americans today think that pursuing their addictive desire will bring them happiness. Kino hangs on to hopes of all the things he can accomplish with the pearl; Americans can easily base their satisfaction on money as well. As is seen in the consequences Kino experiences, this idea is deceptive. And it takes a selfish human nature to believe the falsehood that any material thing will ultimately bring satisfaction.
—Carrie D., 16

Do you notice how much better these two paragraphs flow, and how much easier it is to follow her ideas with these advanced transitions? The author's unique transition phrases - instead of generic transitions - help the reader to follow the author's train of thought.

Between paragraphs, try to borrow a phrase or two from the ending sentence in the preceding paragraph and re-use it in the next paragraph. Look again at the beginning of the second paragraph above. This is a good example of recycling key language in order to connect two paragraphs: This very specific transition sentence - "One example of human selfishness in the culture is in the area of money." - ties back to the last sentence of the preceding paragraph, which talks about the selfish nature of the "real world." That connection is crucial because it takes us out of the book itself and makes us connect the book to modern society, which is the point of this author's paper.

Within paragraphs, for key shifts or additions to your ideas that don't warrant an entirely new paragraph, you may want to add a more sophisticated transition between sentences. Look at the second sentence in bold in the student example: "This epidemic of desire for material things parallels quite closely with Kino's obsession over his pearl." This sentence helps shift the paragraph back to the book so that she can connect the problem in the real world to the lesson in the book.

If these kinds of advanced transitions seem intimidating to you, remember that they take time - and they will emerge as your papers develop from draft to draft. Don't get too impatient with yourself as you write a first draft of a paper; instead, as you revise, notice how much easier it is to craft a targeted transition that guides your reader from idea to idea.

With the complexity of excellent transitions in mind, a great first step to writing your own sophisticated transitions is to study them in the writing of others. When you read news articles and nonfiction books, pay attention to the many different sophisticated transitions. When you read essays by peers, point out great transitions and what makes them work so well. Before you know it, you will be writing sophisticated transitions like a pro!

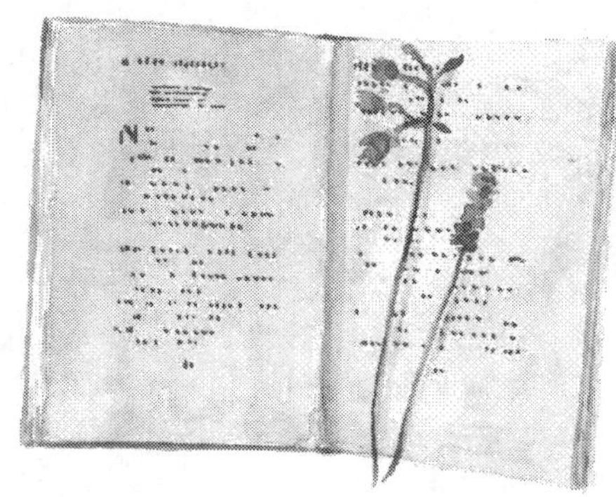

Activities

Key Terms

Define the following key terms: transitions, transitional phrases, known-new contract

Comprehension

1) How do transitions help your writing?
2) Where is the best place to put a sentence that follows the known-new contract?

Practice: Add transitions to the following paragraphs:

1) Playing a team sport will help people become physically stronger, allow people to push themselves mentally, encourage people to communicate and work together with teammates. Moving around while playing a team sport will strengthen the immune system. This will prevent people from some sickness and injuries. When people play a team sport, they will push themselves mentally to become better players. This will give them a positive attitude, so they will work harder on everything they do. Playing a sport can allow players to know each other and become friends. This will help people to communicate and work together with their teammates which will improve communication skill. Team sports will help lots of people in their daily lives and tasks.
2) This year, I took a vacation to California with my mom and younger brother. We flew to California to visit my uncle and cousin. I learned how to surf at Santa Monica Beach. I only rode white water; my uncle and I were drained from the relentless beating of the waves. We traveled to Mission Beach, and I used a wave generator to go wake boarding. Ten people joined me, and we took turns transitioning between wake and boogie boarding. We toured Huntington Beach to celebrate my uncle's girlfriend's birthday. If I could, I would definitely do this vacation again.

Application

1) Write a paragraph about how to make or do something, using transitions between each step.
2) Write an essay about your last vacation, using the known-new contract between paragraphs.

More activities and student examples available at **www.writefromtheheart.org/resourceguide**.

Chapter 7: Introductions and Conclusions

A lot of your time is spent in the planning stages on your thesis statement and your supporting information, and students sometimes view introductions and conclusions as "extra" paragraphs that simply bookend the paper. But they perform an important function in your paper: they bring your reader in and make sure they understand the topic before they see your thesis statement, and then leave them at the end with a way to understand the importance of your topic.

In studying how we communicate, scientists have found two things to be true: we form our impressions quickly, and we remember the last thing we read (or talked about) with a person most clearly. Your introduction is your "first impression" and your conclusion is your "memory maker" to help your readers remember your work.

Because of this, some writers choose to write their introduction and conclusion last. Others like to do it in order with the rest of the paper. Either is fine, but you need to make sure you understand how to make these as effective as possible.

Introductions

When you begin a new essay, the very first paragraph that your reader will encounter is your **introduction**. A good introduction will do three things:

1. It must have an attention getter that capture the readers' attention.
2. It must clearly introduce the topic and any information the reader needs.
3. It must include the thesis statement.

There is not one "right way" to write an introduction, but it <u>must</u> have these three elements.

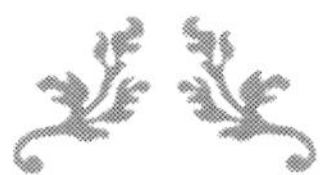

Quotation: Use a well-known quotation that directly relates to your essay, and explain its context and author

Question: Ask a question in the introduction to get your reader thinking, and then answer the question in the rest of your introduction.

Facts or statistics: Use real facts of statistics to grab the attention of your reader

Sensory Details: Tell a mini-story or write a description that directly relates to your topic to draw your reader into your essay creatively before you get to the "meat of your essay."

(For more information on this, see Section 3)

1. Attention Getter

There are several techniques that we can use to grab the attention of our readers.

Each of these are effective ways to begin an essay. Some of them require a little bit of research. Sometimes, you may encounter a situation, such as a standardized test, where you do not have the ability to look up outside information, and you will have to come up with an introduction without any research. In this case, using a mini-story is a very effective way to begin any essay.

For example, if your essay topic was about a career you might want to pursue, you could write about doing something related to the future career. Then, you would incorporate the thesis statement. It might look like this:

As I sit at the table in front of me, I sigh. On it sits a model rocket and its assembly instructions. On the paper is a complicated schematic <u>that shows the rocket and its components. Next to the diagram are</u>

the instructions of how to put the rocket together. The words might as well be Portuguese for how well I understand them. I sigh again and take another shot at trying to decipher the words. They seem to bunch together, and then fall off the page into a pile of senseless jargon. I moan in frustration and push myself away from the table. If I ever want to be a mechanical engineer and design machines, I have to understand machines and their different parts. I know that to become an engineer, I would have to work hard in school to get good grades and at my job to get good pay, but if I make it past the initial trials, I know that it will be worth it. —Caleb S., 14

Do you see how the mini-story directly tied in with the subject of the essay?

Any number of stories might have worked in this situation: studying difficult math, building a go-cart with his dad, or successfully flying the rocket he built. There are endless possibilities! As long as the mini-story directly relates to the topic of the essay, and more specifically the thesis statement, then you can be as creative as you want. However, you still want to be brief. You don't want to confuse your reader into thinking that you are writing a short story instead of an essay. Limit your introduction to a short moment in order to grab the attention of your reader without distracting them from the important points of your topic.

2. Introduces the topic and gives any needed information

Once you have gotten the reader's attention, you need to introduce the topic. Sometimes this element is included and implied in the attention getter and thesis (as in the example above in the second to last sentence), but often you will need to give a little more information about the topic before you give your thesis statement.

"True friends aren't phony with you. They show you who they really are. They're honest with you when it matters most. They never try to deceive you to make themselves seem stronger, more successful, or better than they really are" (Smykowski). This is what Mercutio and Alan are to the main characters in Romeo and Juliet and Kidnapped. Romeo and Juliet is a drama where two people fall in love. The issue is that they're both from families that are in a feud against each other. Even so, they get married. Romeo was banished and in the end, they both committed suicide for each other. Kidnapped is a book about a boy named David. He gets sold into slavery, put on a wanted poster, and files a lawsuit on his uncle. With the help of his older friend Alan, David becomes a man. Although Mercutio and Alan are characters in very different books, they both support the main character with their wits, willingness to fight, and loyalty.

—Isaac F., 14

Notice how this introduction starts with an attention getter (a quote), then explains the topic (two books)—but he needs to make sure the audience remembers what each book is about before he gets to his thesis statement.

The amount of information you need to give in an introduction depends on the topic and what your audience needs to know. The could include: definitions of important words, a summary of an event, a quick plot synopsis of a book, an explanation of what happened right before the event you will be discussing, or a preview of your argument.

3. Thesis Statement

We have already talked about the thesis statement in **Chapter 4**. When you connect your thesis to the introduction paragraph, you might need to reword it a little and add a transition so that it flows smoothly in the paragraph.

Conclusions

A **conclusion** is an important component of your paper, because it is the final impression you leave with your audience - your final words on this topic. Your conclusion ties together your thesis statement and your supporting points and gives your audience a lasting sense of why your topic matters.

Just like an introduction, a conclusion has three elements:

1. Restates your thesis statement
2. Summarizes the main points and ties up loose ends
3. Connects the topic to a larger idea or issue or makes a call to action

Notice that the conclusion is in the opposite order of the introduction—an introduction ends with the thesis statement, but the conclusion starts with it.

1. Restates thesis

Reword your thesis statement from the beginning of the essay. Your thesis statement should not sound exactly the same as it did in the introduction, but it should also not include entirely different ideas! In order to reword your thesis, using a thesaurus is quite helpful.

2. Summarizes the main points and ties up loose ends

This part of your conclusion functions in a similar way as the second part of your introduction—it gives additional information that the reader might need to fully understand your topic.

This is not a place to add new supporting information. Rather, you are summarizing what you said throughout the paper and pulling it all together to show your reader that you have effectively proven your thesis.

3. Connecting the topic to a larger idea/call to action

One way to think about this point is to imagine you are answering the question "So what?" from your readers, or perhaps "Why does this matter and what should I do about it?". You've spent all this time showing or proving your thesis to your readers. But why should they care? How might this topic affect their life, or the lives of those close to them? This is where you tell them!

Different genres of essays will require different kinds of connections to larger topics or call to actions. For example, in a book review of *Anne of Green Gables*, you may want to connect the relevance of the book to the idea that many young women have wild imaginations or feel misunderstood by those around them so they should read the book. In contrast, in a persuasive essay about plastic, you may want to call your readers to action by telling them practical ways to be more eco-conscious when they use plastic.

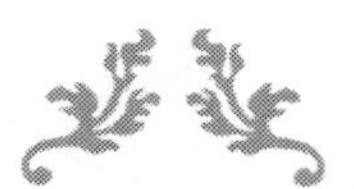

A conclusion is NOT:

- Only one or two sentences
- A place to say everything that you forgot to say in your essay.
- A place to restate every topic sentence in your paper.
- A place to introduce a brand-new idea

Conclusions always leave the reader with a sense of finality. Writers can create that sense by carefully combing through the essay's introduction and seeing if there is any element from the introduction that can be referenced in the conclusion. For example, if you began with a mini-story, you may want to briefly allude back to that or create a "bookend" mini-story to balance out or continue that story. If you began with a quotation or question, you may want to respond to that quote or question in the conclusion, now that the reader is familiar with the topic.

If you can't find a way to connect your conclusion to your introduction, it's quite possible that your introduction needs some more revision. Try going back and revising your introduction so that you CAN make that final connection in your conclusion!

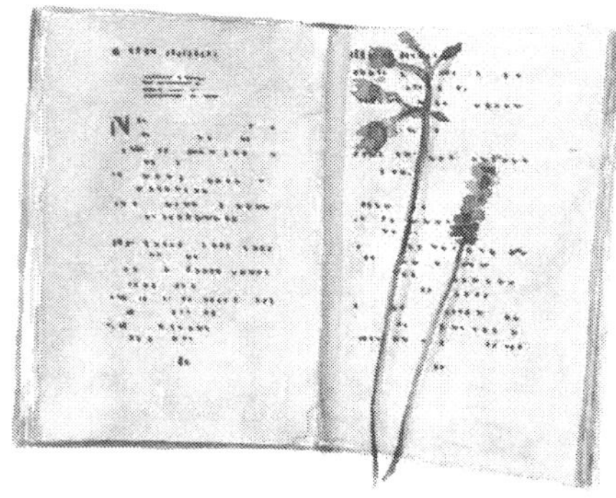

Activities

Key Terms

Define the following key terms: introduction, attention getter, conclusion

Comprehension

1) What are the elements you need in an introduction?
2) What are the elements you need in a conclusion?
3) How are the introduction and conclusion linked?

Practice

For each of these examples, write an attention getter using the technique listed

1) Topic: expanding unemployment benefits
   Technique: Question
2) Topic: Taking care of the elderly
   Technique: mini-story
3) Topic: Abraham Lincoln
   Technique: Quote

Application

1) Find a good introduction in another source (newspaper, magazine, online article, textbook, etc). Then write an explanation about why it is a good example.
2) Find a good conclusion in another source (newspaper, magazine, online article, textbook, etc). Then write an explanation about why it is a good example.
3) Find a good introduction AND conclusion in another source (newspaper, magazine, online article, textbook, etc). Then write an explanation about how they link the two together successfully.

More activities and student examples available at **www.writefromtheheart.org/resourceguide**.

Section 3: Voice Techniques

Mickey Mouse turns to Goofy and says, "Gosh, I guess you're right, pal!"

Porky Pig pops his head through the screen and declares, "Th- Th- That's all folks!"

As you read each of these, did you hear the voice of the speaker? Everyone has a certain way of speaking and putting words together. Your voice is as unique as you are. A strange thing happens when we write, though. Somehow, we have come to believe that our voice only belongs in creative writing—if we are writing a persuasive paper or a research project, it needs to sound "scholarly," which is really code for "cold and removed from the way I actually sound." This is a lie! Unfortunately, it's a lie that is perpetuated by some very well-known writing programs that focus on writing as a "formula" that you learn: understand the parts of writing, plug in a few adjectives, switch out a couple nouns, and voila! You've written a paper.

You might know how to create a piece of writing, but that type of writing is as far from the art of writing as a jar of spaghetti sauce is from an Italian grandmother's secret all-day recipe. You don't want jar of spaghetti sauce writing. You want masterpieces—you want the all-day secret recipe sauce kind of writing! And the great thing about this is that if you add your voice back into writing, suddenly "boring" writing assignments are no longer boring—you don't have to hide who you are when you are writing! This section is going to teach you how to add the spice of your voice into all kinds of writing.

Chapter 8: Elements of Voice

Your voice is what breathes life into your writing. It is what changes your work into an artistic expression of YOU. While structure and organization are both necessary, voice is the spark of life in all your creations. And the great part about voice is that you already have it. You don't need to learn a new skill...you just have to look for opportunities to use it and grow it!

But what exactly is "voice in writing"? **Voice** refers to the mixture of personality, tone, point of view, vocabulary, and syntax that conveys the authorship of a piece of writing. A writer with a well-developed voice can write in any style and it can be identified as their work.

Personality

Personality is the unique piece of you that you bring to everything you create. Just as you have aspects of personality in everyday life, you can highlight those attributes to bring flair and flavor to your writing. Think of how people would describe you and how you would describe yourself. Maybe your math teacher would call you dedicated. Your choir teacher thinks you're dramatic. Your friends would vote you the class clown. You can use those attributes in your writing. Don't be afraid to include your passion, your intensity or your humor in your writing. Own it!

One way to do this is to write like you talk. Make it sound like you. As mentioned in **Chapter 2**, you should have different ways of expressing yourself for your audience. You might think (or say), "Neil Armstrong was so cool! Can you imagine being the first person to walk on the moon?" In your paper, you could write, "Neil Armstrong was an impressive figure, with the unimaginable distinction of being the first person to walk on the moon." Your passion for space and astronauts will come through.

When you finish your assignment and you read through it, it should sound like something you would enjoy reading. Let's say the assignment is to write about the Civil War. There are people who are drawn to facts and figures, and they may include statistics about army size, battles fought, and lives lost in their paper. Other people are drawn to a good story, and they might choose to tell the story of nurse Clara Barton. Someone with a passion for justice might talk about Harriet Tubman's role in the war. And someone with a sense of humor might mention that Mark Twain fired one shot in the war and then left. I tend to be drawn to the unusual and unique. When I was in college, I wrote my senior history project on women who disguised themselves as men and enlisted in the armies of both the North and the South—there were more than 400 of them who successfully fought in battles!

If you are authentic in your writing, you will infuse your writing with your personality and when someone else reads it, it will be like they're getting to know you!

Tone

Have you ever said something to your mom, and she responds with "don't take that tone with me, young lady!" What is she upset about? It's not *what* you said; it's the *way* you said it. That's **tone**.

In order to convey your tone when the reader can't hear you, use word choice, imagery, and details. Tone can change within the same story. There are many examples of tone: scared, excited, sarcastic, depressed, wondering, confused, happy—really, any adjective you can think of! The tone of the piece shows the reader what the author is feeling.

Think of the description of a lovely valley, with the sun gleaming off a slow-moving stream and the sound of birds in the trees. Imagery like this will convey a peaceful tone. But if the author adds in some ominous dark clouds, and a rumble of thunder, the tone has changed to foreboding. Then when the rain comes whipping down and lightning transforms the landscape into something unrecognizable, the author could be showing fear. And when the sun comes out again and water drips from the leaves, he feels relief.

For example, in Edgar Allan Poe's "A Tell-Tale Heart," nervousness and guilt build throughout the story. The emphasis added with capital letters, quick sentences and the repetition of the word "louder" make the reader feel the same emotions as the narrator:

> It was a low, dull, quick sound—much such a sound as a watch makes when enveloped in cotton. I gasped for breath—and yet the officers heard it not. I talked more quickly—more vehemently; but the noise steadily increased. I arose and argued about trifles, in a high key and with violent gesticulations; but the noise steadily increased. Why would they not be gone? I paced the floor to and fro with heavy strides, as if excited to fury by the observations of the men—but the noise steadily increased....What could I do? I foamed—I raved—I swore! I swung the chair upon which I had

> been sitting, and grated it upon the boards, but the noise arose over all and continually increased. It grew louder —louder —louder!

As you write, think about the feeling you want to convey to your audience and make sure to pick adjectives and other words that express that feeling.

Point of View

The **point of view** refers to the perspective the author takes as they write. Which perspective they take is called **person**. A piece of writing can be in either first person, second person or third person. Depending on what style of writing you are doing, you will need to decide which point of view to use, and if it is appropriate to use more than one.

First person uses "I," "me," "my," "mine" and "we" pronouns to narrate the story from the perspective of the main characters. Here's an example from a student paper:

> I slid down onto the ground and curled up in a ball, my anger gone and replaced with raw desperation. A tear dashed down my cheek. The situation felt irreparable. I knew that in thirty minutes I would need to be speaking words in front of an audience, but what those articles would be, evaded me. Tears came more freely now; they slipped off the side of my cheek onto the moistened carpet. —Erin T., 13

This perspective is best utilized in personal narratives and in fictional works. In academic writing, comparative essays - in which the writer makes some sort of decision - typically use the first-person voice. In most other essays, the third-person voice typically works best for beginning writers. Advanced writers do use the first-person voice in parts of some essays, but it is sometimes difficult to avoid "I think" language until you have more practice.

Second person uses "you" pronouns. This is an unusual choice for most narratives. It's harder to establish a connection as an author with your audience when you use "you" pronouns. But when it's done properly it can be very effective. Here's an example from *A Moveable Feast* by Ernest Hemingway:

> You expected to be sad in the fall. Part of you died each year when the leaves fell from the trees and their branches were bare against the wind and the cold, wintery light. But you knew there would always be the spring, as you knew the river would flow again after it was frozen.

Most of the time, you will not use second person in your assignments. Formal papers should not refer to the reader directly, although that can be a hard rule to follow. Sometimes, the writer does not use the pronouns, but the second-person voice is implied. For example, in a recipe for chocolate chip cookies, the directions might say, "Mix the flour, eggs, sugar, vanilla, and butter." The writer of the recipe doesn't say "*You should* mix the flour, eggs, sugar, vanilla, and butter," but the "you" is implied. Implying the "you" is generally considered more acceptable in academic writing.

Typically, the second-person voice works best in letters, directions, and recipes. This perspective usually does not appear in academic writing. If you are making a general statement at the end of an essay, avoid using the second-person voice. For example, if you are writing an essay about the benefits of recycling, at the end of the essay, you may want to encourage your audience to recycle. You might be tempted to say, "You should try recycling. Even small changes to your habits can make a big difference." But this is not the strongest way to write in academic work. Instead of using the second-person voice, you could instead stay in the third-person: "Recycling is worth trying. Even small changes to a person's daily habits can make a big difference."

There are exceptions (like this book, for example!). It is best to discuss this with the teacher who gave the assignment to see how you should handle this.

Third person uses "he/she/they" and "him/her/them" pronouns. Where first person writing allows for a lot of emotional development, third person allows for a great deal of description. The third-person voice works well in nonfiction pieces, essays, fiction, and much more. The third-person voice is extremely versatile, so writers use it quite often.

Third person is used the most often for factual papers. An expository narrator writes in the third-person perspective in a more distant, objective way. Expository narrators are impersonal; they do not know the inner thoughts and feelings of individuals or characters. As a result, expository narrative style is typically not used by writers in fictional works. **See Chapter 14** for more information on using third person in narratives.

However, expository narrative perspective is important in non-fiction works, such as expository essays, textbooks, and directions. News articles are typically great examples of expository narration. Newswriters do not claim to know the emotions of individuals they cover in articles. However, if those individuals share something that they thought or felt during an experience, a journalist can report on that information using a quote. This what third person looks like in a student example from an informative essay on horse-riding:

Exercising is linked to riding horses because if someone gets on a horse and expects to ride perfectly their first time that won't happen! They first need to build up leg and core muscles. This is something that they can either exercise for or just let happen in riding lessons. Many people think that riding horses is easy and doesn't take much effort, but it actually takes a lot of strength and persistence. —Julia R., 11

Every type of writing has a structure that lends itself to a different point of view from the author. As you look at the assignment you are given, make sure to consider what perspective you should be writing from. The sections discussing individual styles of writing (**Section 4**, **Section 5**, and **Section 7**) will help you make those decisions.

Vocabulary

Vocabulary is the list of words you are aware of that you can use to communicate effectively. You may have a list of words that you typically use, a list of words that you know but may not come to mind quickly, and a list of words that you only understand in context. The best way to build your vocabulary is to read more and read different genres. Students are often assigned lists of vocabulary words to memorize but knowing the meaning of omniscient, perplexed or prestidigitation doesn't add any value if you can't employ them in your writing. There are resources to help you, though, and they're as common as your dictionary and your thesaurus.

Vocabulary Tip:
Pick a word that fits your voice.
If the word you choose doesn't sound natural to the way you talk, it will sound ridiculous.

The biggest mistake people make when using a **thesaurus** is choosing a big word, often one with many syllables, to sound intelligent or impressive. Don't do this! You should never use the thesaurus for words you wouldn't use in your normal speech or for words whose definitions you don't know. For example, let's say you have this in your paper: "A storm is coming. Those clouds look dangerous." Dangerous doesn't feel like the right word, so you use the thesaurus. Maybe "threatening" was the word you were looking for, but the thesaurus offers "fatal, perilous, and precarious" as options, and none of these have quite the right meaning. Every word in a thesaurus is *similar* in meaning, but not exactly the *same*. May sure to pick the right one, or you could end up sounding fantastic (an alternate option for silly)!

A thesaurus is a good tool to nudge your memory when a word is on the tip of your tongue. If you find your essays are repetitive and you want to avoid overusing a particular word, you can use the thesaurus to find alternate words with similar meaning. When you want choices for your words or you aren't sure you have the right word and you want to compare it with its synonyms, the thesaurus can be helpful. When you want a strong, precise word, the thesaurus is there for you once again.

Syntax

Syntax is the arrangement of words and phrases to create well-formed sentences in a language. By rearranging the words in a sentence, you can change the emphasis and sometimes the meaning. These three sentences have the same words and essentially the same meaning, but maybe you prefer one of them as sounding "right" compared to the other two.

The dog barked loudly.

Loudly, the dog barked.

The dog loudly barked.

Sometimes, though, moving a word changes the meaning of the sentences. By moving the word "only" in the following sentences, the meaning changes:

- Mrs. Smith liked only the cookies. (Translation: The cookies were the only dessert that Mrs. Smith liked.)
- Only Mrs. Smith liked the cookies. (Translation: No one but Mrs. Smith liked the cookies.)
- Mrs. Smith only liked the cookies. (Translation: Mrs. Smith thought the cookies were mediocre—she liked them, but didn't love them.)

Syntax is a way to help your own natural speaking rhythms come through in your writing. But as you can see from the example above, there are rules for following proper word order depending on the sentence. You can find more information about these grammar rules in **Section 9**.

Activities

Key Terms

Define the following key terms: voice, personality, tone, point of view, first person, second person, third person, vocabulary, syntax

Comprehension

1) What elements combine to make up your voice?
2) Which point of view do you find it easiest to write in—first, second or third person? Why?

Practice

1) Rewrite the Ernest Hemingway quote from *A Moveable Feast* from second person to third.
2) What are five things about yourself that you can incorporate into your writing when appropriate?

Application

1) Create a paragraph the way you talk, then go back and rewrite it with your audience (an adult you know who isn't a family member) in mind.
2) Choose a topic to inform others about—a hobby, an event, a person—and write an essay explaining that topic and why it's important for others to know about it. Include elements of voice.

More activities and student examples available at **www.writefromtheheart.org/resourceguide**.

Chapter 9: Playing with Voice: Descriptive Details

Which is better?

"It was a cold and foggy day."

OR

> It was cold, bleak, biting weather, foggy withal and he could hear the people in the court outside go wheezing up and down, beating their hands upon their breasts, and stamping their feet upon the paving stones to warm them. The city clocks had only just gone three, but it was quite dark already—it had not been light all day—and candles were flaring in the windows of the neighboring offices, like ruddy smears on the palpable air. The fog came pouring in at every chink and keyhole, and was so dense without, that, although the court was of the narrowest, the houses opposite were mere phantoms. — *A Christmas Carol,* by Charles Dickens

Obviously, the second one right? It really gives you a picture of what is happening in the scene, and you can see, hear, and even smell the moment. This is what **descriptive detail** does. When writing, your passage can seem bland without descriptive words and phrases. There are several different ways to add descriptive detail to your work.

Use Your Senses

When someone says, "describe this," beginning writers often only think about what something looks like. But that is only one of the ways you can use your senses to describe. You already know your five senses: hearing, sight, smell, touch, and taste. They're the key to unlocking true communication between

your work and the reader's sensory response. **Sensory details** are descriptive details that utilize each of your five senses (often in combination) to describe something. Take a look at these examples:

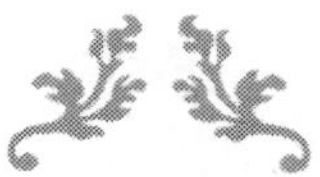

Sight: The sharp-nosed pedestrian marched steadily on, with the blue cloak streaming out behind him like a banner; and the lively infant splashed through the puddles with a duck-like satisfaction pleasant to behold. —"Transcendental Wild Oats," by Louisa May Alcott

Hearing: A light wind began blowing past my ears. It whispered secrets only I could hear. —*The Joy Luck Club*, by Amy Tan

Touch: She held my hand impersonally, as a promise that she'd take care of me in a minute and gave ear to two girls in twin yellow dresses who stopped at the foot of the stairs.
—*The Great Gatsby*, by F. Scott Fitzgerald

Smell: To each other, we were as normal and nice as the smell of bread. We were just a family. In a family, even exaggerations make sense. —*Cider House Rules*, by John Irving

Taste: I perceived I had got in hand a nauseous mess: burnt porridge is almost as bad as rotten potatoes; famine itself soon sickens over it. —*Jane Eyre*, by Charlotte Bronte

When you describe with your senses, try to use more than one of your senses to create a well-rounded scene instead of just a visual. Think of the painter Bob Ross capturing the basics of his subject before he starts to add details, transforming a blank canvas into an intricate scene full of happy little trees. You may think he could be finished countless times, but he continues to add detail and layers onto the canvas until he's satisfied with his masterpiece. Adding more than one sense to your description can take your writing from a stick drawing to a work of art! To help you do this, think about when you look at a landscape. What do you notice? Are there people? What is the background? How does it make you feel? And what's happening now?

Example:

As the boy was walking along the coast of the ocean, he could hear the calm waves and the squawking of the seagulls. Suddenly, he felt a crunch under his feet. He looked down and saw a small piece of plastic. It must have been another plastic bottle someone had littered, he thought to himself.

—Lucas H., 14

Describing People

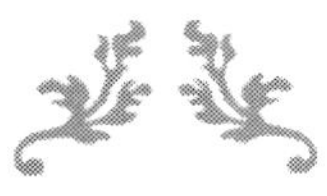

Describe people using action and gestures. Writing with details does not mean writing exactly.

When describing people, you can draw a picture with words that allows the reader to picture the character in their mind. You don't have to describe every little detail—most people will picture something different no matter how much information you give them. Instead, say as much as possible about a person with only a few well-chosen details—and don't just describe their clothes, but other sensory details!

> Aunt Sponge was enormously fat and very short. She had small piggy eyes, a sunken mouth, and one of those white flabby faces that looked exactly as though it had been boiled.
>
> —*James and the Giant Peach*, by Roald Dahl

It's easier to describe gestures, body movements, or actions than to describe faces. This author is describing a character's response to a pretty avenue. Instead of saying, "She looks amazed. Her face was surprised, and she liked the view." This is how she described her:

> Its beauty seemed to strike the child dumb. She leaned back in the buggy, her thin hands clasped before her, her face lifted rapturously to the white splendor above. Even when they had passed out and were driving down the long slope to Newbridge she never moved or spoke. Still with rapt face she gazed afar into the sunset west, with eyes that saw visions trooping splendidly across that glowing background.
>
> —*Anne of Green Gables,* by L.M. Montgomery

Notice how you don't know exactly what this character looks like, but you definitely know how she *feels*, which is the most important thing. However, we got a few details: she's a child, she has thin hands (which means she is probably underweight and skinny), and she has a very expressive face. This is a good example of blending action with details to describe a person. Writing specifically does not mean writing exactly.

This is a common mistake that many writers make. When asked to describe someone, they create a list of specific details and think this is describing. But just listing details does not create a description—combining details with the senses and action does! For example, if you were describing a giant, you could say, "He was seven feet four inches tall." But that's pretty boring. Instead, look at this:

> The Giant was sprinting down the High Street. He was running so fast his black cloak was streaming out behind him like the wings of a bird. Each stride he took was as long as a tennis court. Out of the village he ran, and soon they were racing across the moonlit fields. The hedges dividing the fields were no problem to the Giant. He simply strode over them. A wide river appeared in his path. He crossed it in one flying stride.
>
> —*The BFG,* by Roald Dahl

There's a lot of action here—and the hugeness of this giant is clear by what he is doing rather than giving specific dimensions. An additional note: This quote also uses figurative language, which you can read about in **Chapter 12**.

Describing Places

Many authors forget to describe their characters' surroundings or say the bare minimum. "He walked home." What does this tell the reader? Nothing, really. But setting can be used in several ways to not only make the story interesting, but to add details about the mood or thoughts of a character.

> Archer walked home alone. Darkness was falling when he let himself into his house, and he looked about at the familiar objects in the hall as if he viewed them from the other side of the grave.
>
> —*The Age of Innocence,* by Edith Wharton

Setting can be used to not only give a complete description of the scene but put your reader in the time period or location with the characters. You can choose details within the setting to show your character's mood or personality.

Describing Feelings

The easiest way to convey feelings is to use adverbs, but it isn't the best way. Have you ever read a section of dialogue where every line ends in -ly?

"Thanks," he said gratefully.

"No problem," she replied, airily.

"No, really, I mean it," he said sincerely.

While it tells the reader how the characters are feeling, it's not interesting to read, and it's easy to skip over. Instead, you can describe the feeling using language that describes the feeling rather than states it. Here is an example from a student:

Jim pulled his blanket up over his Mario Kart pajamas and up to his chest. He took a huge sip of hot chocolate and then teased the steam with his breath. Ah, peace and comfort, Jim thought. He flopped his English book upright onto his lap. Suddenly noticing the bus, he took a deep relaxing breath. "Ahhhhh," Jim expressed. The bus came to a screeching stop, and he watched as the children took their heavy burdens upon their backs and boarded the yellow chamber to school. —Noah B., 15

You can see how the character expresses he is happy to be schooling at home without the author ever saying that he was happy.

Using sensory details and body language is a good way to do this. Using figurative language (explained in **Chapter 12**) is a great resource as well.

Describing Action

They say a picture is worth a thousand words. But you can do that with your description. Think of a descriptive passage as a way to take a snapshot of a moment and dive into each detail that makes the picture come alive.

You can use a tiny action to describe a big emotion. Some may be cliche - a single tear running down someone's cheek, closing a book to symbolize the end, seeing someone come towards you and turning away—but they may still be effective. In this example, the character had his feelings hurt. But instead of saying "the boy felt like the girl was mean to him" the author uses an action to show how badly he was hurt:

> The little wretch had done her utmost to hurt her cousin's sensitive though uncultured feelings....He afterwards gathered the books and hurled them on the fire.
>
> —*Wuthering Heights*, by Emily Bronte

In some ways, writing can be more powerful than a picture, because you can combine action with description to express emotion.

Putting It All Together

No matter what your topic, *all* your descriptions should be translated into something your reader can understand and feel through the five senses. If you can master the art of appealing to all five senses, you create a well-rounded conversation between the writing and the reader's imagination. You can describe a setting, a person, and a feeling all while moving the action forward.

By including sensory details, you're no longer talking to the reader; instead, you give the reader a chance to view the world from your eyes. Here's an example from a previous student:

Dinner was ready, and we all gathered around the table. Everything looked great; the table was set neatly, the food was colorful, and everyone was happy. Or, in my case, trying to look happy. I sighed inwardly as I looked down at the food. After a prayer, my heart nearly died as I watched my plate receive a spoonful of the casserole. I could tell it wasn't that big, but I was nervous. It was a looming mountain of pain and suffering. I silently prayed my own prayer as Mrs. Holland set my plate in front of me. I took a deep breath. Then, very quickly, I shoved my fork in my mouth. At first, the pierogies tasted alright; cheese and potato mixed together to create a simple, pleasant taste, but only for a second. The texture made me feel like gagging. It was almost squishy-like and lumpy; I could feel each piece of potato in my mouth, each one daring me to gag. —Benjamin C., 15

Notice how the author uses sensory details and vivid descriptions to create this whole moment of agony. It's very creative, and as a reader, we feel as though we are right there with him!

Using Descriptive Details in Academic Papers

So far, we have been discussing voice using fictional examples or personal stories. But what if we are writing an essay for English, a research paper for history class, or a persuasive letter to the editor? Can we still use descriptive details?

YES!!

This is a big mistake that students make—and a lot of adults, too! Academic writing is often more formal and professional sounding than a fictional story. But that does NOT mean you should lose your voice. Remember from **Chapter 8** that your voice is made up of your personality, tone, point of view, vocabulary, and syntax. Descriptive detail is part of that! Here's a student's opening in an informative paper about competitive dancing:

The dancers were all crowded in the green room with their faces up against the mirrors. Moms had eyeliners in their hands and were cupping their children's faces. The dancers were chatting and putting finishing touches on hair and makeup. Once they were done, the Juniors got everyone in their group together and headed backstage a few numbers before their dance. They joined together in a huddle, leaned in, and put their arms around each other. —Annie H., 12

In your academic writing, look for places to use your senses. Often, this could be in the introduction when you are catching the reader's attention, or at the end when you are explaining why something is important in the real world. But you can put it other places too:

- When you are describing a problem in a persuasive paper, you should make sure your reader understands the emotional impact or consequences in peoples' lives.
- In a research paper, you can use descriptive detail to highlight an important moment in the person's life, or the climax of an event.
- If you are comparing two locations or items or possibilities, you should be using sensory details to describe them.
- When explaining an activity or hobby, you can create a description of what participants are like while they are doing the activity.

But remember: in nonfiction papers, you cannot make up facts. All of your descriptions need to be true and verifiable. You can describe the way a laptop looks and feels, but you cannot describe what Queen Victoria was thinking when she was a child. However, there is a great loophole that a lot of writers love to use: the hypothetical. A **hypothetical example** is a clearly fictional example that is used to explain a situation or a feeling. These need to be marked as clearly fictional using signal words like "imagine..." or "perhaps..." and it is best to add a disclaimer such as "although it is not possible to know for sure.." or "this is just one way that it could have happened..." If you do this, then you CAN create a sensory picture of what Queen Victoria was doing, but you need to make sure you mark it as fictional. Here's what a hypothetical example looks like in a student's paper. Note the underlined sentence begins with "perhaps":

In fact, Queen Victoria had a fonder disposition towards her governess than towards her mother the Duchess. Perhaps Victoria despised her mother's dependence on Sir John Conroy - an overbearing man who had "hopes of exercising power during a regency" (Epton 13). When she was young, she was raised by the 'Kensington System', which involved "sharing a room with her mother and having no time alone" (Williams). The way that she was paraded around grew tiresome to Victoria, and she resented the way she was used.

—Addie D., 16

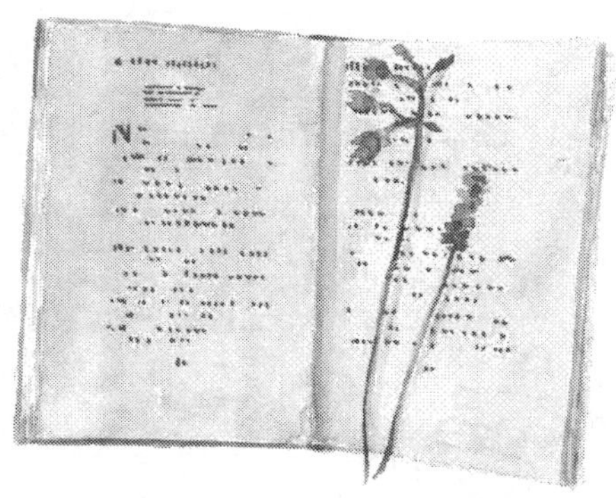

Activities

Key Terms

Define the following key terms: descriptive details, sensory details, hypothetical example

Comprehension

1) Explain the best way to communicate the features and personality of a character in a narrative.
2) What are the areas where sensory details can enhance your narrative?
3) How can you use descriptive details in nonfiction writing?

Practice

1) Write a sentence describing an object you can see from where you're sitting.
2) Write a sentence describing a feeling.

Application

1) Choose a setting and write a paragraph describing it using sensory details.
2) Choose a person and write a paragraph describing them using sensory details.
3) Write an essay explaining which holiday is the best one to celebrate. In your supporting paragraphs, be sure to use descriptive details to make your points come alive.

More activities and student examples available at **www.writefromtheheart.org/resourceguide**.

Chapter 10: Playing with Voice: Inner Ideas

> I first heard of Antonia on what seemed to me an interminable journey across the great midland plain of North America. I was ten years old then; I had lost both my father and mother within a year, and my Virginia relatives were sending me out to my grandparents, who lived in Nebraska.
> —opening lines of *My Antonia* by Willa Cather

What a wonderful way to start a story! We wonder who Antonia is, who this narrator is, and what happened when he moved to Nebraska. The narrator, it is obvious, is flashing back to his youth and pondering his experiences. These **inner ideas** are important in stories and essays because they give the reader a reason to be interested in a character. An inner thought allows you to "climb inside" a character's mind. This technique is especially helpful if you find yourself stuck in linear plot details (this happened, then that, then that). It's fun to put inner ideas into creative writing: a character can talk to herself, or in a memoir you can tell the reader what you were thinking in a specific moment.

In academic papers, it can feel harder to add inner thoughts, since you don't know what exactly what a real person was thinking in a real situation. And since those types of papers are factual, you can't just make something up! But you don't need to abandon this technique of spicing up your writing in essays and research papers— you can play with inner ideas in a factual way, too. In each type of inner idea below, we will look at where it can be used in fictional writing as well as in nonfiction writing. There are four main types of inner ideas that can be used successfully in any type of writing.

Flashback

In a **flashback**, a character (or writer) thinks of something in the past. It is a return to something that happened previously. This is a good way to break up linear order of plot, or to draw connections between something that happens in the present to something that happened in the past.

> Lately, however, this business about being equals started to bother me. It's been on my mind, only I didn't really know it. I just felt a little uneasy about something. And then, about a week ago, it all became clear. —*The Joy Luck Club*, by Amy Tan

In academic papers, we cannot make up flashbacks, but we can use a transition sentence to show the audience that we are going back in time:

> The small, colorful room in Walt Disney's house was very quiet. There was a large desk where Walt Disney was sitting. Imagine: the faint scraping sound of his dull pencil danced on a rough piece of paper. He drew a circular head, a round nose, two small eyes, a long tail, a short, slim body, and finally, big, black ears. Walt had finished one of his most famous cartoon characters, Mickey Mouse. Perhaps Walt thought, "It looks pretty good. I wonder what I should do with it... Maybe I can turn it into an animation! I wonder if people will like it." —Emily H., 13

Flash Forward

In a **flash forward**, the speaker thinks about what the future might hold. It is similar to a flashback, but it is imagining what will come next.

> Antanas was a boy! And he was as tough as a pine-knot, and with the appetite of a wolf. Nothing had hurt him and nothing would hurt him.... The more of a fighter he was, the better—he would need to fight before he got through.
> —*The Jungle*, by Upton Sinclair

In nonfiction papers, this is useful in conclusions, especially for persuasive papers when imaging what the world would look like if the problem was fixed. This can be a hypothetical example, or it can be a quote from someone. It can only be fictional if it is clearly marked as hypothetical.

> Imagine a different scenario. After going home and practicing their individual parts, the student quartet comes together for another rehearsal. They realize their mistake in being unprepared, and they try playing their piece again. This time, they produce a sweet, melodious

sound that floats through the building and amazes passersby. Once they finish the piece, they realize that they have learned to struggle through practice, to work as a team and make beautiful music, and to patiently work through their mistakes. As they lift their instruments to play the piece again, they feel satisfied with their work and ready for their performance a few days later. —Mari S., 13

Internal Debate

In an **internal debate**, the speaker or character wrestles internally with their own thoughts and choices. This is a good way to show inner conflict as well as a way to question the motives of other characters.

> There must be something in books, things we can't imagine, to make a woman stay in a burning house; there must be something there. You don't stay for nothing.
> —*Fahrenheit 451*, by Ray Bradbury

This is a good technique to use when a character is trying to make a decision or is weighed down by their conscience.

In academic writing, we cannot know the inner debates of other people unless they tell us! You cannot make up a conflict unless you find a quote that shows the person was struggling internally. Because of the limits on it, this type of inner idea is rarely used in nonfiction writing. However, you can create a hypothetical situation and then lead into the material from the essay. You must clearly note that it is not real or make sure the reader understands that it is an example. This is a student example from a persuasive paper on preventing traffic jams:

The sounds of car horns are echoing all over the highway. But they are of no avail to the sea of cars blocking the road. The traffic jam stretches for few kilometers. A young office worker on his way to work is sitting exasperated in his car. As he looks around him, he sees no exit from this enormous prison of cars and people. Why doesn't that car in front of me move? This road is supposed to be a highway! This type of problem happens every day on highways across the country. —Jay K., 14

It is clear by that last sentence that this is not a real person but is representative of a larger problem.

Feelings and Emotions

We can use inner ideas to express the emotions of a character or speaker through thought.

> It was not until he happened to need his scissors that the terrible fact burst upon him: Eppie had run out by herself—had perhaps fallen into the Stone Pit. Silas, shaken by the worst fear that could have befallen him, rushed out, calling 'Eppie!'"
>
> —*Silas Marner*, by George Eliot

This is an excellent technique to express what a character is thinking, either when they are alone or when they don't want the other characters to know they are lying or doubting themselves, but you want to let the reader in on that secret.

In academic writing, we again need to express these emotions using a quote or evidence that is factually based. It is certainly acceptable to draw conclusions based on what is logical about human behavior, but it is a good idea to use phrases like "it would appear" or "he must have been..." or "she was probably..." to make it clear that you are drawing a conclusion. For example, Franklin Delano Roosevelt lost both his mother and his wife to an illness in the same day. He forbid anyone to ever speak his wife's name in his presence again. It would be acceptable to say, "FDR was deeply grieved by the death of his wife and never spoke her name again. He must have felt very sad for a long time." This is drawing a conclusion without making anything up. It would NOT be acceptable to *make up* a thought like this: "FDR lost his wife and mother on the same day, and he thought to himself 'I don't think I will ever stop crying because I'm so sad!' and he never said his wife's name again." We don't know what he thought. We could use a quote from a diary or letter if we wanted to, though—that would be a factual feeling or emotion!

Punctuating Inner Ideas

In the English language, there are many punctuation rules, and spoken language requires specific ones (**see Chapter 13**). However, thoughts and feelings can sometimes be unspoken; thus, there is more flexibility. There are three different options you can choose from;

1. Put the thought in quotation marks. Use this if the thought is silent, or if the character is saying it out loud only to himself, not to another character.

You do not have to start a new paragraph unless the thought is interrupted by someone else.

> Shasta's heart gave a great jump and he had to bite his tongue to keep himself from screaming. Next moment he realized what it was: the horns of Tashbaan blowing for the closing of the gates. "Don't be a silly little coward," said Shasta to himself. "Why, it's only the same noise you heard this morning." But there is a great difference between a noise heard letting you in with your friend in the morning, and a noise heard alone at nightfall, shutting you out.
> —*The Horse and His Boy.,* by C.S. Lewis

2. **Put the thought in italics**. When you do this, you do not have to start a new paragraph just for the sake of the thought.

> I could feel everyone staring at me. I swallowed hard and blinked back tears. *If only I could do it over I know I'd make that catch.*
> —*Fudge-a-mania,* by Judy Blume

3. **Use a signal word.** Keep the thought in normal type, don't use quotations, and add a "signal word" such as "thought that," "wondered," or "said to herself."

> Anne sometimes thought wistfully that Marilla was very hard to please and distinctly lacking in sympathy and understanding.
> —*Anne of Green Gables,* by L.M. Montgomery.

Make sure that no matter the option you choose, you pick ONE option and remain consistent throughout the whole piece.

Blending Inner Ideas with Descriptive Details

Once you know how to use inner ideas, you can blend them with descriptive details, and your writing can become even more powerful! Descriptive details help you place the reader into the setting of your story or essay. By giving realistic and specific details, you create a picture in their minds. Inner ideas give you the ability to convey emotions and thoughts that aren't spoken out loud. They give the character a more three-dimensional personality and allow you to reflect or expand on the meaning of previous actions. When you add the two together, it can take your writing to the next level. You can blend them together like this:

> Meg knelt down at her mother's feet. The warmth and light of the kitchen had relaxed her so that her attic fears were gone. The cocoa steamed fragrantly in the saucepan; geraniums bloomed on the window sills and there was a bouquet of tiny yellow chrysanthemums in the center of the table. The curtains, with a

> blue and green geometrical pattern, were drawn, and seemed to reflect their cheerfulness throughout the room. The furnace purred like a great, sleepy animal; the lights glowed with steady radiance; outside, alone in the dark, the wind still battered against the house, but the angry power that had frightened Meg while she was alone in the attic was subdued by the familiar comfort of the kitchen. —*A Wrinkle in Time* by Madeline L'Engle

The first part of the paragraph describes the scene and the end of the paragraph gives you insight into how Meg feels about it.

Inner ideas can also be used to add to the narration, which helps the reader understand what's happening in a story. Take a look at this student example:

Rainbows of clothing swarmed around me. Patterns shifted and swirled, flurrying past my focus. *Where was she?* I stood in the midst of the herd of well-dressed people; my eyes scanned for the small blonde girl with blue eyes. I was beginning to lose hope of catching a glimpse of her sailboat-patterned dress. *There!* To my left, a glimpse of the pale hair peeped through the crowd. I pushed past dizzying waves of texture attached to people, muttering "Excuse me's" as I went. Suddenly, air seemed freer around my being. I was in a clearing of people, and there in the middle was the girl with blue eyes: Rita! —Erin T., 12

Notice that these inner thoughts are not particularly long or detailed. But, they add a lot of value to the moment! For instance, the paragraph opens with a description of a crowded area, but that first inner idea takes it from a simple description to providing the character's motivation: she was looking for someone!

Inner thoughts are an excellent way to provide insight into characters, reveal information, and to push forward the plot. In your own writing, try to use inner ideas when a character is making a decision or wondering about something, to increase the action or tension of a moment, and to frame the personal experience better for the reader.

Activities

Key Terms

Define the following key terms: inner ideas, flashback, flash forward, internal debate

Comprehension

1) Where are good places to add inner ideas?
2) How can you add inner ideas to non-fiction and what do you need to watch out for?

Practice

1) Find an example of each of these inner ideas in something you read: flashback, flash forward, internal debate, and feelings and emotions.
2) Write three versions of the same event to practice all three types of punctuation to add thoughts—quotation marks, italics, and within the text.

Application

1) Write a paragraph about a time you were playing outside that combines inner thoughts with sensory details.
2) Write an essay about the life of a historical person. Start your essay at a later point in their life and use a flashback transition to their childhood. Include either an internal debate or feelings and emotions somewhere else in the paper.

More activities and student examples available at **www.writefromtheheart.org/resourceguide**.

Chapter 11: Playing with Voice: Manipulating Time

You know what's one of my favorite moments in a movie? That moment where time slows down to a crawl. The music gets super intense, or there's a ringing silence filling the air. The actors are moving in slow motion, and there's usually some broken glass shattering or a bullet ripping through the scene, leaving ripples in its wake. It feels so cool to experience a moment in time where everything's basically come to a halt.

It's too bad we can't do that with writing.

Or, can we?

With a few simple techniques, we can alter the way the reader perceives time, no matter how fast they're blazing through the text.

These moments happen when the author uses a variety of techniques to make the moment drawn out, as if it were happening in slow motion. Not only does it help the reader feel the same level of disorientation the main character is feeling, but it also enables the writer to explore every detail: sounds that happen, emotions racing through veins, and visuals that the main character just can't seem to pull their eyes away from. **Slowing time down** allows all this to happen in just a short space of time, creating that slow-motion effect.

We can also do the opposite and **speed time up**. One of the great things about stories is that they skip over the boring bits. No one washes dishes or goes to the bathroom unless it's important. School days can skip from getting off the bus to lunch in the middle of the day to arriving home, and no one misses the things in between. You could cover an entire summer in just a few sentences in a memoir or summarize an entire period of a person's life in a paragraph of a research paper.

But, how do we do it? Here are just a few ways we might stretch time within our writing:

Slowing Time Down

If you want to slow down time:

- Focus on the details. Take time to describe sensory details discussed in **Chapter 9**.
- Slow down the action and build intensity by describing each movement or what every character is doing or thinking.
- Show how the character is experiencing the moment - if it seems to go on forever and they feel hyper aware of every little detail, include that in your explanation.

Remember, you want to use description to explain every moment you are expanding. If you were using a camera, this would be the moment when you freeze the action and examine it from every angle, zooming in and pausing to describe what is happening inside each character's mind. This example is from *Return of the King* by J.R.R. Tolkien:

> A brief vision Sam had of swirling cloud, and in the midst of it towers and battlements, tall as hills, founded upon a mighty mountain-throne above immeasurable pits; great courts and dungeons, eyeless prisons sheer as cliffs, and gaping gates of steel and adamant: and then all passed. Towers fell and mountains slid; walls crumbled and melted, crashing down; vast spires of smoke and spouting steams went billowing up, up, until they toppled like an overwhelming wave, and its wild crest curled and came foaming down upon the land. And then at last over the miles between there came a rumble, rising to a deafening crash and roar; the earth shook, the plain heaved and cracked, and Orodruin reeled. Fire belched from its riven summit. The skies burst into thunder seared with lightning. Down like lashing whips fell a torrent of black rain. And into the heart of the storm, with a cry that pierced all other sounds, tearing the clouds asunder, the Nazgûl came, shooting like flaming bolts, as caught in the fiery ruin of hill and sky they crackled, withered, and went out.

As you read it, can you picture the scene just as if you were watching the movie? The action seems to slow, until the towers start to fall, but you can almost feel them crashing down in slow motion until the "Fire belched" line when the action resumes normal time as the Nazgul come.

Don't rush your important parts! You really want to take the time to describe every movement and feeling. This is a good place to blend descriptive details and inner ideas as well as use figurative language. Some short stories can be pages long, but only take place in a few minutes of real time.

Speeding Time Up

If you want to speed time up, don't focus so much on every little detail. Instead, identify and highlight the important actions and use them as quick sign posts to show the passing of time. It's ok to skip the boring parts!

The key here is to use transition words like "Later that day..." "The next day..." "Next year..." "After twenty years..." Here's an example:

> But, my good master Bates died two years after, and I having few friends, my business began to fail; for my conscience would not suffer me to imitate the bad practice of too many among my brethren. Having therefore consulted with my wife, and some of my acquaintance, I determined to go again to sea. I was surgeon successfully in two ships, and made several voyages, for six years, to East and West Indies, by which I got some addition to my fortune. —*Gulliver's Travels,* by Jonathan Swift

Notice how Swift compresses large amounts of time into a few sentences; he wants to get to the important voyages the story is about instead of wasting time on the six or more years of nothing. But also note that he still uses these sentences to give us important details: this is a man with money issues, few friends, a wife, an education (he's a surgeon) and a love of the sea. He does not simply say, "I got on a boat and sailed for six years after my business went under." He still creates a tone within the sped-up time—this is a man frustrated with trying to make ends meet and wants an adventure, right? You can do the same type of thing with the details you choose to highlight as you speed over years.

One mistake that students sometimes make is in using dialogue. Sometimes, they put a conversation where a quick sentence would work better. For example, a student might write:

> I wanted to go outside and play. I found my mom.
> "Mom, can I go outside?" I asked.
> "Are you finished all your homework?" she replied.
> "Yes. And I did my chores too." I said.
> "Okay, but be back by dinnertime," she said.

This dialogue doesn't reveal anything about the story—which is what is coming when the speaker goes outside! An easy way to speed this up is to write:

I wanted to go outside and play. I told my mom I had finished my homework and chores, and she said I could play until dinner.

This is where it is good to remember the focus of your paper. If you are writing a story, you want to make sure you focus on the main problem the character has and avoid adding unnecessarily long explanations getting to the main part of the action. If you are writing a research paper, you will need to choose what parts of a person's life to highlight and what to skim over.

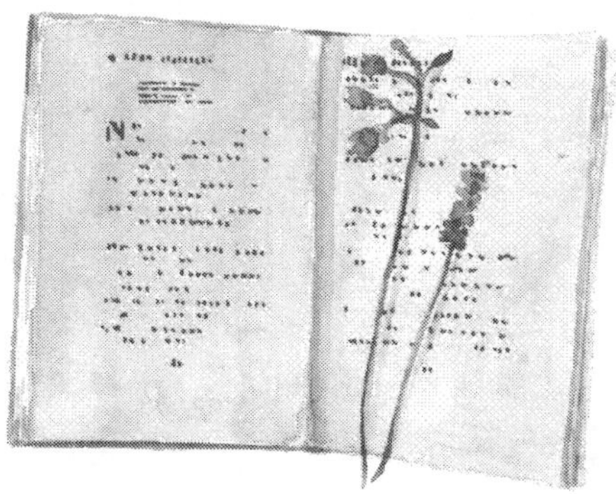

Activities

Key Terms

Define the following key terms: speeding time up, slowing time down

Comprehension

1) What are the ways you can play with time in your writing?
2) What are some ways to speed up time?
3) What are some ways to slow down time?

Practice

1) Slow down a moment and describe it in minute detail. Possible topics: scoring a goal in soccer, watching your cat pounce on a toy, tripping in front of a room full of people, winning an award.
2) Explain what you did on your last vacation in two sentences or less.

Application

1) Write paragraph about a historical figure, highlighting the most important features of their life—stick to only one paragraph!
2) Write an essay about a time when you got life changing news and what happened because of it, making sure to slow down certain moments, and speed up the parts in between.

More activities and student examples available at **www.writefromtheheart.org/resourceguide**.

Chapter 12: Playing with Voice: Figurative Language

Figurative language is language that isn't literal. Instead, the writer uses phrases that are typically used in other contexts to communicate their ideas more memorably and powerfully. It goes beyond the dictionary (or literal) meaning of the word to create a message or idea. It is divided into three categories: words, sounds and concepts.

Words

Some figurative language is all about playing with words and the relationship between them. This collection of tools creates meaning by the way the words interact: creating a connection, a humorous idea, or a picture through the combination.

Metaphors

A **metaphor** is a comparison between two items or phenomena that normally would not be connected using the words *is* or *was*.

My dad *is* an angry volcano.

We *were* couch potatoes all weekend.

Examples:

All the world's a stage / And all the men and women merely, players.
—*As You Like It,* William Shakespeare

All religions, arts and sciences are branches of the same tree.
—Albert Einstein

The sun in the west was a drop of burning gold that slid near and nearer the sill of the world. —*Lord of the Flies*, William Golding

Similes

Like a metaphor, a **simile** is a comparison between two items or phenomena that normally would not be connected but unlike a metaphor, a simile makes the comparison using the words *like* or *as:* As brave as a lion, as busy as a bee, as clear as mud.

Examples:

> Life is like a box of chocolates. —*Forrest Gump*
>
> She entered with ungainly struggle like some huge awkward chicken, torn, squawking, out of its coop.
> —*The Adventure of the Three Gables*, Sir Arthur Conan Doyle
>
> The water made a sound like kittens lapping.
> —*The Yearling*, Marjorie Kinnan Rawlings

Hyperbole

Hyperbole is when you intentionally exaggerate statements or claims in a way that isn't meant to be taken literally in order to emphasize a point.

This weighs a ton!

I'll die of embarrassment!

I haven't seen you in a million years!

Example:

> Well now, one winter it was so cold that all the geese flew backward and all the fish moved south and even the snow turned blue. Late at night, it got so frigid that all spoken words froze solid afore they could be heard. People had to wait until sunup to find out what folks were talking about the night before. —"Babe the Blue Ox," folktale retold by S.E. Schlosser

Idiom

An **idiom** is a group of words that has a meaning that can't be understood from the ordinary meanings of the words in it. Often, we would refer to it as "an expression" and we know that the phrase isn't meant to be taken literally or seriously. Idioms are particularly hard for people who learn English as a second language to grasp, and other languages have their own sayings that would be equally hard for us to understand.

I'm so tired. I have to hit the hay.

With the weather, the game is up in the air.

When he stole my girlfriend, he stabbed me in the back.

That cost an arm and a leg.

I'm all ears.

Examples:

> I tell you that, I'll never look you in the face again: but those that understood him smiled at one another and shook their heads; but, for mine own part, it was Greek to me.
> —*Julius Caesar*, William Shakespeare

Sarcasm

Sarcasm is saying the opposite of what you mean in order to insult someone, convey contempt or irritation, or to add humor. It is sometimes easier to identify sarcasm when someone is speaking versus a written statement. People often joke that there should be a "sarcasm font" to indicate when you aren't being serious. You have to use the context around the phrase to indicate that the phrase is meant to be sarcastic. As you can see in the examples below, italics, capital letters, or quotation marks can also help get the point across.

It's a beautiful day. I *really* want to clean my room, though.

You've been SO helpful.

I had the "brilliant" idea to add the ice after the cup was full and it overflowed onto the table and floor.

Example:

> Thank you for explaining that my eye cancer isn't going to make me deaf. I feel so fortunate that an intellectual giant like yourself would deign to operate on me. —*The Fault in Our Star,* John Green

Pun

A **pun** is a play on words that uses a word that sounds like another or a word that has different possible meanings to make a joke.

The tallest building in town is the library: it has thousands of stories.

Example:

> Alice: "You see the earth takes twenty-four hours to turn round on its axis—"
>
> "Talking of axes," said the Duchess, "chop off her head!"
> —*Alice in Wonderland*, Lewis Carroll

Sounds

This collection of figurative language tools is all about playing with the way words sound. This is often called the **sound quality** of words. Oftentimes, this collection is fun to read out loud, but you can still "hear" the sounds as you read.

Onomatopoeia

Besides being fun to say, an **onomatopoeia** is a word that represents a sound. Zoom, bash, bang, aargh, honk, vroom, pop and shush are all examples of an onomatopoeia.

Example:

> He saw nothing and heard nothing but he could feel his heart pounding and then he heard the clack on stone and the leaping, dropping clicks of a small rock falling.
> —*For Whom the Bell Tolls*, Ernest Hemingway

Alliteration

Alliteration is when all the words in a phrase start with the same letter. Too much alliteration in a row can sound silly, but it can also add emphasis to a poem, or to a phrase or title in a nonfiction work.

She sells seashells by the seashore

Peter Piper picked a peck of pickled peppers.

Example:

> He was four times a father, this fighter prince:
> one by one they entered the world,
> Heorogar, Hrothgar, the good Halga
> and a daughter, I have heard, who was Onela´s queen,
> a balm in bed to the battle-scarred Swede. —*Beowulf*

Assonance

Assonance is the repetition of a vowel sound across several words that are next to or close to each other.

Example:

> Once upon a midnight dreary, while I pondered, weak and weary.
> —"The Raven," Edgar Allen Poe

Consonance

Consonance is the repetition of consonants in words that are next to or close to each other. This may sound similar to alliteration, but consonance can occur in the middle or end of the word—not just the beginning.

Example:

It was many and many a year ago,
In a kingdom by the sea,
That a maiden there lived whom you may know
By the name of Annabel Lee;
And this maiden she lived with no other thought
Than to love and be loved by me.
—"Annabel Lee," Edgar Allen Poe

Concepts

This collection of figurative language tools goes beyond the meaning of the words to create a larger understanding of an idea. Sometimes these ideas are repeated throughout a work to add to a theme.

Personification

Personification is when the author describes an inanimate object as if it had human characteristics. It can also be applied to animals or concepts.

My dog grinned, proud of himself for finding his ball.

The sun smiled down on us as we hiked.

The dancing leaves whirled in the wind.

Example:

> Peace had deserted Devon. Although not in the look of the campus and village; they retained much of their dreaming summer calm. Fall had barely touched the full splendor of the trees, and during the height of the day the sun briefly regained its summertime power. —*A Separate Peace*, John Knowles

Symbolism

Symbolism is using an object or work to represent an abstract idea. An action, person, place, word, or object can all have symbolic meaning. When you want to suggest a certain mood or emotion, you can use symbolism to hint at it, instead of expressing it blatantly. For example, think of the use of colors. Red often represents love or romance. Green represents spring and new beginnings. Black may represent night or death.

Some symbols can be universal and everyone would understand them—a wedding ring represents a married person, a cross represents Christianity or religion, a heart could represent love. But some symbols are specific to a story or work.

In literature, we can analyze symbols that carry throughout the novel to point to larger ideas. In *The Scarlet Letter,* Hester Prynne is a Puritan who has to wear an "A" on her clothes as punishment. It symbolizes her sin for all to see. In *The Great Gastby,* the green light on the far side of the water symbolizes Gatsy's hopes and dreams for the future. In Edgar Allan Poe's poem "The Raven," the black bird symbolizes death and loss.

Paradox

A **paradox** is a statement that seems silly or contradicts itself and reveals a truth. "I must be cruel only to be kind," says Hamlet. Cruel and kind contradict one another. In *Animal Farm* by George Orwell, there's a rule that "All animals are equal, but some are more equal than others." *A Tale of Two Cities* by Charles Dickens starts, "It was the best of times, it was the worst of times." There are several proverbs or sayings that you've probably heard that are paradoxes when you think about it. Less is more. The enemy of my enemy is my friend. Failure leads to success.

Oxymoron

An **oxymoron** is a figure of speech that refers to a set of contradictory words. It may seem similar to a paradox, but a paradox is a statement or argument that seems to be contradictory or go against *common sense*, while an oxymoron is a group of words that are almost exact opposites of each other that create a new meaning.

Some oxymorons are phrases we use all the time: original copies, liquid gas, virtual reality, paid volunteers, old news, seriously funny. Some other examples are a love-hate relationship, absolutely unsure, or deafening silence.

Example:

> Why, then, O brawling love! O loving hate!
> O anything, of nothing first create!
> O heavy lightness! Serious vanity!
> Misshapen chaos of well-seeming forms!
> Feather of lead, bright smoke, cold fire, sick health!
> —*Romeo and Juliet*, William Shakespeare

Activities

Key Terms:

Define the following key terms: figurative language, metaphor, simile, hyperbole, idiom, sarcasm, pun, onomatopoeia, alliteration, assonance, consonance, personification, symbolism, paradox, oxymoron

Comprehension

1) What is the difference between a simile and a metaphor?
2) What is the difference between alliteration, assonance and consonance?
3) When and why would you use figurative language?

Practice

1) Write a sentence that includes one of the figurative language tools in the "words" category.
2) Write a sentence that includes one of the figurative language tools in the "sounds" category.
3) Write a sentence that includes one of the figurative language tools in the "concepts" category.

Application

1) Choose three figurative language tools and write a humorous paragraph of something that happened to you last summer.
2) Write a poem using alliteration.

More activities and student examples available at **www.writefromtheheart.org/resourceguide**.

Chapter 13: Playing with Voice: Dialogue

Dialogue is an important part of any story. It is used when two or more characters talk to each other. It helps define your characters' personalities, moves the plot along and can be one way to "show not tell" the action. When you get it right, dialogue adds drama and interaction between characters to the story, and the mechanics of how to format it shouldn't be distracting to the reader. This chapter should give you the basics on how to create dialogue for yourself.

Making Dialogue Realistic

Dialogue should sound like talking. Each person has a unique way of saying something, and so should the characters in your stories! If you aren't sure if your dialogue sounds realistic, read it out loud. If you stumble over some of the words, it probably doesn't sound the same way people would speak it.

Let's look at this example of a scene from Harper Lee's *To Kill a Mockingbird*.

> Early one morning as we were beginning our day's play in the back yard, Jem and I heard something next door in Miss Rachel Haverford's collard patch. We went to the wire fence to see if there was a puppy—Miss Rachel's rat terrier was expecting—instead we found someone sitting looking at us. Sitting down, he wasn't much higher than the collards. We stared at him until he spoke:
>
> "Hey."
>
> "Hey yourself," said Jem pleasantly.
>
> "I'm Charles Baker Harris," he said. "I can read."
>
> "So what?" I said.

"I just thought you'd like to know I can read. You got anything needs readin' I can do it . . . "

"How old are you," asked Jem, "four-and-a-half?"

"Goin' on seven."

"Shoot no wonder, then," said Jem, jerking his thumb at me. "Scout yonder's been readin' ever since she was born, and she ain't even started to school yet. You look right puny for goin' on seven."

Jem brushed his hair back to get a better look. "Why don't you come over, Charles Baker Harris?" he said. "Lord, what a name."

"'s not any funnier'n yours. Aunt Rachel says your name's Jeremy Atticus Finch."

Jem scowled. "I'm big enough to fit mine," he said. "Your name's longer'n you are. Bet it's a foot longer."

"Folks call me Dill," said Dill, struggling under the fence.

"Do better if you go over it instead of under it," I said. "Where'd you come from?"

Note how this exchange tells us a lot of details about the characters: we can *hear* their childishness, we can get a feel for where they are from, and they each have a different way of talking.

Here are some tips for writing dialogue.

1. Write the dialogue as speakers actually speak. Is your character's personality lazy, sophisticated, techno-geeky, uneducated, highly principled? Can you hear the Southern twang when Charles says, "funnier'n" or Jem says, "longer'n?"

2. There should be a reason for the dialogue that advances the story. In this example, one character's beliefs clash with another character's—we are seeing the beginning either of a childhood friendship, or a lifelong enemy.

3. Keep the conversation brief and moving forward; characters don't have to say everything we do in spoken conversation.

4. Start a new paragraph every time someone new speaks. Identify the speaker <u>if</u> it isn't clear who is talking. Too many "he said's" "she said's" clutter up the story! Notice when Charles talks it rarely says, "He said."

5. Use dialogue to reveal the characters' personalities and their relationship with one another.

Paragraphing Dialogue

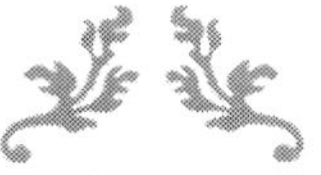

Alternatives to "Said"

- Use a stronger word that shows more action or emotion: scowled, cried, yelled, whispered, whined, yawned, etc.
- Put an action before or after the spoken words instead of a "said."
- Don't put any label for a few lines until it becomes unclear who is speaking.

Dialogue shows conversation between two or more people. Always start a new paragraph *each time* you switch speakers.

In addition, sometimes dialogue is interrupted with a brief description. If the description relates to the quote, keep it in the same paragraph; if the description doesn't relate to the quote, like the bolded line below, make it its own paragraph. The extra empty space gives the reader a very necessary visual break and makes the text appear more digestible.

The Earl was silent for a moment.

"There is something in the stable for you to see first," he said. "Ring the bell."

"If you please," said Fauntleory, with his quick little flush, "I'm very much obliged; but I think I'd better see it tomorrow. She will be expecting me all the time."

"Very well," answered the Earl. "We will order the carriage." Then he added dryly: "It's a pony."

Fauntleroy drew a long breath.

"A pony!" he exclaimed. "Whose pony is it?"

—*Little Lord Fauntleroy,* by Frances Hodgson Burnett

Punctuating Dialogue

Written dialogue consists of two ingredients: a quotation and a dialogue tag. The quote or **quotation**, the part the speaker actually says, is set apart with quotation marks. Ancient Greeks used the curved lines to represent the speaker's lips. The **dialogue tag** is the phrase that tells the reader who is talking or how they spoke; for example, "he said," or "she replied emphatically."

If the dialogue tag appears BEFORE the quote:

- Capitalize the dialogue tag and put a comma at the end of the tag.
- Put quotation marks at the beginning and end of the quote.
- Capitalize the beginning of the quote.
- Put the proper end punctuation *inside* the last set of quotation marks.
- **Example:** My mom said, "The phone's ringing. I bet it's for you!"

If the dialogue tag appears AFTER the quote:

- Put quotation marks at the beginning and end of the quote.
- Capitalize the beginning of the quote.
- *Inside* the closing quotation marks put a comma, exclamation point, or question mark. Never use a period here.
- Add the dialogue tag. Do not capitalize it. Put a period at the end of the tag.
- **Example:** "Your hair is a mess today," announced the freckle-faced boy.

The same rules apply for nonfiction quotes!

If the dialogue tag appears in the MIDDLE of a quoted sentence:

- Put quotation marks at the beginning and end of the first half of the quote.
- At the end of the first half of the quote, put a comma inside the quotation marks.
- Include the dialogue tag. Do not capitalize it. Put a *comma* at the end of it because the quoted sentence isn't finished yet.
- Put quotation marks at the beginning and end of the second half of the quote.

- Do not capitalize the beginning of the second half of the quote unless it's a person's name or the pronoun "I."
- At the end of the second half of the quote, put the proper end punctuation inside the quotation marks.
- **Example:** "Why is it," he wondered out loud, "that every time I get on the computer, time just slips away?"

If the dialogue tag appears in the MIDDLE of the quote AND the first half of the quote is a complete sentence:

- Put quotation marks at the beginning and end of the first half of the quote.
- At the end of the first half of the quote, put a comma inside the quotation marks.
- Include the dialogue tag. Do not capitalize it. Put a *period* at the end of it.
- Put quotation marks at the beginning and end of the second half of the quote.
- Capitalize the beginning of the second half of the quote.
- At the end of the second half of the quote, put the proper end punctuation inside the quotation marks.
- **Example:** "I like eggs," said my sister. "They are the perfect breakfast food."

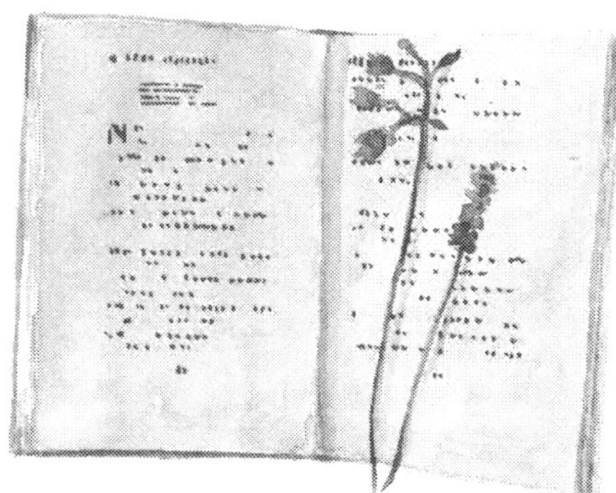

Activities

Key Terms

Define the following key terms: dialogue, quotation, dialogue tag

Comprehension

1) When should you add dialogue?
2) What elements should you cut from your dialogue to keep your story moving along?

Practice

1) Come up with as many verbs as you can to replace "said"—try to come up with at least ten.
2) Start a paragraph in the middle of a conversation with an exciting line of dialogue and then explain what's happening.

Application

1) Write a one-page dialogue between two people where one is telling a story and the other is asking questions. Make sure it's clear who is speaking but don't add "he/she said" after every line.
2) Write a story that includes dialogue between three or more people, where they are trying to solve a problem together. Try to give each speaker their own personality and concerns coming in to this discussion together.

More activities and student examples available at **www.writefromtheheart.org/resourceguide**.

Section 4: Creative Writing Styles

Creative writing is often a favorite type of assignment. You don't have to study for it. You just need to use your imagination! But it can also be more challenging than you think. Even if you love to read, it can be hard to write the type of story you want to create. How do you start? How do you develop characters or advance the plot? How much detail should you use? How do you actually apply writing advice like "show, don't tell," or "hook your readers" or "write about what you know"? By studying the building blocks of writing, we can learn the secrets of creative writing and how to craft a masterful story or poem.

Chapter 14: Narrative

When a writer wants to tell a story, they use a **narrative** writing style. Some narratives are completely fictional, and some are based on real-life events; some take place in outer space while others happen all in a backyard. No matter what happens in a story, or where it takes place, there are things that all stories have in common. Something always happens within the pages: a problem is solved, a lesson is learned, or a relationship is developed. While there are many ways to put a story together, every attempt should have a beginning, a middle, and an end.

Plot

There are several key elements of a narrative plot: Exposition, conflict, rising action, climax, falling action, and resolution. Think of your plot like climbing a mountain: you start off with a character, and they need to solve a problem, come face to face with that problem at the top, and then go down the other side as a new person. We often call this the "story graph" and it looks like this:

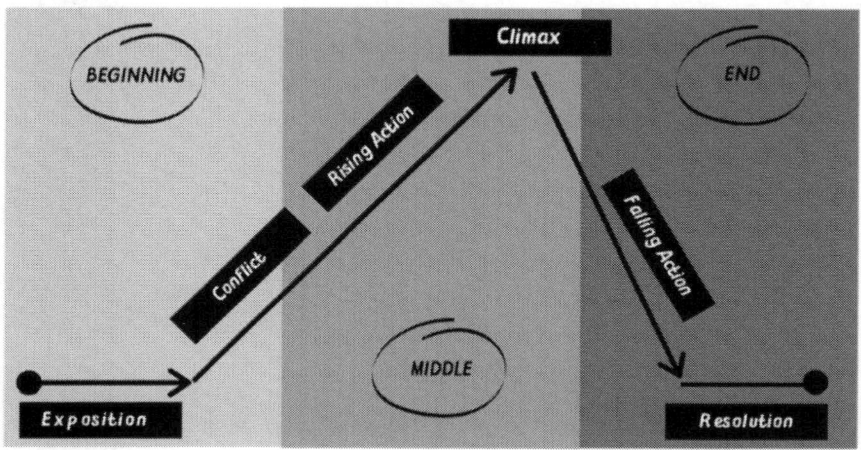

© Write from the Heart

Exposition is the back story, or explanation of all the reader needs to catch up with to understand what's happening in the story. Think of a great beginning in literature:

> It was bright cold day in April, and the clocks were striking thirteen. —*1984*, George Orwell

> Whether I shall turn out to be the hero of my own life, or whether that station will be held by anybody else, these pages must show. — *David Copperfield*, Charles Dickens

> There was a boy called Eustace Clarence Scrubb, and he almost deserved it. —*Voyage of the Dawn Treader,* C.S. Lewis

All of these beginnings draw the reader in, because they immediately fill his or her mind with questions. Who is speaking? Why are they important to the story? Where are we? What is happening? How should we feel? And most importantly, what's going to happen next? The exposition should answer these questions by introducing the characters, describing the setting and establishing the problem in the story.

Conflict is the problem in the narrative. If there is no problem to overcome, there's no reason to tell a story in the first place. This struggle between opposing forces creates the need for a plot and drives the action forward. But every conflict doesn't have to be an actual physical battle. There are six types of conflict that we see in a narrative:

- **Conflict with the self**: the character internal battle that they have to overcome. Examples: Hamlet, Crime & Punishment, The Lion King
- **Conflict with others**: the character must work out issues with other people, but it doesn't always mean that they're fighting. It can apply to stories about romances or friendships. Examples: Charlotte's Web, Hamilton, Romeo & Juliet
- **Conflict with the environment:** the character is trying to survive against something in nature or win a battle with a natural element. Examples: Little House on the Prairie, The Old Man & The Sea, The Lorax
- **Conflict with the supernatural:** the character is fighting off ghosts, dinosaurs, or werewolves; or, the main character has to go on a spiritual journey. Examples: The Odyssey, Lord of the Rings, War of the Worlds
- **Conflict with technology**: the character faces the consequences of technology and must solve a technical problem to survive. Examples: Jurassic Park, The Matrix, Frankenstein

- **Conflict with society:** a character is out of step with the world around them, and they need to decide if they will find a way to fit in, or demand that the society change for them. Examples: To Kill a Mockingbird, Hunger Games, 1984

Sometimes stories have more than one conflict. If you look at *Lord of the Rings,* Frodo faces several of these elements. He is conflicted between his desire to have an adventure or stay safe and, at the end, finishing his quest or keeping the ring for himself. He must work with other hobbits, elves, dwarves, and men to reach his goal. They must battle with orcs, ents, dragons, and Sauron himself! Usually, there are one or two overriding conflicts in a story. Short stories should focus on only one, while novels can have several.

Once your character and his or her situation has been introduced, things should start happening to move the plot forward. This is called **rising action**. You should incorporate a series of incidents that create interest, suspense, and tension. If you think of your story as a mountain, you should be climbing up the side, and each paragraph brings you closer to the top. In the rising action section, the main character will try several different ways to solve the conflict, but none of them will work or be satisfying. The tension should increase with each failed attempt.

The rising action should lead naturally to a **climax** in the action. At the climax, you've reached the peak of the mountain, the most exciting and the most important moment your character will face. This is the moment Little Red Riding Hood says, "What big teeth you have, Grandma!" and the wolf responds, "The better to eat you with, my dear." At the climax, the conflict is finally addressed head-on, and there is a battle or some other confrontation or crisis. The main character wins or loses, makes a decision, or somehow solves or succumbs to the problem.

After the climax, the story doesn't just end. Many things may still need to happen to finish all the plot lines. For example, in *Charlotte's Web,* the climax is often cited as the moment when Wilber wins the prize. However, lots of important things happen after that scene! The plot points after the climax are called **falling action**. If you think about the mountain metaphor, you are now on the other side of the summit and descending, but that doesn't mean you won't face harsh conditions, wildlife, and treacherous descents. The biggest moment that most people remember from *Charlotte's Web* hasn't even happened yet. That's a lot of action to take place, so don't think that the climax means the story is over!

Finally, there is a **resolution,** or the conclusion of the action. The main problem should be resolved. The resolution ties up all the parts and pieces of the plot and hopefully gives the reader a satisfactory ending. This may be a happily ever after, or a not so happily ever after. In *Romeo and Juliet,* the

Capulets and the Montagues make peace, but many of the characters are dead, which is sad. Another way to think about the resolution is to think of it as a scene or scenes of the "new normal" after the character's adventure. It doesn't need to be years in the future, but it should hint toward happiness or something else ominous, or whatever might be coming in this new world.

Setting

The **setting** of a narrative is an important point to analyze. The setting encompasses the time period, physical location, mood, and circumstances of a narrative. Even if you set a scene of dialogue in an ordinary diner, or on a park bench, adding details about the setting can make the reader feel like they're sitting with the characters instead of just reading about it.

Some settings take more explanation than others. Imagine you are writing a scene in a library. You may want to mention the quiet, especially if someone is going to interrupt it in the next moment, but you probably don't need to say much about the setting to paint a picture in the reader's mind. They are familiar with a library. However, if you want to write a sci-fi adventure set in the exploratory base on planet ZX-9, you need to do more to show the reader what the characters' surroundings are like. What does it *look* like? What does it *smell* like? How does stepping outside the safety of the base make the characters *feel*? What can they *hear*?

The setting is also a good place to introduce imagery or themes. In *A Tree Grows in Brooklyn,* the tree outside Francie's window symbolizes the lives of the people living there. In *Wuthering Heights*, the wind-swept, wild weather of the moors reflects the passions and wildness of the characters in the story. If your setting is going to highlight or reflect aspects of the characters or show a theme, make sure you describe those elements well.

While you can have the characters move from setting to setting, be aware of the number of settings—each one is going to take time to describe. If you are writing a short story, limiting the settings is a good way to maximize the room you have for action or dialogue. Any time you change setting, ask yourself if it is helping to move the plot forward or allowing the characters to grow. Sometimes, you can simplify by having the characters return to a setting you already described rather than going to a new setting. You don't want the description of the new setting to distract from an important conversation or plot point!

Characters

Characters are also an integral part of literature. I'm sure we can all think of a character we love from literature...and one we hate! Maybe there's even one we look up to and feel inspired. A character that sticks with us long after we have finished a book is a good example of the process of **characterization.** Characterization begins when the author introduces the character. Introduction might include a physical or emotional description of the character, a look inside their thoughts and feelings or some dialogue that establishes important facts. As the narrative develops, so does the character. Some narratives are more driven by events in the plot. Some are more driven by the development of a character or group of characters. But even books that are plot-driven require characters to advance the plot, so it's important to understand characterization.

The **protagonist** is the main character, the one most of the action is happening to. Many protagonists are heroes, but some may be an anti-hero, like Heathcliff in *Wuthering Heights* or Jack Sparrow in *Pirates of the Caribbean.*

The **antagonist** is the character who opposes the protagonist. If the protagonist is the good guy, the antagonist is the villain.

Some characters do not change significantly in the story, so they are referred to as **static** characters. These characters exist to make stories realistic. If your protagonist goes to class with his friends, the classroom needs to be full of other kids, and one of them might answer the teacher's questions. That character needs to appear realistic, and may add something to the plot, but isn't important to the story in the big picture.

Characters that do change are **dynamic** characters. **Secondary characters** may be sidekicks or have their own interesting side story that isn't as important as the main plot but gets tied in by the end. One way to expose the inner thoughts of a character is to have them confess to a **confidant.** If a character is a confidant, then the protagonist trusts them with their innermost thoughts.

Many stories are not categorized as love stories, but they still include a **love interest** for the main character. The love interest can often be a catalyst to action—either the main character wants to impress her and dedicates his quest to her name, like Penelope in *The Odyssey*, or they may inspire a moment of humor or humanity.

Some characters can be considered a **foil.** The foil could also be the antagonist, but doesn't have to be. A foil, by its nature, reflects the opposite character trait of the protagonist. If you want to show that your main character is brave, it helps to have a character who is cowardly to highlight the difference.

Theme

When you are writing a story, your character has a problem to solve, and the plot is about the conflict that results from that problem. After the climax, the character usually changes somehow. Perhaps they learned a lesson or fixed a character flaw. Sometimes characters don't learn the lesson they are supposed to (a lot of times this is true of the antagonists), but we the readers understand what that bad behavior is telling us to do—we learn what *not* to do from their actions. These lessons or understandings about life is called the **theme**.

The theme of the work is what the story is trying to tell you about life or the human condition. In a fable, it is the "moral of the story"—Aesop's fables even end with the theme written out for you! For example, the theme of "The Tortoise and the Hare" is "Slow and steady wins the race," and the story revolves around that. Longer stories can have more than one theme—different characters and situations might teach the reader a different lesson about life. Short stories usually have one theme.

The theme is often formulated as a sentence. For example, when talking about a theme, instead of saying "the theme is death" you could say, "Each time a friend dies, you lose a bit of yourself." The statement should be enough to explain how the work reveals a truth about human behavior.

Voice

As you write your story, you will want to study **Section 3** of this handbook carefully. Recall that voice refers to the mixture of personality, tone, point of view, vocabulary, and syntax that conveys the authorship of a piece of writing.

All of the voice techniques are excellent tools for making your world come alive. A character should be described using sensory details. The plot should play with time, speeding it up and slowing it down. Figurative language can be used to make a setting flourish. Symbolism should be present throughout the work.

One of the most fun things about writing a story, though, is that you don't have to use your own voice! You can create a character who tells the story, or it can be told by a nonspecific narrator (who isn't you if you don't want it to be). In fact, it doesn't have to be a person at all—one student I had wrote a tale of kitchen disaster, all from the perspective of the coffee maker! The use of a different voice from your own is called **narrative perspective**.

Always remember: No narrative perspective is inherently better than another, but each narrative perspective is often best-suited to particular genres of writing.

When reading your writing assignments, always look for directions about which narrative perspectives you should use. Some assignments and pieces of writing will have no directions about narrative voice; in these instances, it's up to you to use your judgment on which narrative perspective to use. To make your decision, look at examples of writing and think about which

perspective will be both understandable and powerful for your audience. You have several options for a narrative perspective.

Omniscient Narrator (Third-Person Voice)

Omniscient means "all-knowing." An omniscient narrator, then, knows about every individual and event in a story. The omniscient narrator can also read and tell you the thoughts of numerous different characters. The omniscient narrator usually has no connection to any character within that story. Omniscient narrative perspective is probably the most common type of narrator in fictional stories and books. Some examples of books with omniscient narrators include *Charlotte's Web* and *The Chronicles of Narnia*.

Limited Narrator (Third-Person Voice)

Unlike omniscient narrators, limited narrators do not know everything. Instead, they usually only are aware of one or two characters' thoughts and plans, and the narrator's knowledge of other characters and events evolves at the same time that the character discovers information. It is almost like this narrator is a camera on the shoulder of a certain character, with access to only their inner thoughts.

One example of third-person limited narration is *Pride and Prejudice*. In this series, the narrator uses the third-person voice, but the narrator does not know what all the characters are thinking. Rather, the narrator knows what Lizzie, the main character, and her sister are thinking. Because the narrator has this limited perspective, the audience is kept in suspense, and makes wrong assumptions about other characters along with Lizzie.

Limited Narrator (First-Person Voice)

When a story is told by a character from their point of view, they use the first person, and they are limited in their storytelling to what they have actually experienced or been told. They can speculate on why other characters did something or what they were thinking, but they cannot discern their thoughts or know what happened if they weren't present.

The limited narrator could be the main character, telling the reader his or her story as it happened to them, like Jane Eyre in *Jane Eyre*, Pip in *Great Expectations*, or Katniss in *Hunger Games*. It could also be a secondary character, recording the action to share with you, the reader, or reporting what they experienced, like Nick Carroway in *The Great Gatsby*.

Multiple Limited Narrators (First-Person or Third-Person Voice)

Sometimes, an author uses several different narrators throughout a novel (if they are using first-person) or follows several specific characters, switching the shoulder-camera (if they are using third-person). This is the same style of writing as a single limited narrator, but it allows the author to jump inside the head of several different characters throughout the story. Each time the narrator changes, we get information into the thoughts of that particular character, but none of the others.

This is a technique that is used in longer stories only—a novel with chapters, or a series of short stories about interconnected people. It should not be used in short stories, because there isn't enough time to get to know each character the way we need to in order for this technique to work. The *Percy Jackson* series and *Wonder* are written in first-person multiple limited narrator styles—the change in voice and narrator happens in chapter or section breaks. The book *Spoon River Anthology* by Edgar Lee Masters is told in third-person multiple limited narrators—it's a collection of short stories about residents in the town of Spoon River, and every story puts the camera on a different person's shoulder.

Unreliable Narrators (First-Person Voice)

Unreliable narrators inaccurately report information about events or characters. Sometimes, the narrator is intentionally untruthful—perhaps to protect himself/herself or others—but sometimes, the narrator has been given inaccurate or incomplete information, or the narrator has misunderstood someone else. The reader has to listen and figure out what really happened or how other characters really view events. One example of an unreliable narrator in a book for kids is Greg in *Diary of a Wimpy Kid.* Famous examples of unreliable narrators in literature for older readers include Holden Caulfield from *The Catcher in the Rye* and any of the characters in Edgar Allan Poe's short stories.

Types of Narratives

Narrative writing style is used in many different types of writing and can be utilized in lots of different ways.

When we think of fiction, we usually think of a **novel**, which is a book-length story. Novels usually have chapters or sections. There are multiple settings, more than one theme, and a cast of characters. Usually there are several plot lines for the characters (a main plot and several secondary plots). We might also think of **short stories**, which follow the same structure as a novel, but are shorter. They include the elements of plot, theme, and setting, but often have less characters and focus on one main plot.

But there are other types of fiction as well. **Flash Fiction** is even shorter than a short story—usually only about 1000 words. It is not a rushed story—it is complete. But it is a mini-story, a focused-in lens on a character, a moment of crisis. Perhaps a character is trying to make a decision and the whole piece is about that moment. Or maybe it is a meeting of two friends—or even strangers—and that meeting represents a significant moment in their relationship. This type of writing is not intended to be "half-a-story" or an incomplete idea. Generally, your story will need to have some element of growth in self-knowledge to be satisfying to your readers, but you are often only focusing on the climax of a story with only a little bit of background.

Narrative writing style also works well for biographies and personal pieces of writing. A memoir can have elements of a narrative story, but it is something true that happened to the author and they are the narrator of the story. We will talk about memoirs in **Chapter 15**.

Sometimes authors blend true-life stories with fiction and write what is called **creative non-fiction**. Perhaps the story is based on a real incident but is so exaggerated that the real people turn into what feels like fictional characters. The movie *Big Fish* is playing with this idea. Sometimes authors write tall tales about themselves for the sake of a humorous sketch. They swear it's real, but with a wink to the audience. Mark Twain was a master at this type of writing. And sometimes it is completely true but written in a heightened literary style—the author plays with time or dialogue or the syntax of sentences, which makes a real moment take on a literary quality. Annie Dillard used this technique in her famous work *A Pilgrim at Tinker's Creek*.

Student Example #1

Dissatisfied

By Christina N., 17

I couldn't believe I was finally here at the county fair. And that meant one thing to me: cotton candy. As I skipped alongside my parents, I heard the music of the carnival: A tinny tune from the carousel tickled my ears; vendors yelled from all sides trying to sell their food; and the groan of a hundred gears shook the ground. As we walked toward the Ferris wheel, I caught my first glimpse of the sweet sugary spindles. It was beautiful; the rosy pink color was so enticing. I knew I needed to have it.

"Mom, mom," I whined as I tugged on her sleeve to get her attention. "I want that cotton candy," pointing to the overweight old man carrying around the pink and blue fluffs of pure sugar.

"Honey not now," my mom replied. "You've had enough sugar today. Let's go ride the Ferris wheel."

Begrudgingly, I followed my parents, but I couldn't keep my mind off it. Cotton candy was the only thing I wanted. I longingly looked back hoping to catch one last glimpse of it. Suddenly a thought popped into my head. *Why do my parents get to decide if I have cotton candy or not? I want it so I'll have it. I'll just slip off and go get it myself.* Pleased with my brilliant idea I started walking slower than my parents to see if they would notice I was gone. They were deep in the midst of a conversation about how sugar makes children stupid so I slipped away.

I could see the rows of cotton candy bobbing up and down as I wove my way through the crowd. I was getting closer when suddenly I got swept up in a huge group of schoolkids all trying to see a pony doing tricks. I tried to push my way out of the crowd but I was stuck. I was being pulled along sideways as if caught in a riptide. After several minutes of pushing and fighting, I finally felt fresh air on my face. I looked around frantically, searching for the cotton candy. It was nowhere in sight.

I started to panic. I needed to find that cotton candy, but I was lost. I didn't know which way to turn. I started walking, hoping that I was going in the right direction. I passed rows of ring toss games and food stands but found no cotton candy. I started to feel like I was walking in circles. Hadn't I just passed that funnel cake stand? I started to feel scared and lonely. Maybe I should have stayed with my parents.

Just when I thought life couldn't get any worse I felt a tap on my shoulder. *Oh no.*

"Well, well, well, look who it is," called out the leader of the group of mean kids from school.

"What do you want?" I called back as I turned to face them. "Please just go and leave me alone.

"Are you scared?" they taunted.

I didn't wait around to find out what would happen if I was scared. I wheeled around and started sprinting in the opposite direction.

"Get him!" I heard from behind me.

I heard their feet pounding the dusty ground behind me. I ran through the crowd as sweat started forming on my forehead. *I should have tried harder in gym class.* I heard their shouts getting closer. I felt a hand reach out for my shoulder. I ducked hard to the left trying not to think about what would happen if they caught up. With my heart pounding I had my second brilliant thought of the day. *I have no chance of outrunning them so I have to outsmart them. What if I run right for that carnival game and at the last minute duck around it? There are so many of them they won't be able to stop and they'll run right into it.* I headed right towards the nearest game. I could hear the mean kids closing in. At the very last second I swerved to the right around the tent. Oomph. I collided with something soft and squishy.

Questions as you read:

- Who was the main character and what was their problem?
- What is the theme?
- Label the elements of narrative in the story
- Circle two uses of figurative language.
- Underline two sensory details.
- Mark one example of inner thoughts or inner dialogue.

Squinting to see past the bright sunlight, I noticed two things. The mean kids had passed me without noticing I had stopped, and next to me on the ground was the cotton candy man. I had finally found him.

"Sorry about that kid, didn't see ya there. Here, have some cotton candy," he said to me as he handed me one of those beautiful fluffs of sugar. I couldn't believe my good fortune. I had been so eager to find him that I hadn't thought about how I was going to pay for it. As I walked away, cotton candy melting in my mouth, I wondered why I didn't feel happier. I got what I wanted.

Clutching my cotton candy, I started to head back to the Ferris wheel to find my parents. It was easier to find my way back with the giant wheel guiding me. As I circled the base of the ride, I called out for my parents. There was no response. I was alone. I had no idea what to do next. I looked down at the cotton candy in my hand and felt too sick to take another bite.

Student Example #2

February 23, 1945

By Drew H., 15

A field of bright vermillion fluttered gently in the drafty hanger, proclaiming the hope of Germany's rise to the factory guards. As the flag gracefully undulated beneath the drab ceiling of the hanger, I gazed upon the beautiful swastika and thought of the great empire it represented. Looking down from my lofty, windowed observation booth, I surveyed my ragged POW slaves slowly pushing the gleaming grey forms of Messerschmitt Me 410's and Focke-Wulf Ta 152's up the cement ramp from deep underground.

Despite Germany's tactical retreats on the front and the bombings against the city, my production here at the Pforzheim aircraft factory was at a record high. If I kept churning out five planes a week, I would receive my promised promotion: I would become overseer of all the Reich's aircraft plants, reporting directly to the Führer. Standing at Hitler's side, my planes would strike terror into the hearts of the Allies, retaking France and winning the war.

RING! RING! My telephone blared, snapping me out of my trance.

"Hello?" I said, picking up the device.

"Hello, Captain Müller," the voice greeted me urgently, "Sir, American B-21's have been spotted by one of our supply convoys a few minutes away from your position by air."

"What? How many?"

"Around 500, plus a significant fighter escort."

"Oh dear," I murmured, flinging down the phone and sprinting down from my booth.

As the scrawny laborers looked up from the beautiful yellow wingtips of a new fighter, I frantically addressed my guards, "Five hundred enemy bombers are coming; they will be here momentarily!"

As the soldiers stood frozen with frightened awe, I continued, "This is not a drill! Get the planes underground and prepare the exterior flak guns; I want this place on lockdown!"

Immediately, the soldiers opened the gargantuan steel doors of the hanger to prepare the defenses. Others herded the workers into groups and got them moving the planes down the ramp and to safety.

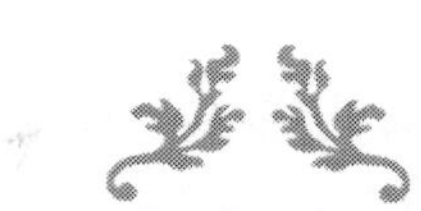

Questions as you read:

- Who was the main character and what was their problem?
- What is the theme?
- Label the elements of narrative in the story
- Circle two uses of figurative language.
- Underline two sensory details.
- Mark one example of inner thoughts or inner dialogue.

Cursing menacingly at the stragglers, I ran outside to oversee the defensive preparations. Already, my men were starting to load the heavy golden shells into the flak guns, aiming their weapons westward, where the moan of aircraft engines could be heard. As the minutes passed, I listened terrified as the moan became a roar; the B-21's were coming into view.

When one of my men shouted at me to get inside, I came to my senses and rushed indoors, adrenaline coursing through my veins. Just as the huge doors of the hanger began to close, the flak guns began tossing their bolts of metallic doom up into the invading bombers.

"Where is our air support?" I wondered aloud, rushing into my booth to oversee the movement of the planes underground. As I mounted the tall staircase to my post, I heard the loud rattle of machine gun fire right outside the doors.

Oh no. The fighters are strafing our guns, I realized. *My defenses won't hold much longer.*

My fears were confirmed when the sound of aircraft engines escalated to hurricane-like volume, and blasts were heard just outside of the compound.

Boom. BOOM. BOOM! The bombs sounded, coming increasingly close.

With a deafening smash, several large chunks of concrete shot to the ground in pieces. The dust only beginning to settle, another bomb hit the roof, knocking me down, cracking the glass of my booth and blowing more of the roof to bits. My ears ringing, another detonation rocked the facility. I heard glass shatter into hundreds of pieces, imbedding crystalline razors into my body. Still reeling from the pain, my booth collapsed, sending me careening towards the rubble below. I felt a jolt of excruciating pain, and then I knew no more.

I awoke laying on the twisted wreckage of one of my fighters; it was dark. Dazed, I saw that my arm was at an impossible angle, my breathing was abnormal, and that I was bleeding from a few glass shards stuck in my body.

Seeing nobody, dead or alive, to help, I ripped my jacket to bandage my cuts and fashion a makeshift sling. I then trudged through the rubble into the bowels my ruined facility, figuring my minions were safe in their subterranean positions. When I finally arrived, I scanned the overturned metal tables and the imposing, mechanical parts to try and locate survivors in the flickering yellow light. Finding no laborers, I stopped my search in horror when I saw one of my guards laying in a pool of blood, his face and body beaten fiercely. Looking up, I saw that my other subordinates shared his fate. All were dead, pummeled with improvised weapons or shot through with their own guns. If that was not enough, all the planes that were brought down before the raid were in shambles, their graceful wings and cockpits smashed. Some had wings or propellers damaged or removed with the very tools used to build them,

others belching smoke out of their hissing engines, and still more were coughing out sparks, blackened by fuel-ignited flames.

Prostrating myself in despair, I wept from the pain of losing my factory, my physical health, and my hope for a greater nation. The attack made me face the truth: Germany stood no chance; we had no defense against the legions of Allies. Our guns and planes were only delaying the inevitable.

Germany cannot win this war, I thought to myself as I lied there, we do not have the strength. The Allies hit us with hundreds of planes, and I can hardly make five a week. It's over for the Reich. All over.

NOTE: Student examples appear in original format and may contain slight grammar errors.

Activities

Key Terms

Define the following key terms: narrative, exposition, conflict, rising action, climax, falling action, resolution, setting, theme, characterization, protagonist, antagonist, static characters, dynamic characters, secondary character, love interest, foil, narrative perspective, omniscient narrator, limited narrator, multiple limited narrators, unreliable narrator, novel, short story, flash fiction, creative nonfiction

Comprehension

1) Explain the best way to communicate the features and personality of a character in a narrative.
2) What makes the climax different from the problems in the rising action?
3) How are the exposition and resolution similar? How are they different?

Practice

1) Answer the question in the sidebar next to Student Example #1.
2) Answer the questions in the sidebar next to Student Example #2.

Application

1) Choose two characters and write a paragraph describing an event from one character's perspective. Then write another paragraph about the same event from the perspective of the other character.
2) Create a fictional short story—make sure to include all the elements of a good narrative!

More activities and student examples available at **www.writefromtheheart.org/resourceguide**.

Chapter 15: Memoir

A **memoir** is a form of autobiographical writing or writing about oneself. Unlike an autobiography, though, which usually covers most of the writer's life, a memoir usually hones in on a particular memory or period in the writer's life. Memoirs are considered a specialized form of narrative writing. Some writers create memoirs that are book-length, but memoirs that are essay-length can be quite powerful.

In these shorter memoirs, the subject matter usually relates to a brief period of time, such as a period of a few weeks, days, or even hours. Some writers choose very short incidents for their memoirs, such as a moment when they experienced some sort of milestone (riding a bicycle for the first time, learning to read, winning an award) or navigated a significant challenge (getting injured, fighting with a friend or sibling, experiencing a tragedy).

In style, memoirs feel a lot like a narrative. You are, after all, telling a story. In real life, though, the elements of narrative are not so neatly seen—our experiences don't always have a clear rising action or resolution. They, do, however, have a beginning, a middle, and an end, and the writer has been changed in some way by the incident; otherwise, it wouldn't be worth writing about!

Ultimately, the writer has a purpose for recollecting this memory: to explore a particular idea, theme, or lesson that has shaped who they are—what they think and believe about themself, others, and the world. For example, a writer may remember the time she successfully performed at her piano recital. That memory could be connected to a larger lesson about how she learned to overcome her fears through the encouragement of family and friends. Another memoir might connect the writer's memory of getting injured in a bicycling accident to the larger theme of learning to be cautious in high-risk situations. Sometimes, at the end of the memoir, a writer might say "Because of this experience, I learned...." Other times, a writer may imply that they learned something through their experience—or that their memory connects with a larger theme.

Elements of a Memoir

Because memoirs are about you and have a story-like quality to them, they share several elements with narratives. Memoirs always include:

- **Setting:** This is where the memory took place.
- **Characterization:** Both you and those with you in this particular memory become the "characters" in the work. You want to make sure you capture everyone's unique personality and explain the relationships between them.
- **Plot:** Memoir focuses on an event or period in someone's life. You need to explain what the problem was and what happened because of it. There should be some sort of conflict, whether it's between two people, with nature, or within yourself.
- **Voice**: Memoirs are written in first person. They should also include lots of description, imagery, and will play with time. Dialogue is necessary.
- **Theme**: The writer is selecting this event or period of time because it was significant, and it changed them. Exactly how it changed them and what they learned from it is the theme. This can be stated or implied.

For more information about these elements, read **Chapter 14** on narrative writing.

Structure of Memoir

When writing a memoir, it is important to create a narrative that follows a clear time sequence. It's okay to have an attention getter that jumps into the action, but it's important to make sure the reader understands what happened at the beginning, middle, and end of the event.

Sometimes a writer will connect several related memories into the same piece in order to better tell the story of the main memory. For example, if a writer is talking about the time she overcame her fear of large audiences by successfully performing at her piano recital, she might also reference or **flashback** to past memories of large audiences, such as the time she froze when reciting a poem or the time her voice cracked during a choir solo. This past experience should help the writer realize something that will help them in their current situation. **See Chapter 10** for more information about inner ideas.

Student Examples

Example #1

Don't Think of Niagara Falls: Lessons Learned in the Pool
By Katie W., 14

It is the sacred job of every mother to teach her children the important lessons of life. Some of these mother lessons are universal: "Drink your milk;" "Mind your manners;" and "Put on fresh underwear every day because you might end up in the hospital." My mom is no exception. She's tried to pass on to me her own personal bits of wisdom, little gems like "Don't blow bubbles during the preacher's sermon," and "Don't share your popsicle with the dog, especially if he just ate rabbit poo in the yard." But my mother hasn't taught me every important lesson. I know I learned at least one of them at a swim meet, the hard way.

Like most Saturdays in my family's life, it was a swim meet Saturday. Deep in concentration, I had been sitting for an entire hour on the hard deck of the indoor pool considering how to go faster in my eight-and-under freestyle race. I was five, and already I hated losing. I wanted shiny, impressive-looking blue ribbons, not those wimpy, forest green sixth place ones that the swimmer who came in last automatically got. But how was I ever supposed to race and win against big, mighty eight-year-olds when I was only five? I needed some secret method, some attack plan. Lately, at practice, my coaches had been talking about "hard work." They said it would eventually make me go faster in my races. But I had found that hard work was just that, hard. It certainly wasn't fun, and I concluded that I wouldn't need hard work if I could find a little shortcut.

As my kindergarten brain mulled over the possibilities of my shortcut strategy, I began to become vaguely aware of growing pressure in another region far to the anatomical south. But before I could take action on that thought, Daniel, my big brother, sauntered over to my fleece blanket.

"Hey, Katie, what's up?" Daniel asked.

I suddenly brightened. Daniel would know what to do! He was an experienced swimmer and way older than me! He was nine.

"Well, I have this problem," I looked up at Daniel hopefully. "I need to go faster in my freestyle, but I don't know how!"

"Ah, yes, this is an interesting dilemma..." Daniel said in his "I'm-superior-over-you" voice. He was always trying to sound smart.

I frowned. I had suddenly become acutely aware of demands of the southern region.

"Stay right there, Daniel," I stammered. "I need to go to the bathroom really badly."

Suddenly Daniel's eyes shone with inspiration.

"Number one or two?"

I held up one chubby finger in response.

"Wait! Don't go to the bathroom! I have an idea!" Daniel exclaimed. Even though Ireally needed to go to the bathroom, I was proud that my older brother, a cool nine-year-old, was giving me advice at a swim meet where his friends were also in attendance.

"What?" I asked with anticipation. "What's the idea?"

"If you don't go to the bathroom, you will go faster in your freestyle! Having to go to the bathroom makes you swim faster," Daniel said, and then he looked at the clock. "You only have ten minutes until your race. You can hold it, right?"

I gulped. This was going to be difficult. "I guess," I mumbled. "Thanks, Daniel."

Two minutes later, I tottered over to the heat bench, the staging area for upcoming events. Normally, I was talkative on the heat bench. But this Saturday, I sat there in silence, just hoping that the next eight minutes would pass quickly. Unfortunately, those eight minutes turned into eighteen.

"We have technical difficulties with the electronic timing system," the announcer boomed over the loudspeaker. "It will be about ten minutes."

As I crouched on the heat bench, I could feel liquid slowly rising and pushing against my abdomen, and I began to deeply regret the three waters I drank that morning. I determinedly tried to focus on pressing my thighs together, until the girl next to me accidentally dropped her yellow Gatorade on the ground. The warm yellow liquid slowly spilled all over the deck, making a "glug, glug" sound as it flowed out of the bottle. I began eying the door to the locker room, where I knew a line of toilets was available as an easy solution to my growing problem.

Wait! What's wrong with you, Katie? I thought, annoyed with my lack of will-power. *This shortcut is going to win you a blue ribbon!* Resolved to "hold it," I clenched my knuckles on the bench until they turned snow white. I tried to take my mind off my desperate need for a job john, but I just ended up remembering some unhelpful memories.

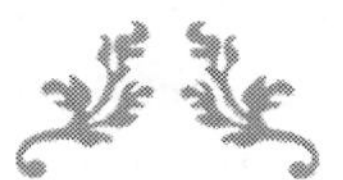

Questions as you read:

- Who were the characters and how could you tell them apart?
- How does the flashback function in the writer's learning?
- What is the problem?
- What is the theme?
- List two sensory details the author had.

I could hear the unmerciful teasing of my brother, many weeks before, when I needed to go to the bathroom at an inopportune time during a long car trip. "Just don't think of Niagara Falls, Katie!" he had taunted, knowing relief was at least a half hour away.

I could also hear my coaches saying, "Katie, you really could go a lot faster in your freestyle if you would work harder at practice."

Then I saw myself, grumbling, "But isn't there an easier way? It hurts to work hard."

"Katie... KATIE!" My mom woke me up from my trance involving number one and my quest to become number one. "Do you want anything to drink?" She was always hounding my brother and me about hydration.

"No!" I said emphatically, with more force than I intended.

"What's wrong?" she asked with a knowing look that was filled with concern. "Do you have to go to the bathroom?"

"No. I'm just not thirsty. That's all," I mumbled convincingly. I was definitely not going to tell my mother about my little plan to go faster. She would not approve.

"Okay," she agreed, while idly shaking the bottle of water that she held.

"Swoosh, swish, swoosh, swish," went the water. I softly groaned as I could feel the rising liquid in my bladder making the same noises.

"Are you *sure* you don't need to go?" my mother asked again.

"YES!" I shouted so loudly that the mother with a sleeping baby nearby shushed me.

Given my dire condition, it seemed to me that the boys' race immediately before my freestyle event went slower than any race has ever gone. It took the 8-and-under boys five minutes to swim one lap of the pool. Or maybe it was twenty seconds, and I just imagined the time was longer because of my desperation. I'll never know for sure. When the boys' race was finally over, I pulled my goggles on with a satisfying "snap," gritted my teeth, and put one foot on the step of the starting block.

Not much longer, Katie. I reminded myself. This strategy is going to make you an Olympian!

"Step up, ladies," the starter said into the microphone attached to the starting equipment.

I stepped onto the block. Instantly I knew I would never be able to bend over and do a regular start without cutting loose. So I put both feet over the edge and crossed my legs. Laughter sounded throughout the pool area. The humid, chlorine-smelling air surrounded me like a blanket. I kept my eyes focused on the wall at the other end of the pool area and didn't dare look at the clear, cool, blue water that was lapping, loudly, against the pool gutter.

"This is one lap of freestyle, ladies," the starter commanded. "Take your marks."

"Beep!" went the starting system. I dove in the water with a splash, and the brisk water rushed around me. My "southern" region felt worse than ever.

How am I ever going to do this? I asked myself.

I need to stop thinking about the toilet! I desperately answered.

So, I tried not to think of Niagara Falls. I tried not to think of leaking water pipes slowly dripping, dripping. I tried not to think of fire hydrants exploding. But I did anyway. I tried to focus on the rhythmic stroking of my arms going "chum, chum, chum," but, at that moment, my mind wasn't interested in my arms one bit. I tried not to think about yellow Gatorade flowing freely out of the dropped bottle. I tried not to think of waves crashing in to the shoreline. I tried not to think of the geyser, Old Faithful, spurting warm water forcefully into the air. I tried, but I did anyway. *Don't think of—* I thought. And then, suddenly, I felt better. My arms "chummed" a few more times, and my hand touched the wall to finish.

I crawled out of the pool feeling like a new person. But, as I looked around, I realized that I'd be getting a forest green ribbon after all. I asked the timer my time.

"Forty seconds," the timer answered.

Darn! I thought. *That's a lousy time!* "Holding it" hadn't helped my time or my place. And it had had other consequences, too.

My mom opened her arms up for a hug, and I ran into them.

"Great job, Katie!" she said as she wrapped me in a towel. "Oh, honey, I, um, noticed your new starting technique. Do you, by any chance, need to go to the bathroom?"

I giggled. "Uh, no. Not anymore."

Her eyes grew wide as she realized what had happened, and she barely managed to utter an answer. "Oh. I see."

As for me, I came to a few realizations myself that day. First, I began to learn that, in swimming and in life, there is no substitute for hard work, and there are no shortcuts to success. After that fateful swimming meet seven years ago, I began to follow the guidance of my coaches by working hard in practice. Over time, that hard work paid off, and I began to earn, without gimmicks or tricks, those beautiful blue ribbons that I had wanted for so long. And yes, along with that lesson of the importance of hard work, I learned another one that ranks right up there with wearing clean underwear and avoiding rabbit poo germs. I learned to always visit the ladies' room before a swimming race!

Example #2

Unraveling Algebra

By Rachel B., 13

I was getting so frustrated that I couldn't think clearly. In the beginning of last school year, I thought that algebra would be easy. I could complete a lesson in about fifteen minutes, and I usually got 100%. But as the year progressed, the problems steadily became more difficult. I especially struggled with the word problems. I would read the problem several times, write an equation, and solve it. When I checked the answer, it would not only be wrong, but so far from the correct solution that I would become even more confused. I'd get the simplest problems wrong. I did my math on the computer, with a program that allowed me to listen to a lecture on the lesson. I could also do the problem sets on the computer. When I had worked the problem, I fast forwarded to the end to check my answer. I went through the motions, listening to the explanation of the problem with eyes glazed over, but I didn't comprehend any of it.

I sat at the kitchen table with my laptop before me, long after my younger siblings had gone to bed, staring intently into space. With my wrinkled and messy paper pinned to the table by my left hand, my right gripping the pencil savagely, I stayed in that position until some noise like the refrigerator turning on jerked me out of my daze. I made a feeble effort to solve the problem but got distracted. A few minutes later, I realized that I had barely finished copying the problem, and in the margins of the paper, I had sketched an intricate picture of my favorite character from the book I was reading. I sighed miserably and rested my forehead on the table. The half-finished word problem glared up at me from the crumpled and eraser-smudged page. I closed my eyes so I couldn't see it. In the living room, my mother's knitting needles clicked and clicked in a steady rhythm, making a soothing noise. I began to daydream...

When I was about five, my mother decided to knit a sweater for me. We drove to a friend's farm, with the autumn foliage transforming the surrounding fields into a patchwork of color. Our friends owned a flock of sheep, and every year they sheared the wool. They sorted the unwashed wool into bags and sent it to a small business in Maine where it was cleaned, spun, and dyed. Later, our friends were sent the final product. Mom decided to get the yarn from them.

While our mothers sat and talked, discussing patterns and needle sizes, I played outside and in the barn with Anna. We had been friends for a while since we were the same age and our mothers got together often. After a while, Mom called me in to pick the color I wanted. There was a large basket of yarn in the corner. I sat down beside it and considered the choices. Then I saw the color I wanted. I pointed to the dark red. It was pure wool, and it felt warm and soft as I held it to my face. I inhaled the smell of wood smoke and sheep, and I didn't think I could wait until my sweater was finished.

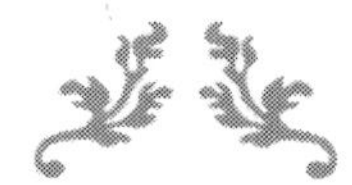

Questions as you read:

- Who were the characters and how could you tell them apart?
- How does the flashback function in the writer's learning?
- What is the problem?
- What is the theme?
- List two sensory details the author had.

As I watched the skeins of red yarn grow smaller and smaller, I decided that I wanted to knit, too. For a while, I was content to sit in my own little rocking chair and knit. I was only knitting short and somewhat uneven rows, but I pretended I was making a sweater for my doll so we could match. Knitting made me feel grown up, "just like Mom," but after a while, I drew tired of the slow progress. My knitting was very tight, and I struggled to push my needle through. It would take me so long to complete a row that I would forget how many stitches I had done. As I struggled to count, the needles would slip out, and my knitting would unravel. I didn't enjoy it anymore. There were other things I wanted to do, and my knitting was set aside and forgotten.

It was several years later, at a women's crafting group, when I started again. An experienced knitter saw my problem and offered some advice. She showed me a better way to cast on and how to hold the yarn firm, but not tight. Her techniques worked. I knit several rows, and within a few days, my knitting loosened and evened out. After a few weeks, I felt confident enough to begin a scarf. I chose a dark red yarn, remembering the sweater I had loved for so long. I worked on the scarf for two months then decided that it would make a nice gift for my grandfather. There was only a short time left before Christmas, so I knit every chance I got. On Christmas Eve, my grandfather was sitting in the living room reading the paper, and I was sprawled beneath the tree, knitting furiously. He noticed me, and asked what I was making.

"Oh, nothing, really," I replied innocently. "Just fooling around with the yarn, I guess."

"Looks pretty," he commented. "I like the colors. You could make a scarf, you know." I couldn't let him guess that it was his Christmas present.

"Yeah, maybe." I tried to sound nonchalant. He might put two and two together and guess that I was making it for him. I tried to divert his attention by changing the subject. "Um, I should get ready for bed now. I'll be back down in a few minutes."

I sprinted upstairs to my room and laid the nearly finished scarf on my bed. For a moment, I stood looking at it. Then I wrapped it around my neck to see how long it was, carefully avoiding the needles. It wasn't scratchy or itchy, but warm and soft. I estimated that I would need to knit half an inch more.

After I cast off, I took stock of my remaining yarn. There was just enough left to make fringe. I carefully measured and cut four-inch lengths, and tied them to the ends of the scarf. I folded it, stuffed it under my bathrobe, and sneaked downstairs. I proudly exhibited it to my mom and grandmother who whispered that it was "just the thing," and, "he'll love it!" Safely back in my room, I wrapped it in holly print wrapping paper. I felt so good. Not only was it a well-made scarf and a thoughtful gift, but it was the first big craft project that I had ever completed.

I started, then sat up, blinking. Thinking hard, I stared at my math paper. Maybe algebra was like knitting—it takes practice and effort to get better at it. When I knit every day, it became easy for me. I built on my skills, each time making a trickier pattern. A short while after I finished my grandfather's scarf, I knit a hat, with hardly any trouble at all. I realized that things don't always come easily. When this happens, I need to persevere through the tough spots and practice until it becomes effortless. I remembered how this happened with my violin. I practiced every day and progressed quickly through the repertoire. As Dr. Suzuki, a great violin teacher, once said, "You don't need to practice every day—only on the days you eat!"

I turned to my algebra with renewed enthusiasm. It was still hard, but I knew that with time, I would master those word problems. Fifteen minutes later, I stiffly stood up, stretched, and grandly presented my mom with the completed, albeit messy, math paper. I couldn't believe it, but I found myself looking forward to tomorrow's algebra.

It is a year later. Algebra has been conquered; the word problems are no longer challenging. Now I face geometry, but I am not dreading it anymore. I know there will be bigger challenges ahead, but I will approach them with the same attitude of "practice, with effort, makes perfect." I am looking forward to joining a math team sometime this school year.

NOTE: Student examples appear in original format and may contain slight grammar errors.

Activities

Key Terms

Define the following key terms: memoir, theme, flashback

Comprehension

1) What is the most important element of a memoir?
2) What narrative techniques should appear in a memoir?

Practice

1) Answer the question in the sidebar next to Student Example #1.
2) Answer the questions in the sidebar next to Student Example #2.

Application

1) Write a paragraph about a memorable family dinner
2) Write an essay about a time you made a mistake and learned from it.

More activities and student examples available at **www.writefromtheheart.org/resourceguide**.

Chapter 16: Poetry

The poem is a special kind of writing. Writing a **poem** is using language and writing structure in a unique way to express a writer's view of the world. There is not a strict set of rules for writing poetically. A poem can rhyme, or not. It can be short, like a haiku, or a book-length epic. It can break all the rules or stick to a strict structure.

However, poets, just like other artists, have their own set of "tools" to use. A sculptor might make an abstract piece or the statue of David, but he still uses the same thing: a hammer and chisel. Maybe one sculptor uses very small tools, and another one works in large, rough style. Poetry works that way, too. Every writer is different, and so is their poetic styling. We all work out of the same toolbox, but the tools we choose to utilize might be different from another poet's.

We will be talking about each of these things in more depth throughout the chapter, but here are the general tools that a poet has at his or her disposal:

- **Sound Quality**—how a poet uses language. This might be rhyming words or matching the first consonants of words in a line. This can also be using onomatopoeia. Language has a sound, even when it is read on the page. For more information about sounds and sound quality in words, refer to **Chapter 12**.
- **Structure**—the way a poem is set up as whole. Does it rhyme? Have three stanzas of four lines each? Do the lines break in strange places? Some structure rules have names (haiku, sonnet), and others are up to the poet (free verse).
- **Word Choice**—what words a poet uses. Porridge is different from cereal. Robin is different from bird. Woman is different from girl. Picking the right verbs, adjectives, adverbs, and nouns can make all the difference in a poem. What you choose depends on your voice, which you can read about in **Chapter 8**.

- **Imagery**—the way a poet creates an emotion or experience within a poem. Explaining an abstract term in concrete language is difficult. I can tell you that I have a green two-wheeler bike with a frayed banana seat, but how do I tell you what it feels like to ride it down the biggest hill in my town? Creating a picture with words or using similes and metaphors are some of the ways a poet can do this. Additional ways to use imagery are discussed in **Section 3**.

As you can see, a lot of these tools are found in the Voice Section. That's because writing poetry is one of the most personal forms of writing and is often described as a "concentrated" form of writing. Every single word matters, and there is often more than one way to understand a line.

For example, take this poem by Percy Shelly, written in 1821.

> The flower that smiles to-day
> To-morrow dies;
> All that we wish to stay
> Tempts and then flies.
> What is this world's delight?
> Lightning that mocks the night,
> Brief even as bright.

On the surface, this poem seems to be about flowers and nature. But what if we think about these items as being metaphors for something else? What if we replace "flower" with "human"? Well, now the poem is maybe about how quickly life goes by, and how something could happen to cut life short—"Lightning" could be an accident, or an illness or anything else like that.

Poets do this all the time. Nature is often a stand-in for our humanity. Here are a few more examples:

> Ah Sun-flower! weary of time,
> Who countest the steps of the Sun:
> Seeking after that sweet golden clime
> Where the travellers journey is done.
> —William Blake

> As for man, his days are like grass;
> he flourishes like a flower of the field;
> for the wind passes over it, and it is gone,
> and its place knows it no more.
> —Psalms of David

You can see here how each of these poems used the same metaphor (flower=human life) but they used different words and structures to show their thoughts. Some of them rhymed, and some didn't. Some played with punctuation and capitalization, while others followed conventional rules. Poetry gives you the freedom to express yourself with many different options.

We covered word choice, imagery, and sound quality in **Section 3** on voice, so in this chapter, we are going to talk a little more about the structure of poetry and what tools you can use to create a poem. It is, after all, the structure of poetry with its line breaks and rhythms that set it apart from other types of writing.

Lines and Stanzas

One of the mysteries of poetry is where and when to put a line break. While some poems have a specific structure, most don't, and where to stop and start each line is up to you. But there are a few things to keep in mind with making these decisions—where you end your lines really does matter!

A **line of poetry** is a group of words that are collected together on one line of the paper. It ends when the poet wants it to end, not where the edge of the paper stops. A line can have one word or many words, and it can end with punctuation or not—all that is up to the poet.

Stanza names

- couplet (2 lines)
- tercet (3 lines)
- quatrain (4 lines)
- cinquain (5 lines)
- sestet (6 lines)
- septet (7 lines)
- octave (8 lines)

A **stanza of poetry** is a collection of lines deliberately put together in a group. There are no spaces between the lines of a stanza, but there IS a space between each stanza in a poem. Some poems only have one stanza, while others can have hundreds. John Milton's famous poem *Paradise Lost* is an epic poem with over 10,000 lines broken up into only ten stanzas!

Types of Line Breaks

Always, at the end of each line, there exists a brief pause. The pause is what creates motion in a poem, a step in the dance of the word. *Where* you put that pause matters.

There are two types of line breaks: end-stopped and enjamb.

An **end-stopped line** is a line that ends in punctuation (a comma, period, comma, or explanation point).

> Shall I compare thee to a summer's day?
> Thou art more lovely and more temperate.
> Rough winds do shake the darling buds of May,
> And summer's lease hath all too short a date.
> —from "Sonnet 18," William Shakespeare

The purpose of an end-stopped line is to give a rhythmic effect, or to end the thought. You slow down at punctuation, so it helps create pacing. An end-stopped line gives the sense of a completed thought within that line. NOTE: Some poets don't use the punctuation, but it is still considered an end-stopped line because it is considered to be a complete thought or phrase (the feeling of end-stop would not lessen, for example, in the poem above if the comma was left out after "May" above).

An **enjambment**, or "ending with an enjamb" is a line that does not end with any punctuation AND continues the thought into the next line. "Enjamb" is French for "crossing over."

> April is the cruelest month, breeding
> Lilacs out of the dead land, mixing
> Memory and desire, stirring
> Dull roots with spring rain.
> Winter kept us warm, covering
> Earth in forgetful snow, feeding
> A little life with dried tubers.
> —from "The Waste Land," TS Eliot

The purpose of an enjambment is to speed up a poem or emphasize a word for comic or emotional effect. It can also help explain complex thoughts across more than one line. NOTE: when you use enjambment, you can still use punctuation, just not at the end of the line.

Let's look again at Eliot's excerpt. How would the poem change if it had been written like this:

> April is the cruelest month,
>
> Breeding lilacs out of the dead land,
>
> Mixing memory and desire,
>
> Stirring dull roots with spring rain.

It changes the meaning, doesn't it? If you look again at the original, he ends every line with an action verb (breeding, mixing, stirring)—this creates a sense of movement, and focuses on the act of growth. When the lines are changed, look at how the focus becomes about cruelty, death, and dull roots. What you put at the end of a line matters!

Tools for Creating Rhythm

Rhythm in music is the beat—it's the thing you clap along to when you listen to a song. Poems also have a **rhythm**, a beat or pace that we can feel as we read. In fact, all songs are actually poems set to music! Some poems have an obvious rhythm (like a Dr. Seuss book), and others deliberately break rhythm patterns to make words or ideas stand out. There are several things you can do to create a rhythm (or avoid creating a rhythm) in your poem.

Meter

One way to create this rhythm is with the syllables in a line. How you use syllables to accent certain sounds is called **meter**. Meter in song is called the "beat." Look at this line from William Shakespeare:

> Shall I compare thee to a summer's day?

Do you hear the beat? One-TWO, three-FOUR, five-SIX, seven-EIGHT, nine-TEN. You can tap your foot along with it. But that beat changes if you switch the words around or use different endings:

> Comparing thee to summer

This doesn't have the same meter. Dr. Seuss does the same thing in his books:

> One fish, two fish, red fish, blue fish.

It's a different meter than Shakespeare, but it has the same effect. It wouldn't read the same if it said:

> Count the fish, red and blue.

Meter has many different styles and combinations, but all of them have to do with how your words create a rhythm. If a line doesn't sound "right" it might be because your meter is different in that line than the others in your poem—try switching the words around or changing the endings to create the same "beat" as the rest of your poem.

And remember, you are allowed to break all the rules of meter to make a poem as well—these types of poems are called **free verse**, and they can't be sung or clapped along with any set "beat."

Repeating Words

Repetition is the using the same word or statement throughout a poem to create meaning or heighten the emotional impact. It could be a repeated word, like this speech from Shakespeare's *Macbeth*:

> Tomorrow and tomorrow and tomorrow,
> Creeps in this petty pace from day to day,

Or it could be a repeated line, like in "Do Not Go Gentle Into That Good Night" by Dylan Thomaas, who repeats the title line four times in his 19 line poem.

A **refrain** is a repeated series of lines that repeat throughout the poem. The chorus of any song is a refrain.

Rhyme

Beginning poets often think that a poem has to rhyme. This is simply not true. A rhyme is only one tool to create structure, not the only tool! A **rhyme** is when two words have corresponding sounds. This most commonly happens at the end of lines, but it can also be done in the middle of lines.

There are two types of rhymes. **Full (or perfect) rhyme** is when vowel and the following consonants rhyme (fish/dish, smiling/filing). **Slant (or half) rhyme** is when the vowels do not match, but the following consonants do (fish/dash, smiling/falling)

Rhyming can also occur in two places. It can be in the same line, called an **internal rhyme**, or it can be at the end of a line, called an **external rhyme**. Edgar Allan Poe uses both in his famous poem "The Raven":

> Once upon a midnight dreary, while I pondered, weak and weary,
> Over many a quaint and curious volume of forgotten **lore**—
> While I nodded, nearly <u>napping</u>, suddenly there came a <u>tapping</u>,
> As of some one gently <u>rapping</u>, <u>rapping</u> at my chamber **door**.
> "'Tis some visitor," I muttered, "<u>tapping</u> at my chamber **door**—
> Only this and nothing **more**."

When a poem has a regular pattern of external rhymes, we call that the poem's **rhyme scheme**. Usually, rhyme schemes are designated by letters (abab, aabb, abacada). Each letter corresponds to the end of the line—if the sound is the same, use the same letter. So for the verse above from "The Raven," the rhyme scheme would be abcbbb. The first three lines are different, so they get their own letters (a, b, and c). But the last three lines match the second line, so we use the letter that we assigned to it—b.

These patterns can be anything that a poet chooses, but certain types of poems have rhyme rules. A limerick has a rhyme pattern of aabba. A Shakespearean sonnet is more complicated and must follow the rhyme scheme of abab cdcd efef gg. Unless you are following a specific form, you are allowed to follow any rhyme scheme you like, or have none at all!

Types of Poems

Blank Verse: A poem that has meter, but no rhyme.

Rhymed Poetry: A poem that rhymes, although the scheme varies.

Free Verse: A poem that has no meter or rhyme.

Epic: A lengthy narrative poem that typically talks about the heroic exploits and adventures of a character from long ago.

Narrative Poetry: A poem that tells a story.

Haiku: A three-line poem with five syllables, seven syllables, and five syllables in the three lines.

Pastoral Poem: A poem that talks about the natural world, rural life, and landscapes.

Sonnet: A 14-line poem that often talks about love and has a rhyme scheme of abab cdcd efef gg.

Ode: A poem that is a tribute to its subject

Limerick: A five-line poem that consists of single stanza, aabba rhyme scheme, and is often humorous

Ballad: A narrative poem that is typically sung—many songs are ballads.

Thinking Poetically

A lot of students are daunted by poetry. It can be hard to find the right rhyme and limiting yourself to words that rhyme can make the poem sound cliché or sing-songy. The more you read poems and experiment with writing your own poems, the more you will be able to communicate through your words. Think about poems that you like—maybe Shel Silverstein, a psalm, or even song lyrics. Think about the emotions that poems can make you feel. And then put your pen to paper and see what you come up with! Have fun with it. Rhyme and don't rhyme. Write in stanzas; write in free verse. Look for inspiration in nature and your feelings. You might find out poems aren't so hard after all!

Questions as you read each poem:

- List one use of figurative language.
- Find one example of using sound quality.
- Name one use of imagery.
- Fine one structural tool the poet employed.
- List two sensory details the author had.

Student Examples

Flying

By Spencer D., 14

Get him! I yelled
As I fly towards the trampoline in my yard like a hawk diving on prey
My very own dragons nest
Learning to fly with my best friend Peter

Shooting through the air
Shiny springs squeaking with every bounce
Fighting dragons who attack our lair
Playing Pokémon between battles

Long abandoned the old sun bleached trampoline sits alone
Rusty weathered springs, threadbare fabric
I see all the fun times I had
And I see how much I have grown up in the last few years

The Cardboard Box

By Allison S., 15

I'm five years old wearing a tutu
And colorful mismatched socks
I'm playing in the living room
With a battered cardboard box

It is..

A ship to sail the weathered seas
A palace with a moat
A table used to serve high teas
A pen to cage a goat

A writing desk to write a poem
A theater for a sock
A tiny fairy's spacious home
A safe with a large lock

A rag doll's storage space for clothes
A brick to build a wall
A dungeon to lock up your foes
A booth to make a call

A house for dolls, a mini fridge
A pot to plant a tree
A princess's fine carriage
A hive for several bees

It used to be all of these things
Imagination had no locks
But now I'm fifteen and all I see
Is a simple cardboard box

Seasons

By: Grace F., 13

You're the snowflake on the window
The snowman in the yard
Your icicle hanging from the gutter
A pond to ice skate on
You're the hot chocolate to warm me up
And the whipped cream floating on top
You're the ornament on the tree
And cookies for Santa

You're the daffodils that are starting to peek
The crocuses starting to bloom
You're the animals peeking out from their homes
The sign of no more snow
You're the sun peeking through the clouds
The kids coming out to play
You're the birds chirping
And the squirrels chattering

You're the sun burning bright
The sprinkler in the front yard
You're the cold waves crashing on the beach
The sand crunching beneath my toes
You're the ice in my lemonade
The sweetener in my tea

The Crash of the Hurricane

By Aidan L., 14

The static of water crackles in one's ears
A vacuum of void consumes everything around it
Constant crashing of tiny buildings
A machine gun onslaught that never ends
A fine mist descends upon the thunder
Calm repetitiveness in a chaotic storm

My Herb Store

By Abigail C., 13

Would you like some spices?
I say to my customer, who is really my mom.
We sell herbal tea, medicine, name anything we have it!
My herb store is in the middle of the country, and it is made of brick and hard work.
I make the two-day trip into town if we run out of spices, but business is booming!
Now, I step into my backyard and see the tumbling pile of bricks that was my herb store.
The piles of paprika and other mysterious powders look like dirt and crumbled charcoal.
The bay leaves and tea leaves have a striking resemblance to stray weeds, pulled out from my backyard. What happened? Why did the magic fade?
My assistant is gone, and so is my childhood.
If I had the chance to bring it all back, I would, oh how I wish I could.

NOTE: Student examples appear in original format and may contain slight grammar errors.

Activities

Key Terms

Define the following key terms: poem, sound quality, structure, word choice, imagery, line, stanza, end-stopped line, enjambment, rhythm, meter, free verse, repetition, refrain, rhyme, full rhyme, slant rhyme, internal rhyme, external rhyme

Comprehension

1) What are the tools you can use to create rhythm in a poem?
2) What is a stanza and how are line breaks important in poetry?

Practice

1) Answer the question in the sidebar next to Student Examples for all five poems.

Application

1) Write a poem with at least four stanzas about something in nature.
2) Write a poem with a refrain.
3) Write a poem about a smell—use as many metaphors and similes as you can to describe it.

More activities and student examples available at **www.writefromtheheart.org/resourceguide**.

Section 5: Academic Writing Styles

Academic writing differs from creative writing because its purpose is to inform or persuade its audience, which means it is more formal. However, just because you are using a more formal voice, that doesn't mean your academic writing needs to be boring. You can use some of the same techniques from creative writing to add interest to your academic writing.

In this section, you will learn how to make your academic writing clear, concise, and backed up by evidence. By defining your focus and using the correct structure, you will find it easier to plan your essays. We will also be mentioning ways to make sure your voice shines in these essays as well.

Chapter 17: Expository Writing

Expository essays are one of the most common genres in academic writing. **Expository** means that the writer is "exposing" the audience to something - explaining or describing his or her topic to the audience. Sometimes this type of writing is called **informative writing.** Common topics of expository writing include things like reporting on historical figures or events, explaining the process of doing something, telling how something works, and describing the way to do something.

The key to writing a strong expository paper is knowing *why* you are writing. A common mistake students make is that they fall into the "I am going to tell you" trap. Imagine your assignment is to write an expository essay informing us about a hobby you like, and you choose gardening. Great! But this is where a lot of students get stuck. What is your thesis? Many think to themselves, "Ummmm...that I like gardening??" and so they write a thesis that reads, "I am going to tell you about gardening." But recall from **Chapter 4** that this is not a thesis statement: it has your topic but doesn't tell us what you are going to show or prove about your topic (and it starts with an "I am going to..." off-limits statement!).

So what do you do? You need to figure out what you are going to show or prove! In expository assignments, this is sometimes stated as "the significance of the topic." Go back to your topic of gardening. What can you show or prove? Lots of things! You could explain the reasons it is enjoyable. You could explain what tools you need to do it well. You could explain different types of gardening. You could explain the different options for things to grow. Whichever you choose will yield a completely different paper, because you will need different supporting points:

Thesis: Gardening is an enjoyable hobby because of the health, environmental, and personal benefits.

> **Supporting points:** health benefits; environmental benefits; personal benefits

Thesis: Gardening is a great hobby if you have the proper tools for each phase of the process.

> **Supporting points:** tools for preparing the garden; tools for maintaining the garden; tools for harvesting the garden

Thesis: Gardening is a hobby anyone can do, no matter what space they have available.

> **Supporting points:** gardening in the yard; container gardening; greenhouse gardening

Thesis: Gardening is a hobby that allows you to grow a variety of plants and vegetables depending on your interests.

> **Supporting points**: vegetable gardening; flower gardening; herb gardening

Do you see how having a thesis that is specific and tells what you are going to show can completely change the content of your paper? All of those choices are excellent for a paper on a hobby. All of them explain *why* you are writing and the significance of your topic to the reader. The same holds true if you are writing a paper for history class about a famous person. You need to know why you are writing and what you are going to show or explain.

Structure of Expository Essays

Expository essays are typically written in the third-person voice (see **Chapter 8**), and they follow a straightforward structure. They include an introduction, several body paragraphs, and a concluding paragraph. Some writers create five-paragraph essays (one introductory paragraph, three body paragraphs, and one concluding paragraph). But as you advance in writing, you might find that each supporting point needs additional paragraphs of explanation. Excellent expository essays can follow a variety of different lengths and formats. For more information on the parts of a draft, see **Section 2**.

In expository essays, opinions are *not* the driving factor—facts are. However, in introductions and conclusions, opinions do make appearances. Usually, when writing in the expository style, it is helpful to give readers a sense of the significance of your topic. For example, if you're writing about how to manage a vegetable garden, why should your reader care about that process? Why is it significant to consider? The introduction and conclusion of the expository essay usually address those questions so that the audience is motivated to read the essay and is able to connect all of the details and explanations of what they read to the larger world.

You should also be writing your expository papers with voice. Remember from **Section 3** that your voice is made up of your personality, tone, point of view, vocabulary, and syntax. All of these should make an appearance in an expository essay. You can also use descriptive details when explaining your topic. Inner ideas should be quotations from experts, hypotheticals, or flashback transitions. And you will probably have to play with time in any paper covering a historical event—remember to focus on the parts of the events that show/prove your thesis statement and shrink down the parts in between.

Expository papers can be called lots of different things: informative paper, definition paper, descriptive paper, and more. Anything that is designed to inform (not persuade) is an expository paper. In fact, a lot of the research papers that will be assigned to you in your high school and even college years will be informative expository papers. You can look at **Section 7** for more information about how to include research in an expository paper.

Student Example #1

The Invention of Bluetooth

By Misa S., 12

A deafening amount of noise fills a hot, stuffy office as most of the people that work there are on a call talking off of wireless headsets. There is a lot of clicking as other people are printing documents off their computer even though the printer is in a different room. These wireless headsets and printers work because of a technology called Bluetooth. The invention of Bluetooth has given people many useful and convenient benefits that they use almost every day.

In 1994, Bluetooth was invented by a Swedish telecommunication company called Ericsson. They wanted to replace the clutter of cords, that were used at the time to communicate between different devices, with a wireless substitute. Other companies such as Nokia and Intel had also started coming up with ideas of connecting devices wirelessly. Two years later, five companies, Ericsson, Nokia, Intel, Toshiba, and IBM, got together and decided to form the Bluetooth Special Interest Group (SIG) which was officially established in 1998 because they realized that in order for them to be able to connect devices from different companies. They decided to collaborate because in order for Bluetooth to work with devices from different companies, it would have to be standardized. SIG released Bluetooth 1.0 Specification was released an year later. By 2001, a mobile phone, a headset, a printer, and several other devices with Bluetooth came out. In 2009, SIG came out with Core Specification Version 3.0 HS. The Core Specification Version 3.0 HS made Bluetooth a high speed technology. An year later, they started using Bluetooth Core Specification Version 4.0, which allowed Bluetooth to be low-energy. By 2014, 90% of mobile phones worldwide had started using Bluetooth.

There are two types of Bluetooth. One type is Basic Rate/Enhanced Data Rate (BR/EDR). BR/EDR uses a continuous wireless connection. BR/EDR sends a steady stream of data like a stream of water continuously flowing into a sink. The other type is Low Energy (LE). LE uses a short-burst wireless connection. LE sends short bursts of data over to the other device. BR/EDR is used for wireless headsets and hands-free, while LE is used for heart monitors and way-finding services. Both types of Bluetooth do similar things, but they are used for their own purposes.

Bluetooth has benefited us in many ways. One way people have been benefited by it is by being able to wirelessly connect devices without any cost. For instance, a phone can be wirelessly connected to a car so that hands-free can be used. This enables people to talk on the phone without even having to get their phone out, which makes driving safer because they are not distracted by holding their phone. An iPad can also be connected to a keyboard by using Bluetooth, so that people can type on a keyboard instead of using the keyboard that pops up on the screen. This makes it easier and faster to type, and it is also less strenuous on their hands. The benefits Bluetooth has given people has made their lives much easier than it would have been without Bluetooth.

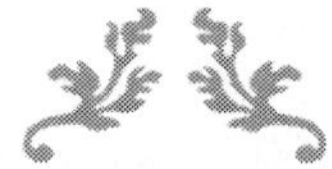

Questions as you read:

- What is the topic of the essay?
- What is the significance of this topic?
- Why does the writer think it's important to talk about it?
- What three points does the writer use to show or explain the thesis?

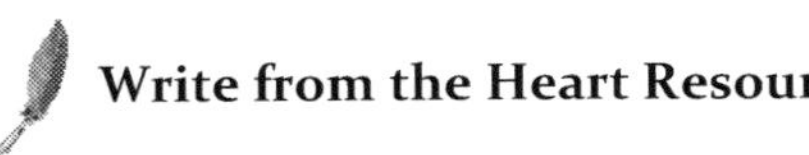

These days many people probably use Bluetooth almost everyday without thinking about how much it has changed their lives. As a result of Bluetooth, people have less untidiness in their houses than they would have had if Bluetooth had not been invented. Even though it is a fairly new invention, it has already impacted us in many ways, and it will probably continue to impact people even more.

Student Example #2

The Importance of Live Theater in Society

Alison S., 15

When most people think of entertainment, they think of a cell phone, a tablet or a movie screen. Their worlds are lit up by these devices which they use as their means of entertaining themselves. They live in a world where entertainment is vastly available and have access to video games, movies, TV shows and so much more without having to do more than unlock a screen.

In a world where entertainment is always at society's finger tips, is live theater necessary? It turns out that theater is actually a great blessing that is underestimated by many people. Theater does so much for society that most people don't even realize. Theater can show an audience a powerful message with the aid of live acting as well as song and dance, can socially enrich society by providing an outlet for self-expression and discovery, and can be used as an extremely powerful tool for education.

Live theater is an asset to society for many reasons, one of these reasons being the powerful messages it gives through song, acting and dance. A story told through these three actions is so much more powerful than any other type of story and can greatly effect an audience. The reason for this is that theater is so much more engaging than any other type of entertainment because it is live and because it is performed by people. Some might argue that movies and TV shows, which are also performed by people, are just as good. However, live theater has a much bigger effect simply because it is live. Broadway musicals cannot be paused or skipped. This makes them so much more engaging than anything shown

on a screen. Theater shows an audience a message through live acting and this can impact an audience greatly. Actions speak louder than words, and theater persuades an audience through showing, rather than telling. Sometimes a singular song or dance performed in a musical theater production can have life changing effects. This is because studies have shown that music has an extremely powerful emotional impact on people. Songs performed onstage, such as "It's Quiet Uptown" from Hamilton are so powerful that they can move an audience to tears. Songs like these have effective melodies and carefully created lyrics designed to move an audience in such a way. Not to mention how the facial expressions acted out by the people singing onstage can seriously cut into an audience member's heart. Such effective musicals have actually caused people to alter their world view.

Questions as you read:

- What is the topic of the essay?
- What is the significance of this topic?
- Why does the writer think it's important to talk about it?
- What three points does the writer use to show or explain the thesis?

Theater also does a lot for society by socially enriching culture. Not only is theater a form of self-expression, but it also helps a lot with self-discovery. Actors report that playing a character and stepping into someone else's shoes has taught them a lot about their own lives and personalities. Someone might not know just how determined and ambitious they are until they play a character such as Alexander in Hamilton. Or maybe an actress had absolutely no clue how much she liked to read until she played Belle in Beauty and the Beast. As actress Stella Adler once said: "The theatre was created to tell people the truth about life and the social situation." Not only does involvement in theater teach the actors more about themselves, but it also unites the audience together in the telling of a story. Theater truly does bring people together in a very special and unique way that not many other entertainment outlets can emulate.

Even though live theater is normally viewed as a source of entertainment, it also multitasks as a powerful education tool. There is so much to be learned about the world, and musicals explore a vast variety of topics and opinions. The new 2015 Musical Hamilton, for example, has enraptured countless teenagers through a unique style of Broadway music and has motivated these young adults to learn more about the American Revolution. Before this musical, founding fathers were just dry old lessons to be learned from history books. Once the story of the revolution was set to music, however, they began to come to life. Jefferson, Washington, Madison and Hamilton are no longer boring dead people with their faces on money. Now they are characters with motivations, deep and carefully researched personalities and entertaining backstories. Never in a million years had anyone imagined that the story of the American Revolution would become such an engaging story for all ages but now, with the help of music and dance, it is an entertaining story full of feuding, romance, and legacy. This is only one example of how educational live theater can be. Musicals like Annie show the devastation of a time period, such as the great depression, by telling a story. There are also musicals such as "Oliver!", the musical adaptation of Charles Dicken's 'Oliver Twist' that come from classic literature and bring dusty old books to life with their powerful impact. A show doesn't have to be just a show. It can also teach an audience an extremely important lesson.

In conclusion, theater does so much more for society than most people give it credit for. It can greatly impact an audience with an effective portrayal of a story told with music and dance as well as providing an outlet for self-expression. Likewise, society should never forget how socially enriching live theater is and how educational it can be. Even though everyone does have access to other methods of entertainment, they should never let the classic art of live theater die.

Note: Student examples appear in original format and may contain slight grammar errors.

Activities

Key Terms

Define the following key terms: expository, informative essay

Comprehension

1) What is the key to writing a successful expository or informative essay?
2) List four different types of essays that would be considered an expository essay

Practice

1) Answer the questions in the sidebar for Student Example #1.
2) Answer the questions in the sidebar for Student Example #2.

Application

1) Write a paragraph explaining the importance of one of the following: brushing your teeth, following your parents' instructions, or eating healthy foods.
2) Choose an activity and write an essay explaining the benefits of participating in that activity.

More activities and student examples available at **www.writefromtheheart.org/resourceguide**.

Chapter 18: Analytical Writing

Analytical essays break down something in smaller parts in order to talk about it. Think of a scientist trying to analyze a blood sample under a microscope to figure out what is making a person sick. They look closely at each piece of the sample: the white blood cells, the red blood cells, and investigate to see if any additional specimens are there that shouldn't be. They count and look closely, trying to understand the whole problem (why the person is sick) by looking at the parts.

That's what analytical writing does. It discusses the parts of something in order to understand the whole. Using these pieces, the writer can explain the importance of doing a task correctly, or why something happened, or what makes a book interesting. There are several types of analytical essays, depending on what you are analyzing.

Process Essay

A **process essay** describes the step-by-step instructions of "how-to" do something or it explains how something was done. Whether your topic is how to bake a cake, bathe a cat, or landscape a yard, your reader should understand what they would need to do. Process essays should be easy to follow and organized to ensure the reader can follow the steps.

There are two types of process essays. **Directional process essays** give instructions or steps on how to accomplish a specific task. These are essays about "how to" do something like create a great birthday party or apply first aid when someone is choking. **Informational process essays** explain or analyze a process that was already done. An example would be how the Grand Canyon was formed—this isn't something the reader can re-create, but you can explain in steps how it happened.

The key for writing a process essay is, once again, in the thesis. A process paper's thesis needs to explain what you are going to show or prove. It could discuss the significance of the process or why following the steps are important.

Examples:

> Baking a cake is a simple process but following the steps carefully will help any baker successfully create a beautiful dessert.
>
> To avoid accidents while hunting, it is important to follow the proper steps for cleaning and maintaining your hunting equipment.
>
> 
>
> The formation of the Grand Canyon was a combination of time and natural processes that created a natural wonder.

The next part of writing a process essay is selecting your supporting points. Obviously, these will be the steps of the process. But how do you organize them? Let's look at the topic of baking a cake. What are the steps to the process?

Read the recipe
Gather ingredients
Get your supplies
Preheat the oven
Mix together dry ingredients
Mix wet ingredients
Blend wet and dry together
Add any special ingredients
Prepare pans
Pour batter in the pans
Put in the oven
Bake according to recipe
Test for doneness
Remove from oven
Let cool
Ice the cake

That's a lot of steps! Some of them might only need one sentence of explanation, but others might need several sentences. And usually an essay has 3-4 supporting points, not 16!! You can't really make a paragraph about each one. So what do you do? Organize the steps into larger parts or segments. In this case, you might organize your paper into the following sections: Preparing to Bake, Mixing the Ingredients, and Baking. You could take that last step and add a fourth point of Finishing Touches and add additional tips about decorating as well. Since you already wrote out all the steps, you know exactly what to put in each section!

The last part is to remember the purpose of this paper in your organization and transitions. Because it's a process, everything should be in chronological order, and your transitions should show the shift from each step and section. First, second, next, then, and last are good words. Try to change the words you use, so every paragraph doesn't start with "then..." You can also use phrases that refer back to the last step: "After mixing the wet ingredients..." Don't forget transitions from one paragraph to the next. Don't number the steps.

Look back at this section: I just wrote a process paper on "how to write a process paper"! I had an introduction and a thesis (Process essays should be easy to follow and organized to ensure the reader can follow the steps.) I explained any terms and what they were, and then listed the steps to writing one in three sections:

1. Understand your purpose
    a. Decide what type of process essay
    b. Write a strong thesis
2. Deciding on your support paragraphs
    a. List out your steps
    b. Organize into sections
3. Organizing the draft
    a. Order
    b. Transitions

And this last paragraph, reviewing all my points and wrapping things up, is my conclusion! Note: you would not put an outline in your conclusion, but I did for instructional purposes.

Tips:

- Include all steps—even things that seem obvious to you
- Explain why each step is necessary and include common mistakes to avoid if applicable.
- Define any terms the reader may not know.
- Offer clear descriptions of tools or materials.
- Don't switch pronouns—if you start in first person ("I"), stay in first person. Don't change to second person ("you") halfway through.
- Make sure you write with voice—it should be an essay, not an instruction manual

Student Example #1

How to Study

By Dahye L., 12

Studying. Everyone has a different idea about it! But how does it make you feel? Excited, or droopy? If you feel droopy, have you tried the RRR method? If you haven't tried it or heard of it, there is an easy way to learn how to study. When studying, it is important for us to be ready, recapitulate, and rest.

The first step you need to do in order to study, which is the most important and easiest, is to be ready. Know what you're studying. To know what you're studying means to know what subject you are studying. Are you studying for science or is it for math? Once you know the main topic, you will know the follow-up topics you are learning. For example, is it earth and space science or life science? Is it about graphs or algebra?

The other thing you need to do to get ready is to collect the materials you need to study. Things such as your textbooks, notebooks, pencils, or any other thing you need should be nearby. After you have done that, put away anything that can possibly distract you. Things like your phone and laptop should be placed aside unless needed. And if those things are needed for some reason, it may be a good idea to put incoming messages on mute, so that you will not be tempted to check who it's from and what it is about, which will likely lead you out of your study.

Now that you're all set up, set a timer for 45 minutes and start studying. Setting a timer can be useful so that you don't wander off so often you don't get as much study as you had planned, or so that you can concentrate on studying rather than keep looking at the time to see how much you have studied. this is where you recapitulate. Recapitulating means summarizing and restating the main points. When studying, write notes, review the facts, and say things out loud to remember better. And if someone near you is studying the same thing, it would be an advantageous idea to study together by teaching the subject to each other, which is another great way to remember the subject. But please note that people have different characteristics that for some people group studies are more beneficial, and for some studying alone is better.

Then when the timer rings, it's time for your 15 minutes break! Set a timer for 15 minutes and rest by closing your eyes, drinking cool water, or anything that pleases you. Resting is very important when studying because when resting, it allows your body and mind to refresh, which will give you a fresh start in the next 45 minutes of studying.

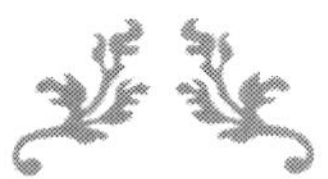

Questions as you read:

- Is this essay discussing directional or informational process?
- What three stages or sections did they break the process up into?
- List the transitions used in this essay.
- What is the significance of this topic? Why does the writer think it's important to talk about it?

But if these steps still do not help you to study, you could try something a bit different. You could try resting 20 minutes and studying 40 minutes, or maybe listen to classical music when studying. You also could go somewhere very quiet if you are very sensitive to the slightest sounds. Or change the time you study to early in the morning, or maybe late at night, just that you find the perfect studying time for yourself. Another great idea would be to study right after exercising. But just be sure there is nothing very exciting that is to happen later because then, it may distract your studying.

There are so many ways you can study, but it is important to find the best way for you. But whatever you do, be ready for what is to come, recapitulate what you are studying, and rest once in a while. If you struggle with studying, try it with the RRR method!

Cause-Effect Essays

Cause-effect essays look at a specific event or situation. It either explains the circumstances leading to that event, or it predicts what will happen as the result of a current situation. Cause-effect essays tend to be informative, factual, and detailed.

Your thesis statement should state what you are going to show or prove. It does not just explain what happened before or after an event in time. Instead it tells about HOW or WHY the causes lead to the event (or HOW or WHY the event had specific effects). Here is a picture of an event/situation and what the causes/effects look like:

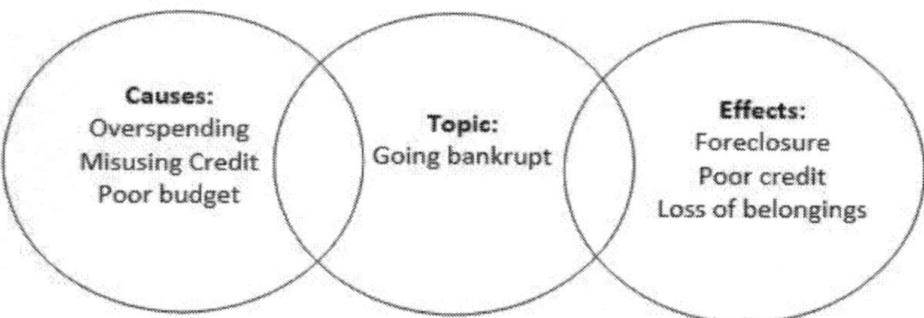

If you were going to write an essay on how someone ends up in bankruptcy, you could write a thesis that explains the causes:

The main causes of bankruptcy are all related to mismanaging one's money.

Your support would be three sections explaining the three causes: overspending, misusing credit, and poor budget.

If you were going to write an essay explaining the effects of the situation of bankruptcy, you could write a thesis like this:

Declaring bankruptcy has an impact on all financial areas of a person's life.

Notice that "reasons" and "impact" are just another way to say "cause" or "effect." Your support would be three sections explaining the three effects: foreclosure, poor credit, loss of belongings.

Usually, these essays talk about *either* the causes or effects of something. On rare occasions, you might talk about both, but this is not common.

Student Example #2

Ocean Pollution

By Timothy C., 15

Trash floated on the surface of the Pacific Ocean, seemingly for miles. The clear remains of coke bottles and plastic garbage bags creates a vast landscape across the clear blue water. The once refreshing smell of salt, now is polluted with the smell of waste, and baked plastic. The blanket of waste blocks the sunlight from reaching the algae and plankton that make their home below the surface. Plastic bags can be mistaken for jellyfish and end up inside the animals which have called this ocean home for centuries.

But ocean pollution doesn't just affect the surface, *One Green Planet*, a news website dedicated to making a healthier world, estimates that nearly 70% of the trash sinks to the bottom of the ocean, affecting the marine life below the surface. But ocean pollution can be seen everywhere. Most of this massive problem however, can be traced back to three main causes: plastics and non-recyclable materials, oil spills, and deep-sea mining.

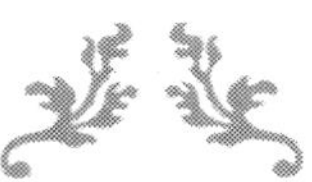

Questions as you read:

- Is this essay discussing the causes or the effects of the topic?
- What three causes or effects did they list?
- List the transitions used in this essay.
- What is the significance of this topic? Why does the writer think it's important to talk about it?

Evidence of the ocean's problem can be seen at beaches around the world, where trash stretches across the coastline, or the dunes of the surrounding area for miles, robbing the landscape of its natural beauty. Obviously trash on the beach isn't ocean pollution, but as soon as the rain comes, or the tide washes up, the trash is eventually washed into the ocean. After months of traveling through the water, the garbage normally makes its way into one of three water gyres. Giant areas of circulating ocean currents, that bring trash, and

other waste into their zones and trap them inside a type of border line. These giant areas are found in the centers of the world's oceans, the first of which is in the Pacific Ocean, the best known of them all. The Great Pacific Garbage Patch or GPGP. This zone is the biggest of the three, estimated at around twice the size of Texas! The other two large gyres are located in the Indian Ocean, and The Atlantic Ocean. These patches however, are still very big, and are composed of the same substances as the Pacific gyre. Almost all of which come from ocean pollution! But what causes this great problem?

Non-recyclable materials can be traced back as the greatest source of ocean pollution. It starts with something as simple as a person not picking up their plastic water bottle, styrofoam cup, or one-use plastic bag, while they're lounging by a river or beach. In fact, according to *Made For Minds*, 90% of all plastic pollution can be traced back to just 10 rivers! All of which are found in Asia or Africa! These rivers are such huge contributors, because of the massive populations that live on their banks. With so many people, pollution is inevitable. After exiting these rivers, the plastic will float around the earth and most likely end up in one of three gyres. But it's not just plastic that ends up there.

The gyres are also filled with gallons of oil from oil spills around the world. Oil spills are a type of major scale disaster that spread tons of gallons of oil into rivers or oceans. The oil from these disasters normally also end up one of the gyres. adding to the already gathering masses of trash. These spills commonly result from a mistake in/on barges, refinery facilities, and tankers. Sadly it isn't all by accident, some people illegally dump crude oil into the ocean because they'd rather not spend money on decomposing their waste oil. According to the International Tanker Owners Pollution Federation Limited, 1.7 billion gallons of oil were lost to the seas from 1970-2009. If every gallon equaled one foot, the amount of oil in the ocean would be able to wrap around the world approximately 13 times! Not only is it harmful to the environment, but oil is also very difficult to clean up, once it has entered the oceans.

Another cause of ocean pollution is deep-sea mining. Deep-sea mining is exactly what it sounds like. Mining underwater for gold and other metals, that can no longer be found on the surface. This idea at first, appears amazing. After all, why not mine the metal that's just sitting there? But it isn't that simple. This process takes place 200m below the surface of the ocean where animals are not use to seeing light and are specially adapted for darkness. Mining the depths of the ocean with giant drills, sends vibrations into the ground, floods the area with light, and destroys habitats. Killing the animals that live where areas are being drilled, and flattening their homes. Rewriting the ecosystems of deep-sea creatures.

The gyres in the ocean are spreading exponentially everyday, and something needs to be done to stop them. These giant "Islands" of trash are killing animals, destroying plankton, and obliterating habitats. If all the plankton is destroyed, the animals that feed off them, like fish or dolphins, cannot find food and die. Slowly the death tolls climb up the food chain. Until, sooner or later this earth is losing entire species to extinction. But there is hope!

Organizations like 4Ocean and The Ocean Cleanup are doing their best to rid the seas of waste, but everyone can do something to help. For example, 4Ocean sells bracelets made from recycled ocean plastic and glass for $20. Each purchase is guaranteed to clear 1 lb. of trash from the ocean. If every person in America bought a bracelet from 4Ocean, 327 million pounds of garbage would be cleared from the ocean. And while this sounds like an enormous amount, it isn't even 1/20 of the amount of trash that enters the ocean each year! And although stopping this problem sounds daunting, it can be stopped if we all contribute. An easy way people can help out, is by doing something as simple as not littering in rivers or creeks. Or cleaning up trash you find in, or around bodies of water. Clean water isn't out of reach! Together everyone can help stop trashing our oceans, and make the world's waters beautiful again.

Literary Analysis Essays

Literary analysis means closely studying a fictional text, interpreting its meaning, and exploring why the author made certain choices. This is not just a summary of the plot or a book report, but is looking at the the parts of a work to understand something deeper about it. It can be applied to any form of writing—novels, short stories, poems, plays, etc.

A good way to think of literary analysis is that it is the opposite of narrative writing, which you learned about in **Chapter 14**. Instead of building the story with plot, characters, themes, and settings, you are breaking the story apart to show or explain to the reader how the story developed.

Some ways that you can analyze a story are:

- Talk about a specific character and how they changed throughout the story.
- Explain what the theme is and how events in the plot reveal that theme.
- Show how the setting forced certain things to happen in the plot.
- Talk about how two characters who are opposites reveal the right and wrong way to do something.
- Pick a symbol and look at the places that it showed up in the story to reveal an idea.
- Look at the point of view and show how this style increased suspense or connection for the reader.

There are many ways you can use literary analysis in academic writing. You could write a short analysis explaining a character's change for a literature class. You could write a comparison paper where you compare/contrast literary elements in two books. You could write a review of a book you read, explaining to an audience why you would or wouldn't recommend it. In high school and college, literary analysis often uses a critical approach, meaning the author looks at the work with a specific idea in mind—they might analyze the economic values of a work, or how women are treated in a novel. When you take classes studying literature specifically, you will learn the skills for how to do this well.

In any literary analysis, you are looking at the pieces of a fictional work to explain some sort of larger idea that the pieces reveal. Whether it's about a character or setting or plot, the thesis tells the reader what the larger idea is that you will show or explain. Your supporting points are examples from the story that add up to create that larger idea. If a character changes, you should talk about what they were like in the beginning, middle and end. If you are discussing a theme or a symbol, you might pick three events or moments when this is revealed. Often, in this type of writing, you should assume that your audience has also read the story and is looking for a deeper understanding of the story, so it's okay to spoil the ending (unless you are writing a review or recommendation). Your conclusion should include telling your audience why this analysis is important: what does this theme teach us, or what does the character changing help us understand about life? Think about what the book or story is trying to get its audience to learn and highlight that in your conclusion.

Literary Analysis vs. Book Reports

Early in your school years, you may have written a book report. A report summarizes all the key details of the plot, characters, setting, conflict, and resolution. A book *report* is NOT the same as literary analysis. A report simply labels all the pieces; a literary analysis takes all those pieces and draws a conclusion about a larger idea. Literary analysis takes the parts to explain what the characters reveal about a theme, or to compare two works, or to recommend a work to an audience. A book report simply summarizes the whole plot of the book without actively evaluating it.

Student Example #3

Pip's Eerie Adventure: *Great Expectations*

By Anna L., 16

"Think for a moment of the long chain of iron or gold of thorns or flowers, that would never have bound you, but for the formation of the first link on one memorable day" (67). Thus, begins the journey with Philip Pirrip, nicknamed "Pip." In Charles Dickens' novel, *Great Expectations,* Pip undergoes many adventures. He's an orphaned boy living with Mr. and Mrs. Joe Gargery, his sister and her blacksmith husband. One day he meets wealthy, elderly Miss Havisham and that first link on that day begins the tale. Nevertheless, what masterfully ties the whole story together is Dicken's use of Gothic themes throughout. He utilizes setting, high emotion, and psychological themes to make the novel Gothic. Therefore, *Great Expectations* by Charles Dickens is an excellent book to read for a straightforward example of Gothic themes in literature.

Oftentimes, Gothic authors use the setting to give a tale an eerie feel most readers enjoy. *Great Expectations* is no different. The setting is the most memorable Gothic theme used throughout *Great Expectations.* From the whispering wind through the marshes at night to the creaky, candle-lit manor, Dickens' settings give one the shivers! The book opens in a graveyard on a gloomy night, as tombstones and graves are exactly what Gothic authors are proud to write about! These authors also enjoy describing candle-lit castles because the old and unknown add an eerie feel. Dickens has characteristics analogous to castles placed in some homes for the same purpose. Pip's friend "Wemmick's house was a little wooden cottage" which had a bridge that "crossed a chasm about four feet wide" exactly like a castle's drawbridge (195)! Even Miss Havisham's manor is described like a castle with "mysterious passages of an unknown house" lit by candles (54). Dickens keeps one on edge with descriptions of the settings and encompasses a Gothic theme in the process!

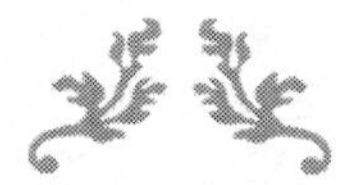

Questions as you read:

- What element of narrative did the author choose to discuss?
- What larger idea are they trying to show or explain?
- List the three moments from the book that they chose to support their thesis.
- What does the author say this analysis helps us understand?

Great Expectations also incorporates the Gothic theme of characters having high, or overdramatic emotions. This causes characters to have outbursts, sudden mood changes, or brooding natures adding to the tension Gothic authors love. Pip is habitually quiet so his emotions aren't frequently expressed in speech. However, as the tale is told from his perspective, the reader knows what's going on inside his head and understands Pip's emotions are simply ineffable. Moreover, his lack of speech typically shows just how much he's brooding inside. But even Pip has his own passionate outbursts. In one such intractable eruption, it's shown just how much he loves Estella, a beautiful girl, when he claims that she's "part of my existence, part of myself" (345). Other characters are passionate, too. Miss Havisham, in one extreme debacle, "wrung her hands...crushed her white hair, and returned to...cry over and over again" (377). Another example of this theme is how Pip's Uncle Joe is incredibly loving towards Pip and therefore impacts both him and the plot of *Great Expectations* considerably. Joe's love makes Pip, also in an outburst, whisper behind Joe's back, "O God bless him! O God bless this gentle Christian man! (439)"

Psychological themes, including the struggle of desire versus duty, searching for often intangible things, or isolation, are also highly prevalent in *Great Expectations*. Pip struggles with desire versus duty when he contemplates leaving home to become a gentleman. He thinks he can't be content with the blacksmith trade he's destined for, because though he "had liked it once...once was not now" (99). One sees Pip struggling with his desire to be a gentleman against his duty of his blacksmith job with Joe. Moreover, the theme of searching is tied into the desire versus duty theme when Pip desperately searches for the answer to that dilemma and is left to ponder and brood like many Gothic characters. Lastly, isolation is seen when Miss Havisham shuts herself off from the outside world in her manor due to grief. There are even severe consequences for "in seclusion...her mind, brooding solitary, had grown diseased" (377-378). Her diseased mind leads her to act crazy, further giving a Gothic feel to Dickens' tale.

To be Gothic, a story must encompass many characteristics. *Great Expectations* incorporates many such themes which make it the novel it is. The main themes include the settings, dramatic emotions, and psychological themes. Due to this, *Great Expectations* by Charles Dickens is a tremendous book to study for a simple model of Gothic themes in literature. Dickens even reintroduces characters from the beginning of the story later on, adding a mysterious atmosphere often seen in Gothic novels. Some may be concerned that this will confuse the tale, but Dickens masterfully describes his characters so one easily remembers them and their mysterious ambiance. If you choose to read *Great Expectations*, see if you can find more examples of these Gothic themes throughout Pip's eerie adventure!

NOTE::Student examples appear in original format and may contain slight grammar errors].

Activities

Key Terms

Define the following key terms: analytical essay, process essay, directional process essay, informational process essay, cause-effect essay, literary analysis essay

Comprehension

1) Why should a writer use analytical writing?
2) What is the best way to organize the steps in a process paper?

Practice

1) Answer the questions in the sidebar for Student Example #1.
2) Answer the questions in the sidebar for Student Example #2.
3) Answer the questions in the sidebar for Student Example #3.

Application

1) Write a paragraph where you explain the process of washing your hands properly.
2) Choose a novel and analyze the work using one of the elements of literary analysis.

More activities and student examples available at **www.writefromtheheart.org/resourceguide**.

Chapter 19: Comparison Writing

In a **comparison** essay, the writer compares and contrasts two items. In other words, the writer notices the similarities (**comparing**) as well as the differences (**contrasting**) between the two items. The items compared and contrasted in the essay could include ideas, opportunities, books, films, time periods, and more.

Why does the writer compare and contrast? Often, the essay allows the writer to draw a conclusion about the two items. For example, the author might need to make a decision between two opportunities or decide whether a book or movie version of a story is better. In more advanced writing, the author might be making a scholarly argument about how two time periods or works of literature are similar or different.

In all comparison essays, it's important to plan your essay carefully. There are many, many different qualities of most items you will compare, but it's important to think about which qualities most clearly show the main similarities *and* differences between the items you compare. If there are no differences, how will you decide between the two? If there are no similarities, you likely don't even need to carefully consider this decision. Choose a topic for your essay that will include both similarities and differences.

For example, if my essay is about my decision to either get a summer job at a fast food restaurant or work at a grocery store, I could list off every single quality of each experience. Here are some things I could compare:

Location
Pay
Working environment
Difficulty

Flexibility of scheduling
Enjoyment of the job
Knowledge of the companies

Not all those qualities are important, though. Perhaps the fast food job is located on Main Street, and the grocery store job is located on Elm Street. Is that an important quality to mention for each job? It depends. The location *could* be relevant. If location doesn't matter as I make my decision, then I probably shouldn't include it in my essay. But maybe it does. Perhaps I can walk or ride my bicycle to Main Street, but I would need to ask a family member to drive me to the job on Elm Street. If so, location might be a key element to show the *contrast* between the two opportunities. Or, perhaps the location of both jobs is close enough for me to walk or ride my bicycle without needing to ask family members to drop me off. That might be a key *similarity* between the two jobs.

The best way to figure out what to discuss in a comparison essay is to spend some time brainstorming. List all the attributes that are similar and different. Then group them into three categories—these become your three supporting points. For example, I could look at my list and combine difficulty and enjoyment of the job together under the heading of "how much I will like it" or "personal satisfaction." Working environment and scheduling and knowledge of the companies could all be grouped as "environment." Pay might be a big enough item that it would deserve its own supporting point.

Then, you want to decide what your thesis will be. A thesis for a comparison paper should include what you are comparing (your topic) and the conclusion you drew (what you will show or prove).

> **Example:** While both the book and movie version of *Wonder* were well done, the book is a better choice to look at first.

However, when your conclusion includes a *decision*, you should use a **general thesis** in the introduction and a **specific thesis** in the conclusion. When you are weighing two options, you don't want to tell the readers up front your decision, or they won't need to read your paper! A general thesis solves that problem: you state your topic, and without revealing the decision, you list *how* you drew your conclusions. Then in your specific thesis, you reveal the decision.

General thesis: When deciding what my summer job should be, I need to consider the pay, the environment, and the satisfaction I will get working at either Tom's Fast Food or Smith's Supermarket.

Specific thesis: Based on the pay, the environment, and my own preferences, it makes the most sense for me to work at Smith's Supermarket rather than Tom's Fast Food.

Be careful with your thesis! A general thesis does NOT mean you say Tom's Fast Food and Smith's Supermarket have a lot of similarities and differences." This doesn't explain anything about my conclusions, or how I came to that decision! This is not a thesis—it's a statement.

Structure of Comparison Essays

Regardless of the author's purpose for writing, all comparison essays follow one of two main formats: the whole-to-whole format (sometimes called the block format) or the point-to-point format (sometimes called the subject-to-subject format).

In **whole-to-whole format**, the writer considers one side or item completely, and the writer summarizes the 3-4 key qualities of that first item. Then, the writer considers the second side or item, summarizing all the key qualities of that item focusing on the same 3-4 qualities in the same order. This form uses phrases throughout such as "unlike Item #1, this item..." and "There is no difference between this item and the other..." The conclusion sums up the similarities and differences and includes the specific thesis.

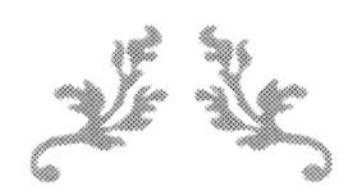

Make sure to keep the ORDER items are discussed the same throughout the essay!

For example, using the decision about choosing between a grocery store and fast food restaurant for a summer job, in the body paragraphs of the essay, the writer would first summarize the key qualities (pay, environment, and personal satisfaction) of the grocery store job. Then, after one to two paragraphs summarizing the grocery store job, the writer would shift focus to the fast food job and would summarize all of the key qualities (pay, environment, and personal satisfaction) of the fast food job. In the conclusion, they would summarize those key qualities and identify how the elements of the fast food job are similar and/or different from the elements of the grocery store job and include a specific thesis.

In **point-to-point format**, the writer identifies the 3-4 key qualities to consider and uses those key qualities as the main points of the essay. In each point, the writer summarizes how a key quality relates to both of the two objects being considered.

For example, using the same summer job decision, the writer would write one body paragraph about the pay of each job opportunity and how it is similar or different. Then, in the next paragraph, the writer would summarize how the jobs are similar or different in terms of environment. Finally, the author would summarize how the jobs are similar or different in terms of personal satisfaction. In the conclusion, they would summarize those key qualities and identify how the elements of the fast food job are similar and/or different from the elements of the grocery store job and include a specific thesis.

Sample Outlines

Whole-to-whole Format—compares 3-4 points by looking at Thing #1 first, then looking at Thing #2.

I. Introduction

- a. Attention Getter
- b. Topic information
- c. Thesis statement—general (tell what you are comparing and what you hope to discover)

II. Thing #1

- a. Point 1
- b. Point 2
- c. Point 3
- d. Point 4 (optional)

III. Thing #2

- a. Point 1
- b. Point 2
- c. Point 3
- d. Point 4 (optional)

IV. Conclusion

- a. Restate thesis with a decision, if applicable
- b. Sum up points
- c. Further thoughts: What do these differences and similarities reveal? What can be discovered by looking at these things side by side?

Point-to-point Format—compares three to four points by looking at each point and discussing it for both Thing #1 and Thing #2.

I. Introduction

- a. Attention Getter
- b. Topic information

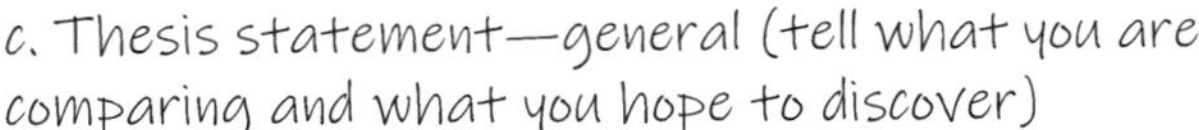

- c. Thesis statement—general (tell what you are comparing and what you hope to discover)

II. Point 1

- a. Thing #1
- b. Thing #2

III. Point 2

- a. Thing #1
- b. Thing #2

IV. Point 3

- a. Thing #1
- b. Thing #2

V. Point 4 (optional)

- a. Thing #1
- b. Thing #2

VI. Conclusion

- a. Restate thesis with a decision, if applicable
- b. Sum up points
- c. Further thoughts: What do these differences and similarities reveal? What can be discovered by looking at these things side by side?

Student Example #1

Piano or Oboe

Charlotte S., 12

"So, Charlotte, what did you think of the orchestra concert?" my mom asks me. I can tell she is hinting to me that she wants me to play oboe, like my sister.

"I liked it, I guess, but piano is still my top instrument," I shrug. My mom sighs. Ever since my musically talented sister had taken up oboe, as well as piano, my mom had wanted me to do the same. I, on the other hand, preferred to stick to piano.

"Just think about it, please?" I could tell my mom REALLY wanted me to do oboe by the tone in her voice.

"Ok, Mom, I will, but I won't promise anything!"

To give some background information, I have been playing piano for seven years. A few years ago my sister, who is a very good musician, took up oboe as well as piano. My mom saw how much my sister enjoyed oboe, and decided she would like me to try it. But I wasn't so hot about that idea. I decided I would have to think about the pros and cons of adding oboe to my instruments, or continuing to concentrate more on piano. I would have to take into consideration my opportunities, time, and teaching options.

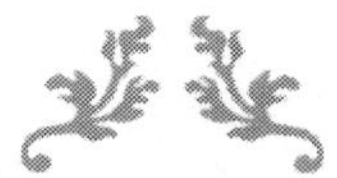

Questions as you read:

- What are the two things being compared?
- What three categories of similarity/difference are they using?
- What is the decision? Where is that revealed?
- What format was this paper written in (point to point or whole to whole)?

First, I should think about the different opportunities I would get with each instrument. With just piano as my instrument, I could focus more on learning about piano, and maybe get a college scholarship in piano. I could play in concerts and accompany my choir. If I added oboe, I would not have as much time to study piano, but I would get a whole other instrument's worth of opportunities. There is a demand for oboe players in my area, and if I played oboe, I would get to be in orchestras and possibly get a scholarship to college. The thing is, I would have to practice extremely hard and spend a ton of time on oboe. That would definitely affect my other opportunities in other areas, not just music.

I also have to remember that I don't have time to do everything! Although I like to be organized (it helps me to think straight), I would not have as much time to organize myself if I spent more time on music. That is why time is an important factor in my decision. I already spend at least thirty minutes a day on piano. I have learned from my sister that when practicing oboe, thirty minutes won't cut it. That means I might spend an hour and a half a day on practicing my instruments. Going into eighth grade, I will have a lot more homework, which means it might be difficult to spend time on two instruments.

Teaching opportunities are not something to be overlooked while making this decision. My current piano teacher studied piano all through college, but if I study diligently, I might pass my teacher in knowledge. Then I would have to find another teacher for piano, which I do not want to do, because I like my current teacher. Adding oboe could mean I would have to find some sort of income to pay for an oboe teacher. We do have an oboe teacher that lives down the street from us, and she taught my sister. My sister paid for her lessons by babysitting the teacher's kids, but I don't think I want to do that.

A few days after the conversation with my mom about me taking up oboe, I came close to making my final decision. Well, I really am interested in trying oboe, but with where I am in school, I think that, time wise, it would be best not to do oboe. I also know that I love piano, whereas I am not positive I would at all enjoy oboe. Learning new techniques and finding a new teacher would complicate matters. As I pondered the pros and cons of my decision, I made up my mind. At least this year, I will not take oboe and will concentrate on piano. Mom will understand my decision, and I think she will be glad not to be stressed about another instrument, just like me.

After comparing opportunities, time, and teaching options, I think that adding oboe to my agenda would create more stress than it is

worth, so I think that I will continue to study just piano. Even though there is a demand for oboists, I feel like it would be hard to learn a brand new instrument while trying to keep up with my homework and playing piano. Maybe someday I will decide that I want to try a new instrument, but at this point in my life, I think the better decision would be to deepen my knowledge in piano.

Student Example #2

Buy it or Make it?

By Maria H., 14

It was a cold and snowy January day, one week before my older sister's birthday. I really wanted to get her a birthday present, so I went to my mom for input as to what I should do. I walked downstairs and found her on the couch reading a book.

"Hey mom, I really want to get something for Karen's birthday. Like a present or something."

She looked up, and said, "You can make her a present or buy it, your choice, kiddo."

I thanked her. I walked back upstairs, sat on my red fuzzy penguin blanket, and thought for a while. *Should I buy Karen a present, or should I make it?* Deciding whether to buy a present for my sister or to make it: I will have to consider the cost, time, and which kind of gift my sister would appreciate more.

If I were to buy a present, I would probably spend $10-20+. The amount would also depend on how many things I would get her. I could get her many little things or I could get her one big thing that would cost more than $20. If I bought her something, she would probably appreciate clothes, gift cards for clothing stores, or shoes.

Next, I will consider how long it would take me to get the present. It would take at least 30-45 minutes to get to a store and to buy a present. I would go to a general merchandise store because they have most everything. Then I would have to find a parking place, get in the store, pick a present, wait in the cashier line, and finally walk out. Then,

I would make the car ride back. Depending on traffic, it could take a longer or shorter period of time.

Lastly, I will consider what Karen's reaction would be. I would take the time to go out to a store and buy a present. She would probably be thankful, knowing that I was thoughtful in getting her something for her birthday. She would acknowledge me buying jeans and sweatshirts for her because she loves clothes.

Making a present, the cost would depend on what I want to do. If it is a wooden puzzle, I would need a piece of plywood, a piece of pressed wood, a plywood saw, blades, sanding paper, wood glue, acrylic wood paint, and varnish. I would spend at least $10-$15 for the materials. Making something more simple than a puzzle out of wood would cost around $5. I would use a cutting tool and a sanding tool because I have these tools. It would cost $10-$15 to make a craft such as painting, a Popsicle stick construction, or a coloring etc. The materials I would need for a craft would be paper, wood, paint, glue, etc.

Once I have decided what to do, I would consider how long it would take to make the present. It normally takes around 4-6 hours cutting out the pieces from the wood, sanding them, and painting them. It would take longer because I would have to wait until the paint or wood glue dries. It would take three days if I worked on it at least two hours every day. The total number of days it would take to complete an entire puzzle would be around 3-4 days.

Lastly, I would regard whether Karen would better appreciate a homemade present. Since I would make a present personally for Karen,

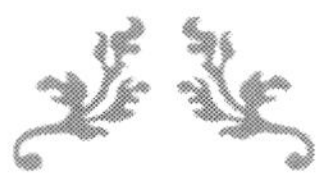

Questions as you read:

- What are the two things being compared?
- What three categories of similarity/difference are they using?
- What is the decision? Where is that revealed?
- What format was this paper written in (point to point or whole to whole)?

I think she would like this more. She would probably enjoy homemade things and think that they are special since I took the time to make them. She also loves doing puzzles, so this would be a personally special present to her.

In conclusion, I think making a present is a little cheaper than buying one. It would probably take a little more time, but I'm sure that Karen would appreciate a homemade present better than a bought one since it was made specifically, personally, and thoughtfully for her.

I ran downstairs and snatched a pencil and some paper. Then, I took my pencil and drew a simple blueprint. It would be a square shaped puzzle with a picture of an elephant because she loves elephants. I had a lot of planning to do for making my sister a large wooden puzzle!

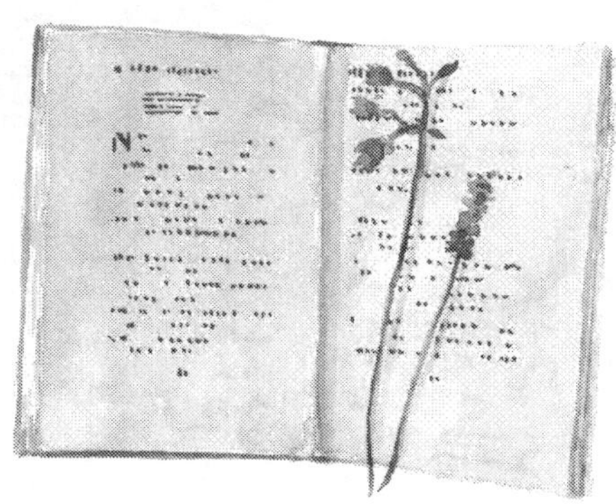

NOTE: Student examples appear in original format and may contain slight grammar errors.

Activities

Key Terms

Define the following key terms: comparison essay, comparing, contrasting, general thesis, specific thesis, whole-to-whole format, point-to-point format

Comprehension

1) Imagine you are going to write a paper comparing a laptop to a desktop computer for your next purchase. What three categories would you use to compare them?
2) Organize these elements into a whole-to-whole format AND a point-to-point format. Make sure to include a general thesis and a specific thesis.
    a. Topic: What should I do for my birthday—go to a restaurant and movie, or have a party at home?
    b. Qualities to compare: cost, activities, who I can invite
    c. Decision: party at home

Practice

1) Answer the question in the sidebar next to Student Example #1.
2) Answer the questions in the sidebar next to Student Example #2.

Application

1) Write a paragraph where you compare one of the following: talking vs. texting, winter vs summer, handwriting vs. typing
2) Imagine you were given $200. Write an essay about two different things you could do with the money and compare/contrast them, revealing your decision at the end with a specific thesis.

More activities and student examples available at **www.writefromtheheart.org/resourceguide**.

Chapter 20: Persuasive Writing

Persuasive essays are pieces written to convince the audience to agree with a particular argument and, often, take a particular course of action because of that argument. In order to convince the audience to agree, the writer uses writing techniques and evidence to build a compelling argument. There are several parts to a successful argument that should be included in your essay in order to have an effective persuasive argument.

Elements of Persuasion

In a persuasive essay, there are five elements needed to make sure that you have a strong argument. These parts are layered within the parts of a draft you already know. Your essay will still have an introduction that includes an attention getter and thesis, several supporting body paragraphs, and a conclusion that includes a restatement of the thesis and concluding thoughts. To review the parts of a draft, see **Section 2**.

Opinion

With a persuasive paper, your **opinion** on the topic is the most important part of your argument: you are trying to convince your audience to agree with you! Your opinion is what you are trying to prove about the topic. You should already have this if you have a strong thesis statement. A persuasive thesis statement will tell the audience what needs to be done to fix a problem, what belief they should hold about an idea, or what action they should take on an issue.

Examples:

> The potholes on Route 156 are dangerous to drivers, and the township needs to prioritize their repair.
>
> Free public transportation would benefit the city.

> Every parent should insist their child take a second language in high school.

Opinions in strong thesis statements will also be specific. It is not possible to cover a large political or social issue like racism or climate change in one essay—there are people who write whole books on those subjects! However, it is possible to write about a specific law and why it should be passed, or an event that people should attend in support of a cause. Just because an issue is large doesn't mean you should avoid it, but you need to make sure you narrow your specific topic for the assignment.

Backing

A good persuasive argument can include your thoughts, but when you are making an argument, most people want more than just opinions. This is where backing comes in. **Backing** refers to the evidence provided to support the persuasive argument. This is what you use to defend your position and prove that your perspective is the correct one.

There are four different types of evidence you can use. **Statistical evidence** is data that shows percentages, survey numbers, or monetary costs associated with the problem or solution. **Testimonial evidence** is information that comes from an expert in a field related to the topic, or a reliable source (newspaper, website) that has done research on the topic. **Analogical evidence** is a comparison to something similar that worked in another situation. **Anecdotal evidence** is telling personal experiences (yours or someone else's) as proof of a problem or a solution that works.

The evidence you give can be either coming from a positive or negative perspective. For example, if you were trying to persuade your town to install bike racks at the playground, you could say, "We should have bike racks and the playground because having racks will encourage people to ride their bikes." This is **positive backing** because it solves a problem or tells a benefit. You could also say, "Not having racks leaves bikes open to theft." This is **negative backing** because it highlights an existing problem or explains a detriment if the problem isn't fixed. Either form of backing is appropriate; there's nothing wrong with providing negative evidence. Just think of this type of backing as telling people what not to do. That can be very effective.

Qualifiers

You want to avoid saying "always" and "never" and instead use a qualifier. **Qualifiers** are words like: sometimes, often, a few, perhaps, etc. They create flexibility within your argument and allow for alternate explanations. For example, if you said to your mom, "I *always* do my chores as soon as you ask me to, so I have shown responsibility" she would only need to come up with

ONE time when you didn't do your chores when you were asked, and your whole argument isn't any good. But, if you said, "I usually do my chores as soon as you ask me to, so I have shown responsibility" she would need to come up with many, many times you failed to disprove that you "usually" do something and so your argument is stronger!

Concessions and Rebuttals

A **concession** is an acknowledgement of what the "other side" is saying and acknowledging that it can be a legitimate argument in some cases. It is usually followed by a **rebuttal**, a counter-argument that explains why your argument is different, or why that concession is unimportant in the big picture.

Example:

> There is a chance that putting bike racks in at the playground could be a safety hazard if children played on them in an unsafe manner. But the health benefits of encouraging children to ride to the park would far outweigh these risks.

The first sentence is your concession. The second sentence is your rebuttal. Conceding a point shows that you truly understand both sides of the argument and have formed an intelligent opinion after weighing the evidence, which makes you sound believable. It also responds to objections before the other side makes them, which makes your argument stronger.

Note the way that these two concepts are introduced with transitions. The concession starts with phrases like: it could be that, there are times when, perhaps, sometimes, it is true that. This is followed by a summary of what the other side might argue. Then the rebuttal is introduced with a contrasting transition such as: however, but, except, still. The writer then counters the argument.

Call to Action

Persuasive writing typically concludes with a call to action. A **call to action** is an appeal to readers at the end of the piece of writing to do something that connects with the writer's argument. For example, in a piece written to try to get a bike rack at the playground, the writer could suggest that readers write to their council representative, sign a petition, or attend a town council meeting. All these things are actions that the audience could do to help fix the problem.

Your call to action should be clear and direct and something that the audience can do. You also should make sure you explain why the call to action would benefit the audience, their community, or people they care about.

Appeals to the Audience

In addition to the elements of persuasion, you want to appeal to every aspect of the reader: their heart, their mind, and their wisdom/character. When an audience is considering your opinion, they want to understand your reasoning with their intellect, but they also want to feel good about their decision and believe that it is a wise choice. Aristotle, a Greek philosopher and one of the most famous persuasive teachers of all time, labeled these appeals pathos, logos, and ethos.

Pathos

Pathos is the term we use to refer to an emotional appeal. "Pathos" is the root word that creates the English words empathy and sympathy. These types of appeals are appeals to the heart. When the writer of a persuasive argument uses emotional language to get readers to feel a certain way about the topic, they are relying on pathos.

Pathos can be very effective! Think about little kids trying to convince their parents that they need a puppy or a treat—those big eyes, the droopy lip and the whiny "please!" are all appeals to the parent's emotions. But professionals rely on pathos as well. Dr. Martin Luther King Jr. expressed his frustration, fears and hopes in vivid language in his famous "I Have a Dream" speech. Telling a story about someone who lost something or was harmed can be pathos, and so can a story about a person who was successful because of the solution you are offering—both appeal to an emotion.

This type of writing catches the attention of readers and causes them to connect emotionally with the writer, allowing the argument an opportunity to persuade. Often, writers use pathos in the introduction's attention getter. Sometimes sad or angry emotions are appealed to in the conclusion when the writer talks about the dangers of not accepting a certain solution. But pathos can certainly be used in the supporting points of the paper at times as well.

Logos

Logos is a persuasive appeal to the mind or a reader's logic. Logical appeals use evidence, facts, and expert opinions to establish an argument. Most of your backing will be based on logos.

One specific type of logos is arguing from example. When you have only this sort of logos, it is called an illustration essay. **Illustration essays** aim to prove an argument through extended examples. These use key examples from personal experience, research, popular media, history, and current events to serve as the main substance of body paragraphs. For example, in an essay arguing about greed in the United States, the writer might use examples of reality television stars' feuds over money. Unlike a more traditional argumentative essay, which might include short pieces of information gathered together, an illustrative essay instead focuses on extended examples in order to prove the overarching argument. An illustration essay might still use statistics and other data, but it is within a specific example. Let's say that your topic is why going to college straight out of high school isn't the best choice for every student. You can include an examples of students who took a year off, students who started at a community college until they knew what major they wanted, students who went to technical school for a two-year degree to pursue jobs like HVAC, certified nursing assistant, and welding (group these examples together), and conclude that alternatives to college save money and can still lead to lucrative jobs and strong career paths, as shown by your examples.

Ethos

Ethos is an ethical appeal. Ethos builds on the character of the writer in order to persuade the readers. An author may appeal to their own position—perhaps they remind readers that they have a degree in a certain field or experience in a certain job. An author may talk about personal experience that they have had with the topic to show that they have first-hand knowledge of the problem. When a child asks for a puppy and gives their parent a list of reasons why they are ready to care for a dog, they're using ethos. When you're reading a textbook or other book for school, you may notice information about the author in the first section or on the back—this is an appeal to ethos. This information typically includes the educational degrees, professional status and publishing experience of the author. They're telling you exactly why you should trust them to teach you what you need to know.

Student Example #1

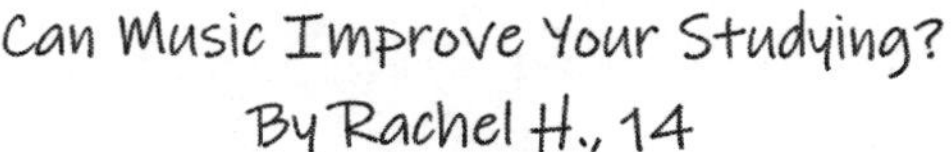
Can Music Improve Your Studying?
By Rachel H., 14

At HSA school, headphones in the study hall are discouraged strongly. Students work on their schoolwork in silence, not an earbud in sight. However, allowing students to listen to music in the study hall could produce some unexpected benefits, and the rules should be changed.

Music has been proven to have a positive effect on people by lifting their spirits. Whether it's singing a soft lullaby to a child or singing along with the radio when traveling, this curious effect music has on moods has a relatively simple explanation. Certain types of music are shown to make a person more cheerful and relaxed by lowering a person's cortisol levels. The hormone that is usually responsible for feelings of stress and anxiety. Dr. Alice Cash of HealingMusicEnterprise once said— "Music naturally relaxes the mind and the body. When the muscles relax to a certain point, the body slows down on cortisol production and eventually stops."

These categories of music have been shown to make students more focused and motivated because they are in a good mood. Which helps them endure studying for long periods. On the other hand, people who are in bad moods are less likely to be able to study. Christian Jarrett, in BPS Research Digest, states— "There's some evidence that being in a bad mood is distracting because it takes mental effort to deal with unpleasant emotions. Being in a good mood, by contrast, is thought to be energizing." It seems that lifting your spirits can do more than anyone would've thought. However, some might object to this idea of music for studying, because not all students find it helpful. They could find it distracting from the work in front of them. Nevertheless, there is a solution to this problem, have the students listen to music wearing headphones, to spare any easily-distracted students from having to listen to the other fellow scholar's music. Another advantage of this system is that it establishes equity among students, even with the ones that prefer music, every kid gets to work in their ideal environment without disturbing each other.

An additional bonus to listening to music was discovered by an analysis done in France, which was published in Learning and Individual Differences. This study found that students listening to classical music in a lecture did better on the quiz as opposed to the students that attended the presentation without music. The people leading the review deduced that the music played put them at ease. Making them more receptive to information and helping them remember the contents of the lecture more clearly.

Another reason why people might object is that some surveys have shown that loud music with lyrics can have a harmful effect on students, rendering their studying ineffective. It might be that some people can't

try to listen to the lyrics of a song and study at the same time. However, this obstacle can be easily avoided if students substitute loud, harsh music for calm, soft music. With pre-approved playlists so that the students can be sure of which songs won't be harmful to them, and teachers can make sure the students are listening to stuff that will benefit them.

It's evident that, despite differences in the students, the majority of them would profit from being allowed to play music when attending study hall. Even if some students don't find it particularly convenient. The option to listen to music that could be beneficial to them should be something available to all students.

Questions as you read:

- What is the author's opinion?
- What type of evidence did the author use?
- Circle at least three qualifiers.
- Mark the concession with a star and put brackets around the transitions into the concession and the rebuttal.
- Underline the call to action.
- List a way the author used pathos, ethos, and logos.

Student Example #2

A Tiny Ball of Fluff For All

By Anna G., 13

It is a magical experience to raise a chicken from a tiny ball of fluff to a trusted friend who allows a child to reach under her velvety belly and grasp a warm, freshly laid egg. In Warwick, Rhode Island, children will never have that experience. Here, it is against the law to own a chicken. This law should be amended to allow the people of Warwick to own chickens.

There is no fresher food than what comes from your own backyard. Many backyard chicken enthusiasts say that the eggs are tastier than those from grocery stores. Since backyard chickens eat vegetation, their eggs have 60% more vitamin A, three times as much vitamin E, and one-fourth less statured fat. Not to mention that they are far tastier than eggs from the large egg industries that only feed their chickens corn (and abuse their chickens).

But chickens do not just lay eggs, they are also a natural defense against insects and their compost is amazing for a yard or garden. That aspect of sustainability is why farm-to-table supporters are so encouraging of backyard chickens. Following that trend of farm-to-table, Rhode Islanders are now bringing chickens home to roost. As Douglas Stuchel, a chef and assistant professor at Johnson and Wales University, says, "We are in a society that wants more farm-to-table."

Questions as you read:

- What is the author's opinion?
- What type of evidence did the author use?
- Circle at least three qualifiers.
- Mark the concession with a star and put brackets around the transitions into the concession and the rebuttal.
- Underline the call to action.
- List a way the author used pathos, ethos, and logos.

While Warwick residents are unable to take part in the farm-to-table movement, other Rhode Island cities are supporting fresh, nutritious, locally grown food. Because of these benefits, Providence, the most urban city in Rhode Island, has changed the law in favor of chicken enthusiasts. For the first time, residents are able to raise up to six chickens and have the benefit of fresh eggs. Barrington, one of the wealthiest cities in Rhode Island, followed suit, as did Bristol, North Smithfield, and West Warwick. Providence's environmental sustainability plan's goal is to ensure that "every resident has access to safe, fresh, affordable, nutritious and culturally appropriate food, regardless of income or race." The town of Warwick should follow these cities' examples and give its residents the same benefits.

Bans on backyard chickens began with New York City in 1877, followed by Boston in 1896. Both cities were motivated by concerns over unsanitary backyard chicken slaughter. Over time, however, slaughter of backyard chickens has all but vanished and is still banned in most communities. However, there are still worries about the smell and noise of owning chickens. To avoid the smell, all that needs to be done is to clean the chicken's coop regularly. As for the noise, the only chickens that are loud are roosters. Cities that have allowed chickens have successfully protected the rights of non-chicken owners by limiting the number of chickens that can be kept, prohibiting roosters, and enforcing standards of care.

The residents of Warwick should be allowed to own chickens. As Ken Ayars, Chief of the Rhode Island Department of Environmental Management said, "The arguments against it [raising chickens], so far, haven't been, to us, scientifically based." The law against keeping chickens should be amended.

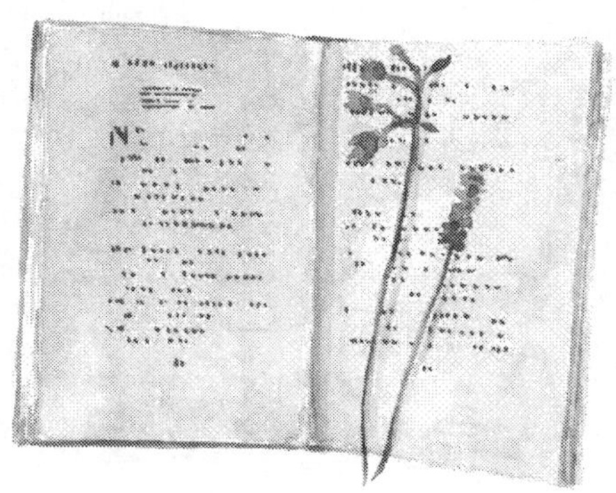

NOTE: Student examples appear in original format and may contain slight grammar errors.

Activities

Key Terms

Define the following key terms: persuasive essays, opinion, backing, statistical evidence, testimonial evidence, anecdotal evidence, analogical evidence, positive backing, negative backing, qualifiers, concession, rebuttal, call to action, pathos, logos, ethos

Comprehension

1) Which type of evidence do you think is the weakest, and why? The strongest?
2) Why is a concession and rebuttal important in a persuasive essay?

Practice

1) Answer the question in the sidebar next to Student Example #1.
2) Answer the questions in the sidebar next to Student Example #2.

Application

1) Write a paragraph trying to convince your parents about something.
2) Choose a problem affecting your local community right now. Write a persuasive essay about how to fix this problem with your local community as your audience.

More activities and student examples available at **www.writefromtheheart.org/resourceguide**.

Chapter 21: Essay Tests

At some point in your high school or college career, you will be asked to take an essay test. An essay test is used to evaluate your writing skills and your ability to fully answer a question in written form. These tests are often called **standardized essay tests**, because everyone is asked the same (or standard) question. It is a specialized form of writing, generally only used in academic arenas, like high school and college classes as well as on certain applications for jobs, scholarships, or grants. If you take the SATs or ACTs to apply for college, you will likely take a test like this.

These types of essays can be stressful for students because of the way they are administered: they are a graded test, and they are usually timed. But that doesn't mean you need to be intimidated! If you have been practicing your writing skills, you should be prepared. The readers of these essays are looking to see your writing skills. Even though you're often being asked to give your opinion, the tester doesn't grade you on your opinion. Instead, they want to see a well-written essay: it should have an engaging introduction (attention getter and thesis), several well-developed supporting paragraphs, and a conclusion that restates the thesis and summarizes the essay. See **Section 2** for more information about the parts of an essay.

With that in mind, there are several things you can do to make sure you are successful in writing these types of essays.

Make sure to answer the prompt

Standardized essay tests always ask a question. They clearly tell you what to do and how to answer the question well. Look for the **directive word**. A directive word will "direct" you to the kind of essay you are expected to create. Examples of directive words are: compare, analyze, choose a position, give your opinion about, agree/disagree, discuss, justify, illustrate. Your thesis should specifically answer the directive given in the question. If you do not answer the directive, it doesn't matter how beautifully you wrote the essay; you won't get full credit because you didn't answer the question.

> Example: Read the following passage and agree or disagree with the author's position.

In this question, you are expected to agree or disagree—it wants you to defend a side. You should pick a side and use persuasive techniques to defend your answer. Any time you see the words "agree or disagree" or "give your opinion about" the reader is looking for you to defend a position. Even if you don't have an opinion, still choose one! Remember, you are showing off your writing skills, not your personal beliefs. An essay that gives both sides of an issue is NOT answering the prompt, and you will not get a good score.

> Example: Read the following passage and analyze how the author came to their position.

This question looks similar to the previous question, but it's not. Look at the directive word: analyze. Analytical essays break down something into parts and look at how those pieces work together. This question is NOT asking your opinion at all. If you answered this question by agreeing or disagreeing with the author, you would not get a good score. Instead, you should be looking at the elements of persuasion in the essay and explaining how the author used them in *their* argument.

The best way to make sure you answer the prompt is to create a strong thesis that answers the directive word. Then make sure your supporting points connect with your thesis.

Always write an outline

Because you have a limited amount of time to compose the test, you may feel tempted to skip the planning stage. Don't do it!! Always take the first 5-10 minutes of the time given to plan out your essay with a mini-outline. This ensures that you do have a thesis and three strong points.

The other use for an outline is to show the reader where you were going if you run out of time. An outlined third point and conclusion at the end of the essay is going to show the reader what you had planned; this will not get you full credit for the essay, but it might get you a few more points than if you simply left your essay unfinished.

Use your voice to stand out

The idea of a standardized essay is that it makes it easier for a reader to grade everyone using "standard" requirements. The downside of this is that the person grading the essays is going to read essay upon essay about exactly the same thing. That means your essay could get lost in a sea of others. If you start with a dry introduction, your paper is not going to be remembered. But if you start with an engaging attention getter, the bored reader is going to perk up and read your essay with more interest.

Often, there is a portion of the grade that is assigned for "well-crafted writing" or "strong voice" or "shows skill in writing." This is where your voice can earn you points. Adding sensory details or a personal connection in the introduction and writing with developed vocabulary and syntax will get you noticed.

Develop your support with accuracy and depth

There is nothing worse for an essay grader than to read a great opening and thesis, followed by generic supporting paragraphs that simply repeat the same thing over and over. There are several ways you can avoid this pitfall.

Make sure you have at least three points. Two is okay in a pinch if they are well developed, but three is better. This is where taking the time to do a little outline at the beginning will really pay off!

It is always better to give an example or a quotation. Even if they are short, an example will show that you have thought about the question. And if you are given a passage to read, make sure to directly quote it at least once in your essay—this shows off your writing skills and helps you answer the prompt well, all at the same time!

When in doubt, qualify. If you can't remember where an event occurred in a play, don't guess and say "Act II." Instead say "Toward the beginning of the play." If you can't remember which character said something, don't assign it to a specific person. Say instead "One of the characters claimed." If you are talking about a historical event but can't remember the year it happened, don't guess. Instead say "in the 1800s" or "before the first World War."

Remember that the point of this essay is to show your writing skills and having well developed points is a big part of this.

Manage your time properly

It can be intimidating to have a clock ticking as you write. But take a deep breath and stay calm! If you have a plan going into the test, you can manage the time easily.

First, look at the number of questions and the amount of time you have. Divide your time up among them and keep your eye on the clock. If you figure out that you have 30 minutes for each question, when the thirty minutes is up for the first question, stop and move on to the next question. In almost all cases, two partially completed questions will get you more points than one completed question and an unanswered one. The exception to this is if one question is weighted more than another—always do the one worth the most points first and finish it.

Budget planning time for each essay at the beginning. Usually you should give yourself about 5-10 minutes for planning. If you have more than one essay to complete, how you plan is up to you. Some students like to read all the questions first and make all their outlines at the start, then write each essay. Other students prefer to outline and write one full essay and then move on to the next. Either method is fine—it's a good idea to practice at home before a big test to see which one works better for you!

Most tests do not require you to answer the essays in order. It is worth reading through them and picking the order for yourself. Many students like to start with the question they are most confident about first, because it will write more quickly and will give them energy to write the harder essay. Others like to start with the harder essay to get it out of the way. Whichever you choose, make sure to keep an eye on the clock and move on if you are at the end of the amount of time you gave yourself. You can always come back and finish if you have extra time at the end.

Always budget 5-10 minutes at the end for "clean up tasks." If you have not finished your essay, write out the rest of your outline at the bottom of the essay. This shows the reader/grader that you knew where you were going with your thoughts. If all you do is put "I ran out of time!" the grader won't know the final great point you had but didn't have time to write. Although you won't get full credit, often a grader will be able to see your thought process more clearly and give you partial credit for your ideas. You also want to use these last few minutes to re-read your essay. Check for any spelling or grammar errors. Sometimes you left out a word accidentally. Fix any last-minute errors.

Student Example #1

Question: Describe how to manage one of the following: stress, stage fright, homesickness, or an irrational fear.

Answer

By Sarah S., 16

My mouth is dry as I peek out at the audience. *That's a lot of people!* My hands shake ever more furiously. I straighten the hem of my costume and try to remember how to inhale. I fiddle with the ring on my left index finger. I spin it round and round in never ending ellipses.

"You ok?" Asks the actor who plays my daughter. The strap of her pinafore is twisted and I unconsciously reach out to straighten it with trembling fingers.

I give her a tight-lipped smile, "I'll be fine." My brain however, is screaming the opposite.

Stage fright is a very common fear. In the US, the number one fear among adults is public speaking. As an actor, I have been in many productions and have gotten stage fright many times. Public speaking and acting is second nature to me but it still, at times, makes me nervous. Recently, I obtained my first lead role in a play. I was not that nervous though, for three reasons. I remembered to breathe, I knew my part very well, and I thought rationally. Armed with these three aids, I nailed my first lead role.

Questions as you read:

- What is the directive word?
- Underline the student's thesis.
- What supporting points did the student use?
- How did the student use voice to stand out?

It sounds obvious, but breathing is very important. Not only does it help keep us alive, but strategic breathing can calm overexcited nerves. Deep, relaxing breathes are scientifically proven to calm the body and mind and lower the heart rate. We breathe deeply while sleeping, and if we mimic this while awake it helps relax us. Many people who experience stage fright tend to hyperventilate. Hyperventilating is very bad both for your body and for acting. While hyperventilating, the brain goes into panic mode and starts sending more endorphins to make you feel even more anxious. It is also hard to sing and act when you are breathing that fast. So, it is important to be mindful of your breathing and try to stay relaxed.

A common reason for stage fright is because we feel underprepared. Take control before the fear sets in. Learn your lines. Practice your harmonies. Practice, practice, practice. As I stated previously, I recently acted in my first lead role. This was in a three woman show that was a coming of age story about space. As a play with only three actors, everyone had a lot of lines. I had long, chunky, and difficult to memorize monologues. In the show, I had many long monologues where I was the only one onstage. This was a very new concept to me as I am used to playing ensemble roles. I had never had that much time onstage by myself before and it was quite terrifying, initially, for me to think about. So, I practiced. I stayed up late every night practicing my lines. I would recite my monologues in the shower, the car, and even at the doctors' office. I may have occasionally looked like a madwoman, muttering lines to myself in the corner, but it paid off. By the time the show premiered, I was barely even nervous.

Another important trick for overcoming stage fright is to think rationally. Ask yourself questions. Will stuttering on a line really be the end of the world? Will messing up really change my life at all? What's the worst thing that could happen? Is it realistic that that could happen? Try and get yourself to think rationally. This isn't the end of the world. It isn't even close. It's just a play/musical/recital/other. All of those things are fun if you let yourself enjoy it. So, have fun! Think rationally! And remember that this isn't the start of the apocalypse.

I stare at the dusty wood floor trying to get into character. My eyes fall shut as I breathe deeply. *I can do this. I practiced all of this a billion times.* I open my eyes and step out onto the unlit stage. I can feel the presence of the audience. I can feel myself change from the nervous actor to the over-worked mom. I stare into the distance as the lights come up. *I am ready.* My lips open to say my first line almost automatically.

Stage fright is a common ailment of many who need to be onstage. It is however, not contagious or deadly and easily treated. With precise breathing, preparedness, and rational thoughts it can be completely eradicated. And ultimately performance isn't about the audience. It isn't about the reviews and critics. It's about the emotions and relationships of people on a stage. It's about the realness of people that in an hour or two you end up in tears. Stage fright is unnecessary as it distracts from your fellow actors and yourself. So I recommend these three tips and I hope it makes your performances even more legendary.

Student Example #2

Question: Which is more beneficial, winning or losing? Choose one and defend your answer.

Answer

By Lucas H., 12

The score is 58 to 60 on the score board at the end of a basketball championship game. There are three seconds left on the clock and white has the ball. Three, two, one, a player on the white team chucks a half-court shot, and the ball flies toward the basketball hoop. The ball bounces on the hoop once, twice, and on the third bounce the ball fall straight through the hoop. The crowd cheers loudly for the white team while the black team shakes hands with the winning team. Winning can be very exciting but it is not the only thing that matters in a competition. The training process has greater benefits than winning, and a player can still have fun with his teammates and will learn more valuable lessons when he loses.

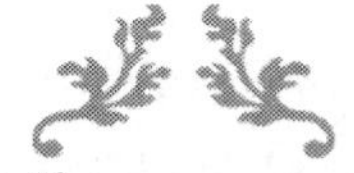

Questions as you read:

- What is the directive word?
- Underline the student's thesis.
- What supporting points did the student use?
- How did the student use voice to stand out?

While many people think winning is the only thing that matters, training actually matters more for a player. Training can make a player physically stronger by exercising his muscles daily. Many good skills can be developed by repeating practices in training. Training will also allow players to become good friends with his teammates and have a strong friendship by spending time with each other. The process of training is more important than winning.

When a team loses, the players may be discouraged but they can still have fun during the game. The player and the audience can enjoy playing and watching the competition. Teammates will support and encourage each other during the game. They will also help each other reach the same goal by working together. Having fun is when a team of players help each other and it's better than winning.

A team can be disappointed when they lose but they can learn more than the winners. They can figure out what made them lose and they can improve the next time they play. They can also learn from the winners and use their strategy to their advantage. Once a team loses, the players can learn to be humble. They can also encourage others who lose by saying kind words to them. Losing may be difficult but it will teach a player more valuable lessons than winning.

Winning can be exciting but it is not the only thing that matters in a game. Training is more important than winning because training can make a player physically stronger and a better player. If a team loses they can still have fun with the competition and can learn to be humble. Winning is not the only thing that matters because there are other aspects that make a good player.

NOTE: Student examples appear in original format and may contain slight grammar errors.

Activities

Key Terms

Define the following key terms: standardized essay test, directive word

Comprehension

1) What does a directive word help you do?
2) What are some things you can do to make sure you finish your essay in the time you are given?
3) What is the best way to manage your time if you need to write more than one essay?

Practice

1) Answer the question in the sidebar next to Student Example #1.
2) Answer the questions in the sidebar next to Student Example #2.

Application

1) Time yourself for one hour and answer the following essay question: What are the most important qualities for a friend to have?
2) Time yourself for an hour and a half (1.5 hours) and answer the following two questions:
    a. Agree or disagree with this quote: "A good traveller has no fixed plans and is not intent on arriving."—Lao Tzu
    b. Imagine your neighborhood has an increased problem with graffiti. Write an essay explaining how this problem should be solved.

More activities and student examples available at **www.writefromtheheart.org/resourceguide**.

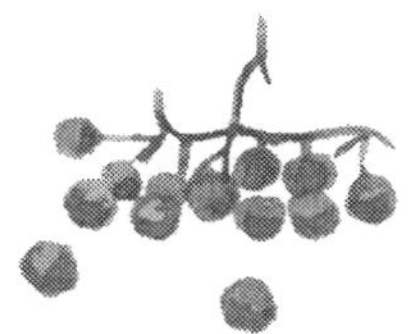

Section 6:
Revising and Editing Tools

Revising and editing are the final steps in the writing process but are arguably the most important. This is where your essay goes from "draft" to finished "paper."

It is also the most overlooked part of the writing process. Many students write a first draft—sometimes quickly the night before an assignment is due—and then have no time for revising or editing. They read through the paper quickly to check for grammar errors and then turn it in. This is one of the worst mistakes a writer can make. A draft is not a completed paper. Even professional writers revise their work!

The revising and editing process is made up of several separate steps. Although you may hear some individuals use the terms "editing" and "revision" without distinction, it is very helpful to keep the two terms separate in your mind. Revising a draft is where you take the time to evaluate what you wrote and fill in the gaps, move pieces around, and remove things that aren't necessary. In contrast, editing is focused on correcting a writer's work in each sentence to follow proper rules related to grammar, punctuation, and other conventions of writing. Together, they are often referred to as the "revision process," but there are multiple steps to this process.

The process of revising and editing is how you hone your writing skills and take your work from draft to polished final product. This section will lay out the tools to help you do that successfully.

Chapter 22: Revising a Draft

The word "revision" can be broken into two parts: "re" and "vision." When you break it up, it is clear what the word actually means: "To see again." **Revising** a piece of writing is exactly that: seeing your whole piece with new eyes and making changes in keeping with what you notice.

In other words, revision is a process related to the entire piece of writing, rather than just a few sentences. Revision is *not* a process of making grammar corrections to the piece of writing. Instead, revision is a process of identifying the overall strengths, weaknesses, and main points of the piece. While revision can focus on clarifying individual sentences, revision is never limited to just those sentences. In fact, sometimes, revising can result in removing, rearranging, or adding entire paragraphs. If you're revising a paper and need to make such extensive changes, don't be alarmed. Advanced writers make extensive changes to pieces of writing, and some works look completely different from the first draft to the final draft.

The first step in this process is **self-revising**: this is when you look at your own draft and begin to pull it apart with a critical eye and evaluate where it needs improvement. It is a good idea to wait at least a day or two before you self-revise a draft. The break from your draft will help you see it with new eyes. There are several things that you can do to evaluate your work.

Testing your Thesis

When you are revising a paper with a thesis statement, an important tool for revision is **testing your thesis statement**. Sometimes, writers begin the writing process with a strong thesis statement, but their evidence and arguments within the paper ultimately send their paper in a different direction than the original thesis statement. Other times, writers begin the writing process with a weak or undeveloped thesis statement, but the paper's main points and evidence become quite well-developed. In both cases, the thesis statement needs to be revised.

To test your thesis statement, ask the following questions:

- Does my thesis statement take a position?
- Does your thesis make an argument, or is it simply a statement?
- Is my thesis statement specific enough?
- Does my thesis statement reflect the arguments and evidence that I made throughout the essay?

If your thesis statement uses vague adjectives or verbs, then it likely isn't specific enough. For example, if you write, "The Battle of Gettysburg was important to history," what does important mean? What period of history are you referencing? What about that battle made it important? In this case, you will need to revise your thesis statement to be more specific. For example, you might revise the example above to instead read, "The location, outcome, and rhetoric of the Battle of Gettysburg shaped the course of American history by accelerating the end of the Civil War."

If your audience were to read your thesis statement and then ask the question, "So what?", then you likely need to revise your thesis statement so that it clearly shows the importance of the topic that you are writing about.

Sometimes when you start writing an essay, the argument develops in a way that you weren't expecting. That's okay! When you start a first draft, your thesis is called a "preliminary thesis" for just this reason—you are expected to adjust it in the revision process!

You want to make sure that your thesis covers all the points in your essay. Perhaps you started with a preliminary thesis that said, "Pool safety is important so that everyone is safe." This is a fine thesis statement. Your first point in the paper was about protecting swimmers and your second point was about preventing accidents—both of those are about safety, so that's fine. But perhaps your third point was about how following the rules lets parents enjoy themselves too because they aren't busy worrying and reminding you what to do. This isn't really reflected in your thesis, so you will need to change it slightly. This can be done by specifically listing the points in the thesis or making a general statement that includes the whole argument.

Examples of a revised thesis:

Making sure safety rules are followed around pools will protect swimmers, prevent accidents, and ensure everyone can have fun.

Following all the safety rules at the pool is required in order to have a safe and fun experience.

Both examples are strong and work well. The first one lists the three supporting points (protect swimmers, prevent accidents, ensure everyone can have fun). The second one covers all three points with the phrase "a safe and fun experience." Either one is acceptable.

There are times where you have a strong thesis, but a supporting point goes completely off topic. When you look at it, you realize you would need to make a really complicated thesis statement in order to make your paper work. If you are struggling with how to fit it in, it is a good idea to consider cutting the paragraph and rewriting a new point that does fit the thesis. This is a large change to a draft, and happens rarely, but it is good to consider if you are really struggling to get the thesis to work. This is also a good time to ask someone else's opinion before you make this type of change—sometimes someone else can help you change the wording of either the thesis or the paragraph without having to rewrite the entire section.

Once you've asked all these questions and accordingly revised your thesis statement and essay, you can take a deep breath! Your thesis statement is likely quite strong, and your essay reflects that thesis statement. If you need to review the requirements for a thesis statement, make sure to review **Chapter 4**.

Improving Development

When we write, we are putting thoughts from our head onto paper. But our thoughts move faster than our fingers can type. Sometimes, the picture or idea we had in our head doesn't get transcribed onto the page the way we had hoped. Adding details during the revision process can help!

This part of revision is called looking at the **development** of the paper: how your argument, description, or story is put together overall. Is it understandable, or are there steps or pieces missing? Is everything explained fully, or are more details needed? Are there extra details that distract from the argument or story? All these questions will help you develop your paper smoothly from start to finish.

Adding Details

To add more detail to your writing, there are several different techniques to try.

Consider Additional Voice Techniques

Is there a moment or moments where you can play with senses? What about inner ideas or time? Do you need more dialogue? Is there a place where you can add a language tool like simile, metaphor, personification, alliteration, or onomatopoeia? Remember that you should still be using these techniques in your academic writing—you can add quotations, figurative language, factual descriptions, and many other techniques. Spend some time reviewing the techniques discussed in **Section 3** and consider adding more details using voice.

Consider Specificity

Sometimes adding concrete details to a paper increases the reader's understanding. In a narrative, is there a place where you can add a specific list of items for dramatic effect? For example, instead of just talking about how the main character was sad and tired when she went to the grocery store and looked for the items she needed, you might instead list off all of the items that she had to find in the store. For example: "She searched the store for cleaning supplies, dog food, and soy sauce - all of the expensive items that were hard to find. It was exhausting." Adding the list of items creates a concrete reality to an abstract idea like "tired."

You can do the same thing in expository or persuasive writing. Instead of just giving a statistic, add a specific example of a person who is part of that statistic and what that looked like in their life. Precise details are a way of showing the reader that you are telling the truth. Be careful with this though—don't make up specifics that aren't true. And don't use them if they would confuse or distract your reader from your point.

You can also add specificity with your word choice. Try to avoid vague words like "big," "beautiful," "stuff," and "things." If you use generic adjectives and nouns, try replacing them with a word picture or a list to show your reader what you mean instead of simply telling them.

Consider Expanding Examples

Sometimes writers are so familiar with an example that they use that they don't explain it enough. Ask yourself if you need to add details to an example. For instance, this was a paragraph in a student's first draft:

> Riding horses teaches you about safety because horses are such large animals. Horses are prey animals, so they can get spooked easily. It is important that you learn safety before interacting with them. Dori Truman, a horse teacher in Port Deposit, Maryland, says, "It is important to learn how to handle yourself around large animals so you know what and what not to do."

Obviously, she knows a lot about horses and how to be responsible around them...but she doesn't actually explain to her reader how to be safe! Here is how she expanded her example so that it was clear what to do and not do around horses:

Riding horses teaches you about safety. Because they are such large animals, it's important to be careful. Make sure to always wear closed toed shoes so your toes don't get trampled from the horse's hooves. You should not crawl under the horse and never walk around the rear end of a horse. Since horses can't see their rumps, when they get scared they kick with their rear legs. Learning about horse safety is important because horses are prey animals, so they can get spooked easily. It is important that you learn safety before interacting with them. Dori Truman, a horse teacher in Port Deposit, Maryland, says, "It is important to learn how to act around large animals so one knows what and what not to do." —Julia R., 11

This second version is much better because the reader knows exactly what safety precautions to take around horses. Adding to your examples can help your reader understand your point much more easily.

Cutting Back

Cutting back writing takes time, but the process of cutting down writing ultimately results in a clearer, more powerful piece of writing. Too many adjectives or too much information in the wrong place can slow things down and make it boring to read your work. Writers often have to consider word and length limits for their pieces as well. Here are some simple tips on knowing when and where to snip away.

Take out the Boring Bits

This is especially common at the beginning of stories or papers. You need to introduce characters or your topic, but you don't need to start from the very beginning.

Example:

Mary woke up at 6 am and opened her bright blue eyes. Her curly brown hair was a messy mop on top of her head, and her pajamas were bunched up. She got out of bed and went to the bathroom, being careful not to disturb Chase the dog, Molly the cat, or her three roommates, Chelsea, Meghan, and Amanda, who were all 22 or 23, like her, and had graduated nursing school last year together.

This is one of the errors mentioned in **Section 3**: describing something with too much exact detail that the point is buried.

After cuts and revisions:

Mary slammed her hand down on the alarm and stumbled out of bed, tripping over her dog, Chase. She tried to stifle her gasp of surprise so she didn't wake her roommates. She couldn't be late for her hospital shift again.

This second paragraph uses specific word choices to convey haste. Some of the other details, like her hair color or her roommates" names, if it's important to the story, could be added in at a later point.

This is particularly true of dialogue: you don't always have to put in the responses, especially if the piece of dialogue is just "Okay" or "Sure." Remember, you don't have to represent the whole conversation, and you can speed up the conversation to include the important parts and leave out the boring bits.

Take out Useless Adjectives

Descriptive writing isn't necessarily flowery or over the top. Say enough to paint a picture but take out repetitive or extra descriptors.

Example:

The shining sun glistened down on the glimmering bay, reflecting brightly off the glittering ships with diamondlike rays.

That's so many adjectives! It makes the sentence difficult to read and the value of the picture is lost.

After cuts and revisions:

The sun reflected off the ships with the intensity of a laser.

Notice that this second sentence uses a metaphor (sun=laser) instead of all the adjectives. Often, switching out overly flowery words with a piece of figurative language will solve the problem.

Take out Repetition

Sometimes repetition happens because your paper isn't organized well. If your paper isn't organized, it can be easy to say the same thing several times without realizing it.

See how those two sentences above sound repetitive? Using the same word over and over indicates that the sentences can be combined to eliminate the repetition:

Sometimes repetition happens because your paper isn't organized well, so it can be easy to say the same thing several times without realizing it.

This can happen in narrative writing as well. When a writer tries to give detail, they end up explaining something in a repetitive way with the same word, or even several synonyms, that makes the writing sound clunky.

First attempt:

It was a small white dog, tiny at probably only twelve pounds, and more round than long, with longish eggshell colored hair and a pink belly and a long tail who loved to nip and bite at guests when they entered the house.

After cuts and revisions:

It was a small white dog, a real ankle-biter.

Take out Anything That Doesn't Support the Thesis or the Plot

In fiction, you might have an idea that is fantastic—maybe it's the history between two characters, or a secret past that someone has. It may seem like some of your best writing, but if it doesn't fit the story, save it for another time. You should not focus on a scene that does nothing to advance the action or connect to a plot point later in the story.

The same is true in academic writing. You may have found the most interesting fact you've ever read, but if it has nothing to do with your paper topic, you can cut it.

An example of this occurred in a student paper recently. The story was about a girl in an orphanage who was trying to figure out what happened to her parents. Her best friend was helping her, and they were stopped at every turn by a mean orphanage director. In the climactic scene, when the main character discovers her heritage, her best friend also discovers that the director is her mother! That's a lot of discoveries!! It was a great idea but having both of those things happening at the same time meant that the main character's story had to share the spotlight with the other plotline that wasn't really set up. In revisions, the student simply made the best friend the director's daughter from the start. This was a hard change because it meant a cool surprise was lost, but it allowed her to focus on the main character and have the best friend struggle with loyalty throughout the story instead, which made for a more interesting plot in the long run. That story went on to win an award in a national contest—it was a good change!

Checking Organization

Organization relates to both the order of your paper, and how well you transition between sentences and paragraphs. You might have the most brilliant points, but if they are scattered throughout the paper and your readers can't follow your argument, you won't be effective.

The first thing you want to check in your organization is each paragraph. Is the paragraph fully developed? You should have a topic sentence, three or four supporting details, and a final sentence to help shift to the next paragraph. Sometimes in a first draft, you might write a sentence in an early paragraph that actually belongs in a later paragraph because you more fully develop that idea later on. Move the sentence to the correct paragraph or eliminate it if it is no longer necessary. In fiction, you will want to check each paragraph to make sure you are following dialogue rules.

The next thing you want to check is the order of your paragraphs. Do they have a logical progression? Every type of writing has specific rules for organization, so you want to make sure that you follow that properly. For example, if you are writing a memoir or a process paper, you should be writing in chronological order. If you are writing a comparison paper, you need to make sure you are following the proper whole-to-whole or point-to-point formatting. You might need to switch sentences around in a paragraph or move a whole paragraph so that you follow the requirements of that style of writing.

The last piece you want to look at is your transitions. Did you follow the known-new rule when you moved from known information to new information? You might also need to add transition phrases at the beginning of paragraphs.

If you need help with transitions and making sure your paragraphs are organized well, make sure to review **Section 2** for more help.

Self-Reflection

Self-revising can be difficult because it's hard to see our own errors or gaps in writing—if I wrote something, I know what I meant, so how do I know if it makes sense or not? That's why it's important to include the next step of the writing process, revising with a partner, which we will discuss in **Chapter 23**.

But reading and evaluating your own work is a very important first step. You might not catch all the problems, but with continued practice in revision, you will start to get a sense that something is just a little "off" about a section of writing. You might not know how to fix it right away but identifying those problem areas and experimenting with changes will help you be better prepared as you work with a partner.

After you have revised your draft to the best of your ability, it's time to reflect on what you still think needs work. This is called **self-reflection**. In order to get the most out of a collaboration, you should come to your partner with questions about your draft. Ask about those wonky paragraphs that just don't sound quite right. Double check that you tested your thesis correctly. Make sure that your information is clear and understandable.

Good Questions to Ask in Self-Reflection:

You want to avoid general questions like "Is my paper good?" or "Am I missing anything?" These indicate that you didn't really revise the paper yourself. It also won't get you the information you need. A general question will get a general answer. When you ask specific questions, it helps your partner pay close attention to the parts you need the most help with!

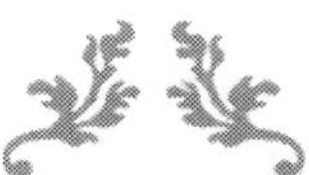

- How can I reword my thesis to make sure it encompasses my entire paper?
- Did I explain this portion clearly enough?
- This section sounds like I'm just reporting facts. How can I make it come alive?
- These two paragraphs don't seem to be flowing smoothly—what am I missing?
- Should I add a quote or statistic to this paragraph?

Student Example

My Adventure at Kennywood

By Abigail C., 13

Note: This is Abigail's first draft, before revisions.

"I'm so excited to go to Kennywood tomorrow!" I told my brother Timothy.

"Me too! I'm a little bit nervous though; I haven't been on a roller coaster before." he replied.

"Yeah me too. I'm not going to ride a really big one." I ended our conversation.

The big day was here! At last we pulled in to the vast parking lot and could see the terrifying heights and slopes of the metal monsters. My courage faded and my legs began to melt into jello.

"Let's go on the skyrocket!" one kid said. The group agreed and we walked toward the line.

The tall, twisty giant loomed overhead. "I'm not so sure about this," I tried to protest, but my friends pressured me to keep moving. When we entered the line I realized I didn't have a partner. "Oh well, I guess I can't ride it!" I thought, with mingled feelings of relief and disappointment. As I made my way back downstream the crowded stairway, my mom and sister Rachel were walking up the stairs. "What are you doing?" Rachel asked.

"I decided not to ride it," I replied.

"Oh come on, why not?" she persisted.

"I don't really want to; and I don't have a partner anyway." I attempted at closing my case.

"I'll go with you!" she lead me toward the car.

With trembling fingers I buckled myself into the seat. "I don't want to do this," I stated with a grimace. "It'll be fun!" Rachel attempted to encourage me. All of the sudden, the cars started slowly moving forward. "No, no no!" I was terrified. It was too late to turn back now.

Blast off! As the cars straightened out the turn, we suddenly felt a boost of momentum. The speed had gone from 0 to 50mph in three seconds. I screamed like I had never screamed before. I looked at Rachel expecting her to be as terrified as I was, but she was laughing! Spiraling upside down, I wondered if I would ever be on solid ground again.

At last the ending track came into sight. It felt like my stomach had completely gone! I attempted to walk down the stairs, and I realized that I was very dizzy! "Wow." I said shakily.

"Haha, your face was so funny! You looked absolutely terrified! And the moment it started you screamed a lot!" she said.

"Oh! I thought you would be scared too!"

"Me too, but I guess laughing at you made it easier; it kind of distracted me from being scared!" we walked away.

"Wow! I can't believe I did that!" I shuddered. "I'm glad I went on it though; if I hadn't I probably would have wondered what it was like for a while. With that we walked away to the next adventure.

Questions as you read:

- Where did they add details?
- What areas of help did the student identify in self-reflection?
- What types of questions did they ask?

Second Draft: After Revisions, and including underlined self-reflection questions for her partner

"I'm so excited to go to Kennywood Park tomorrow!" I told my brother Timothy.

"Me too! I'm a little bit nervous though; I haven't been on a roller coaster before." he replied.

"Yeah me too. I'm not going to ride a really big one." I ended our conversation.

The big day was here! I awoke at 6:00 am, ready to start a new adventure! As we packed the car with coolers and supplies necessary for a fun-filled day, I noticed the clock steadily ticking away. I wondered if we would get there on time. Soon enough the car was full and we were on the road to Kennywood! My nerves were steadily climbing, and our car drew closer and closer. At last we pulled in to the vast parking lot and could see the terrifying heights and slopes of the metal monsters. My courage faded and my legs began to melt into jello. We walked under the big yellow sign that read, 'Kennywood' and joined the rest of our group. The group was composed of kids from our summer camp, and some loved thrilling rides; some did not.

"Let's go on the skyrocket!" one kid said. The group agreed and we walked toward the rollercoaster's line.

The tall, twisty giant loomed overhead. "I'm not so sure about this," I tried to protest, but my friends pressured me to keep moving. When we entered the line I realized I didn't have a partner. "Oh well, I guess I can't ride it!" I thought, with mingled feelings of relief and disappointment. As I made my way back downstream the crowded stairway, my mom and sister Rachel were walking up the stairs. "What are you doing?" Rachel asked. <u>Is my dialogue paragraphed correctly?</u>

"I decided not to ride it," I replied.

"Oh come on, why not?" she persisted.

"I don't really want to; and I don't have a partner anyway." I attempted at closing my case.

"I'll go with you!" she lead me toward the car. <u>Do I make it clear why I changed my mind?</u>

With trembling fingers I buckled myself into the seat. "I don't want to do this," I stated with a grimace. "It'll be fun!" Rachel attempted to encourage me. All of the sudden, the cars started slowly moving forward. My whole body was shaking, my heart was racing, and my nerves were escalating. "No, no no!" I was terrified. It was too late to turn back now. We slowly rounded a corner; anticipation building. My hands were sweaty and I held tight to Rachel's hand. My grip was like iron.

Blast off! As the cars straightened out the turn, we suddenly felt a boost of momentum. The speed had gone from 0 to 50mph in three seconds. I screamed like I had never screamed before. We zoomed toward the incline of what looked like 90°. Shooting up the sky-scraping height, my sense of gravity had gone haywire. In just a few seconds, the cars slowed down and I opened my eyes. That was a mistake. As I opened them I saw how high I was, I heaved difficult breaths of air. I looked at Rachel expecting her to be as terrified as I was, but she was laughing! I didn't get to ask her what was so funny, because all of the sudden, we dropped. Down the enormous, vertical hill. Plummeting toward the ground, I let out a long-winded scream. Suddenly I felt the ride twist and turn through big loops. Spiraling upside down, I wondered if I would ever be on solid ground again. **Do I use too many adjectives to describe my fear?**

At last the ending track came into sight. I was beginning to recover from the shock and terror that had enveloped me for the entirety of the ride. I laughed a little, and was glad when the car came to a complete stop. Still trembling, I stepped out of the car. It felt like my stomach had completely gone! I attempted to walk down the stairs, and I realized that I was very dizzy!

"Wow." I said shakily.

"Did you like it?" said my sister Rachel.

"I think so, but I'm not sure. I am definitely glad that I did it, but I'm not sure I would do it again!" Rachel laughed.

"Oh yeah, what were you laughing at?" I asked.

"What? Oh! Well I guess I was laughing at you!"

"Me? Why?" I was surprised.

"Haha, your face was so funny! You looked absolutely terrified! And the moment it started you screamed a lot!" she said.

"Oh! I thought you would be scared too!"

"Me too, but I guess laughing at you made it easier; it kind of distracted me from being scared!" we walked away.

"Wow! I can't believe I did that!" I shuddered. "I'm glad I went on it though; if I hadn't I probably would have wondered what it was like for a while. With that we walked away to the next adventure. **Do I need to explain my lesson more?**

Activities

Key Terms

Define the following key terms: revising, self-revising, testing your thesis, development, organization, self-reflection

Comprehension

1) What is the difference between revising and editing?
2) What sorts of questions show that you have done self-reflection?

Practice

1) Answer the questions in the sidebar for Student Example #1.

Application

1) Choose an essay that you have completed for another application in Section 4 or Section 5 and complete a self-revision on it. Make sure to ask self-reflective questions in preparation for a partner.

More activities and student examples available at **www.writefromtheheart.org/resourceguide**.

Chapter 23: Revising with a Partner

When you finish a piece of writing, it can feel like you poured your blood, sweat, and tears into crafting this magnificent creation. When people give constructive criticism, it feels like they're attacking you and your choices. But there's an element we can't forget about in writing: while we are expressing ourselves, we are doing it FOR an audience. It's art, meant to be enjoyed by others.

Now, certainly, we can create art without the input of others. But part of the process is making sure we are communicating clearly—we want others to understand what we are trying to say. That's where revising with a partner comes in. Writing is a community activity and interacting with someone else in the draft stage will always help you become a better writer.

Part of it is practical. You have probably read the same paragraph and the same sentence dozens of times, and this can cause you to think it looks right, even when it doesn't. Maybe you have minor errors. Perhaps you used "brooch" instead of "broach the subject." Maybe you have two *the*s in the same sentence. Maybe you're missing an article or a whole phrase at the end of a paragraph. And maybe an entire point from your outline got deleted and the conclusion doesn't make sense. It's always good to get a second (or third) set of eyes on your work.

The other part is artistic. If you are trying to persuade an audience, it's a good thing to test out your argument and see what feedback they give you. Sometimes when you are close to something, you don't see the gaps. I like to call this "point jumping." If A leads to B which leads to C in our argument, sometimes when you write (because we think faster than we write), you will only write out A and C, because it makes sense to you. If we have someone else read your paper, they can say, "I understand this, but how did you come to this conclusion?" and you can add in the additional information so that the point is more convincing.

Or perhaps you are writing a short story and you know the characters really well. Perhaps you didn't explain their relationship well enough, or you created a scene without introducing all the people in it. Having someone else read the story and say, "Who is this person?" will help you create a better scenario for your characters.

When you get feedback, whether it's positive or meant to be a helpful suggestion, remember, you are still the author, and you have the power to make the change, or decide not to. However, if an outside person is confused or doesn't understand what you're trying to convey, you might want to look closer at your words to see if you can communicate better. Writers who wait to get feedback until a final draft are missing out on an important step in their growth, and it will take them a lot longer to improve their skills than writers who take time to collaborate with others throughout the writing process.

Finding a Partner

Looking for someone to read your early drafts can be intimidating, but it is not something you should skip. Your work will be read eventually (even if it's just by a teacher), so showing it to someone before you turn it in for a grade or for publication can only improve it.

The first step in finding a partner is making sure you are prepared. You don't want to show someone a half-finished draft, unless you are completely stuck and need help figuring out what to do next. But it is not going to be helpful to get feedback on half of a story or paper you just haven't finished typing out—how will they be able to tell you if your argument makes sense or if the characters are fully developed if they don't have the whole piece? Make sure you have finished your draft AND you have revised it yourself, as explained in **Chapter 22**. Come to the partner with your best version and questions you have about problem areas.

But who can you ask? A lot of people take writing classes or attend workshops for this exact reason. It's a lot easier to trade papers with someone else doing the same assignment as you than to ask someone randomly. Even professional writers have weekend workshops where they bring their work to trade and revise with the help of others.

Look for classes for students your age—there are many online groups that do this, as well as professional online classes for credit (Write from the Heart offers both workshops and full credit classes that do this very thing!). Classroom peers know the assignment and they know what to look for to help you improve your grade. Point out the areas where you're struggling or where you think you could improve, and they may be able to help you solve the problem. Make sure if you are investigating online services, you ask if they

offer peer interactions or revision help during the writing process—some services only offer teacher input on final drafts at the end of the project and don't have peer interactions at all. You want to find something that offers help during the project as well as an evaluation at the end of it.

Even if you aren't taking a class that offers revisions as part of the program, you can always ask the teacher for help before the paper is due. Try to turn in a draft before the final paper is due. Pay close attention to what the teacher is asking you to revise. Their suggestions are probably based on the requirements of the assignment and the rubric you will be graded against. If they are asking for more information or telling you to change something, it may be an area where you will lose points without revisions.

If you are writing on your own, make your own group of writers. Some students attend co-ops or after school programs, and many start their own writing clubs with their friends! There are free online groups you can join as well where you can post your work and get feedback. Often this is not going to be as specific as a classroom or a teacher, but they can come up with some great ideas to help you. These types of groups work best with creative writing—most people don't enjoy reading other people's class assignments for fun!

Parents and siblings are also a great blank slate to test your work against. They represent a random wider audience without prior knowledge of what you're trying to accomplish. It's extremely important to make sure you have done a good self-reflection before you go to them, because family members tend to be more generic than other groups. They want to encourage you and say nice things, so they will often just look at grammar and not the structure. But if you ask specific questions about certain areas, they will feel freer to tell you if they were confused or you were missing something. It will also prompt them to give you specific suggestions.

Don't look at feedback as a negative experience but a system of checks and balances to help you identify something you may have missed. It's your opportunity to tweak minor mistakes (or major ones) and create a strong piece of writing.

Reviewing a Partner

Now it's your turn! How do you help someone improve their writing? First, review the assignment. Make sure they are completing the requirements. Does their fictional story answer have a beginning, middle and end? Is there a conflict, climax, and resolution? Does their essay have a thesis, a developed body with at least three points and a strong conclusion? Do their arguments make sense? Are they missing any information or citations? The more you practice the techniques in this book, the easier it will be for you to recognize them (or notice if they're missing) in someone else's work.

Make sure you point out anything that doesn't make sense to you, or if an argument isn't strong or seems to be missing information. They probably won't phrase things the way you would, but they should still be communicating effectively. Focus on the structure and development of the work. Don't worry too much about grammar at this point, because they might revise the whole section and those sentences might not even exist anymore. Instead follow these tips.

Be honest. It is not helpful to tell someone their work is great or incredible when it really needs work. You are falsely building them up to a possible larger embarrassment later. It is far better to be honest than to be nice. However, being honest does equal being mean. You can still be honest and kind at the same time. For example, if someone said, "Does this shirt make me look fat?" you could say "Ewww gross, yes!! Blech!" or you could say, "It doesn't really compliment your figure...maybe try the blue one instead?" Both are honest, but the second one considers the person's feelings.

You can do the same in your critiques. If they have organization problems, you don't have to say, "This is a terrible mess and doesn't follow the rules!" Instead, you could say, "You switch your order of points between these two paragraphs. They need to be in the same order in both to follow comparison rules." If you have something negative to say, don't be mean. Be honest, but be kind.

Offer constructive criticism. Offering feedback like this takes skill and practice but has many benefits. **Constructive criticism** is not ripping apart someone's work but is offering help to improve or further develop their writing. The best way to do this is to provide specific suggestions and recommendations. Instead of saying, "Add more detail" you could say "Describe what you are thinking and feeling in this moment—use sensory details to help us be immersed in it too!" Telling someone to add more detail is not helpful, because they obviously thought they already had enough detail or don't know how to add more. Giving them specific suggestions will enable them to do that.

Point out the good things they did, too. There are lots of proverbs and sayings that highlight this: you catch more flies with honey, a spoonful of sugar helps the medicine go down. Don't forget to congratulate them for the things they did well. This will serve to encourage them as well as remind them that you are here to help, not tear down. Try to give just as many compliments as suggestions. You could tell them a specific part was engaging or well written, or include both a compliment and a suggestion together: "I love the

way you describe your mom—I can totally see her face in this moment! You should try to do the same thing for your dad, too."

Ask quality questions. One of the very best tools for revising your own writing—or helping a partner to revise his or her writing—is by asking questions throughout the piece. This is an excellent way to help someone see exactly what is missing. **Quality questions** are those questions that begin with who, what, where, when, why, and how. A quality question cannot be answered with "yes," "no," or just a couple of words. Instead, a quality question typically requires a sentence to several sentences of development to adequately respond. This also helps them be specific about their details—answering a "why" question will automatically mean they are adding more information.

Example:

On Thursday, we were playing musical horses. We had to get on the horses with no tack as fast as we could, before the opposing teams did. **How did the game work? How many people were on each team? How many horses? Where were you standing and where were the horses?** I looked at my partner, standing in the middle of the round arena, and Miss Hannah, who stopped the music.

"Riley!" I called to her when the music stopped. She dashed over **over where?** and I jumped down, **down from what?** ready to boost her up on the pony.

Notice the questions in bold. They all ask questions that help the writer add more details and development to her narrative. The answers to each question would help make this story more complete.

If you have a revision peer to trade assignments with, you will both improve through the process. Revising with a partner allows you to grow your skills in both in your own work and in your understanding of the concepts of what makes writing better.

Student Example

Note: this is a partner response to the self-reflection that this student did at the end of ***Chapter 22****. The questions that she asked are still underlined, and the partner's feedback is bolded.*

My Adventure at Kennywood

By Abigail C., 13

"I'm so excited to go to Kennywood Park tomorrow!" I told my brother Timothy.

"Me too! I'm a little bit nervous though; I haven't been on a roller coaster before. " he replied.

"Yeah me too. I'm not going to ride a really big one." I ended our conversation.

The big day was here! I awoke at 6:00 am, ready to start a new adventure! As we packed the car with coolers and supplies necessary for a fun-filled day, I noticed the clock steadily ticking away. I wondered if we would get there on time. Soon enough the car was full and we were on the road to Kennywood! My nerves were steadily climbing, and our car drew closer and closer. **What were you thinking in the car ride? What were you nervous about?** At last we pulled in to the vast parking lot and could see the terrifying heights and slopes of the metal monsters. My courage faded and my legs began to melt into jello. We walked under the big yellow sign that read, 'Kennywood' and joined the rest of our group. The group was composed of kids from our summer camp, and some loved thrilling rides; some did not. **This is an excellent summary without getting too caught up in extra details that don't matter.**

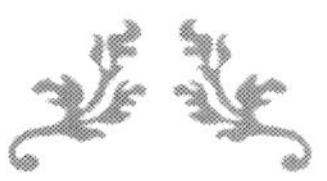

Questions as you read:

- List two of the questions the partner asked.
- What encouraging comments did they make?
- How did the partner give the author options without telling her what to write?

"Let's go on the skyrocket!" one kid said. The group agreed and we walked toward the rollercoaster's line.

The tall, twisty giant loomed overhead. **New paragraph** "I'm not so sure about this," I tried to protest, but my friends pressured me to

keep moving. **New paragraph** When we entered the line I realized I didn't have a partner. "Oh well, I guess I can't ride it!" I thought, with mingled feelings of relief and disappointment. **New paragraph** As I made my way back downstream the crowded stairway, my mom and sister Rachel were walking up the stairs. **New paragraph** "What are you doing?" Rachel asked. Is my dialogue paragraphed correctly? **No—see my notes**

"I decided not to ride it," I replied.

"Oh come on, why not?" she persisted.

"I don't really want to; and I don't have a partner anyway." I attempted at closing my case. **Great dialogue tag!!**

"I'll go with you!" she lead me toward the car. Do I make it clear why I changed my mind? Not really. You should say here why you let her lead you—what made you change your mind? It could be something as simple as "I figured if my sister was with me, I could be braver" (I know there's definitely something about doing something scary with your parents or siblings that makes it easier than with your friends sometimes! It's happened to me!)

With trembling fingers I buckled myself into the seat. **New paragraph** "I don't want to do this," I stated with a grimace. "It'll be fun!" Rachel attempted to encourage me. **New paragraph** All of the sudden, the cars started slowly moving forward. My whole body was shaking, my heart was racing, and my nerves were escalating. "No, no no!" I was terrified. It was too late to turn back now. We slowly rounded a corner; anticipation building. My hands were sweaty and I held tight to Rachel's hand. My grip was like iron. **Great description here!**

Blast off! As the cars straightened out the turn, we suddenly felt a boost of momentum. The speed had gone from 0 to 50mph in three seconds. I screamed like I had never screamed before. We zoomed toward the incline of what looked like 90°. **it's better in a paper like this to write out "90 degrees"** Shooting up the sky-scraping height, my sense of gravity had gone haywire. In just a few seconds, the cars slowed down and I opened my eyes. That was a mistake. **Where were you at this moment? The top of a hill?** As I opened them I saw how high I was,

I heaved difficult breaths of air. I looked at Rachel expecting her to be as terrified as I was, but she was laughing! I didn't get to ask her what was so funny, because all of the sudden, we dropped. Down the enormous, vertical hill. Plummeting toward the ground, I let out a long-winded scream. Suddenly I felt the ride twist and turn through big loops. Spiraling upside down, I wondered if I would ever be on solid ground again. <u>Do I use too many adjectives to describe my fear?</u> **No! I think you did a great job with this!**

At last the ending track came into sight. I was beginning to recover from the shock and terror that had enveloped me for the entirety of the ride. I laughed a little, and was glad when the car came to a complete stop. Still trembling, I stepped out of the car. It felt like my stomach had completely gone! I attempted to walk down the stairs, and I realized that I was very dizzy!

"Wow." I said shakily.

"Did you like it?" said my sister Rachel.

"I think so, but I'm not sure. I am definitely glad that I did it, but I'm not sure I would do it again!" Rachel laughed.

"Oh yeah, what were you laughing at?" I asked.

"What? Oh! Well I guess I was laughing at you!"

"Me? Why?" I was surprised.

"Haha, your face was so funny! You looked absolutely terrified! And the moment it started you screamed a lot!" she said.

"Oh! I thought you would be scared too!"

"Me too, but I guess laughing at you made it easier; it kind of distracted me from being scared!" we walked away.

"Wow! I can't believe I did that!" I shuddered. "I'm glad I went on it though; if I hadn't I probably would have wondered what it was like for a while. **New paragraph** With that we walked away to the next adventure. <u>Do I need to explain my lesson more?</u> **Yes...You need another paragraph here telling what you learned. What did you realize? What did you take into other situations and apply there?**

Activities

Key Terms

Define the following key terms: constructive criticism, quality questions

Comprehension

1) Where can you give encouraging feedback in a partner's essay?
2) Why should you be honest with a partner, and what is the best way to do it?

Practice

1) Answer the questions in the sidebar for Student Example #1.

Application

1) Find a partner to ask for revisions. Use the paper you prepared at the end of **Chapter 22** if you would like. If you desire, find a group that you can do this with permanently—a class, a group, an online collaborative.
2) Offer feedback to a friend for their writing. Practice the techniques offered in this chapter.

More activities and student examples available at **www.writefromtheheart.org/resourceguide**.

Chapter 24: Editing

The last step in the writing process is editing. **Editing** is focused on correcting a writer's work in each sentence to follow proper rules related to grammar, spelling, punctuation, capitalization, and other conventions of writing. Unlike revision, which focuses on structure, organization, and voice, the editing process asks the writer to move slowly through their piece, sentence by sentence, from beginning to end, to see how to create the most correct language possible.

While it might be tempting to complete this step at the same time as whole-paper revisions, this is actually a waste of time. If you are revising paragraphs correctly, that means you are adding sentences, cutting extra phrases, and reorganizing your paper. It's possible that a grammar error that is there at the beginning of the process gets fixed naturally, or perhaps the error gets eliminated because you cut that sentence completely. Additionally, if you add extra details, you have not checked those sentences for errors. It's more time-consuming to try to go back through and remember what you checked or didn't check; just ignore grammar for the most part until the editing step. Certainly, if you happen to notice something, fix it when you see it! But don't spend the time carefully reading for grammar until your other revisions are completely finished.

Just like with revisions, it's a good idea to ask someone else to read through your paper to check for errors. This is especially helpful if you know you are weak in a certain grammar area, like fragments or missing commas: it might be harder for you to notice these errors. Offer to read over their paper as well, if they have one. Looking for grammar errors in someone else's work has been proven to be a highly effective way to strengthen your own grammar skills.

As you go through the editing step, though, you don't want to just look for grammar mistakes. There are five areas to focus on that will make your paper a stronger final draft.

Sentence Errors

Sentence errors include things like fragments, run-ons, comma splices, misplaced or dangling modifiers, unclear pronoun references, problems with subject-verb agreement, and errors in parallelism. All of these are explained in **Chapter 33** with examples of how to correct them. The more practice you have identifying these errors, the easier it will be to see them in your own work. If you are particularly weak in this area, I would recommend that you read through your paper once looking just for these errors, and then looking again for the rest of the editing items. Getting help from a partner or a parent to walk you through these areas will also help you grow.

Sentence Variety

One of the wonderful things about the English language is all the ways that we can put sentences together. When we first learn how to write sentences, we are taught to have a subject then a verb. But as we mature, we discover that there are a variety of phrases, clauses, and other interjections we can add to our sentences to make them more interesting. As you edit, consider the variety you have. Review **Chapter 32** on sentences and sentence structure for ideas of ways you can create more interesting sentences.

Ways to Add Variety

- Change where clauses or phrases appear in the sentence
- Combine two sentences together with punctuation
- Use intentional fragments for emphasis
- Change a declarative sentence to an imperative or interrogative
- Vary the first word of your sentences by inverting them or adding a phrase

Punctuation and Other Conventions

After sentence errors, this is usually the area of biggest struggle for students. **Conventions** refers to the use of proper punctuation and spelling in your sentences. Some worry about where to put commas, while others don't know how to properly use semicolons. Review **Chapter 34** and **Chapter 35** for help with commas, capitalization, titles, hyphens, dashes, semicolons, colons, and many other types of conventions.

You also want to review your spelling throughout your paper. A modern spellchecker is extremely useful for almost all errors, but it won't catch things like using the wrong spelling of a word (like typing "roll" instead of "role" or "bear" instead of "bare"). Double checking spelling of commonly misused words is always a good idea.

Wordiness or Vagueness

Wordiness and vagueness can happen on the sentence level and correcting this is covered in the grammar section in **Chapter 33**. But this can also happen within sentences as well. Sometimes wordiness could be using too many adjectives to describe an item. Usually this means you need to pick a more precise adjective that covers more attributes. For example, you could say "the small infinitesimal teeny tiny piece of lint" or you could say "the microscopic piece of lint." Vagueness, too, usually happens by not being precise. Avoid words like "stuff" or "things" or "etc." Use specific nouns instead.

Thesaurus Check

The very last editing check you want to do is look at your word choices themselves. If you have vague words, or even just boring words, use your thesaurus and replace them! For example, there are so many synonyms for the word "huge"—use one you like better!

Remember that vocabulary is one of the elements of voice, so use the thesaurus wisely to truly represent you as a writer. Review **Chapter 8** for more help with thesaurus choices.

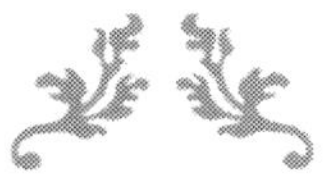

Thirty Synonyms for Huge

colossal, enormous, extensive, gargantuan, gigantic, humongous, vast, whopping, immense, magnificent, mammoth, massive, monstrous, monumental, epic, tremendous, bulky, elephantine, immeasurable, jumbo, mountainous, oversized, planetary, titanic, walloping, cosmic, weighty, Herculean, hulking, astronomical

Student Example

*Note: this example is the final copy of Abigail's paper that was revised in **Chapter 22** and **Chapter 23**.*

The bolded words are ones she replaced with a thesaurus. One spelling error was fixed. Did you notice it before? She used "lead" instead of "led" in earlier versions of the sentence "she lead me toward the car." It is fixed in this version. The other editing corrections are underlined. You can also observe her additional revisions after her partner's comments in ***Chapter 23****.*

My Adventure at Kennywood

By Abigail C., 13

"I'm so excited to go to Kennywood Park tomorrow!" I told my brother, Timothy.

"Me too! I'm a little bit nervous though; I haven't been on a roller coaster before," he replied.

"Yeah me too. I'm not going to ride a really big one." I ended our conversation.

The big day was here! I awoke at 6:00 am, ready to start a new adventure! As we packed the car with coolers and supplies necessary for a fun-filled day, I noticed the clock steadily ticking away. I wondered if we would get there on time. Soon enough the car was full and we were on the road to Kennywood! My nerves were steadily climbing as our car drew closer and closer. I worried about being pressured to go on giant rides.

At last we pulled into the vast parking lot and could see the terrifying heights and slopes of the metal monsters. My courage faded, and my legs began to melt into jello. We walked under the big yellow sign that read 'Kennywood' and joined the rest of our group. The group was composed of kids from our summer camp; some loved thrilling rides, and some did not.

"Let's go on the skyrocket!" one kid said. The group agreed, and we walked toward the rollercoaster's line. I didn't want to be left out, so I was forced to go with them.

Questions as you read:

- Do you think she made good choices with her thesaurus words? Why or why not?
- What was the grammar error that she had to fix the most?
- Give an example of sentence variety.

The **sky-scraping**, twisty giant loomed overhead.

"I'm not so sure about this," I tried to protest, but my friends pressured me to keep moving.

When we entered the line I realized I didn't have a partner. "Oh well, I guess I can't ride it!" I thought, with mingled feelings of relief and disappointment.

As I made my way back downstream the crowded stairway, my mom and sister, Rachel, were walking up the stairs.

"What are you doing?" Rachel asked.

"I decided not to ride it," I replied.

"Oh come on, why not?" she persisted.

"I don't really want to, and I don't have a partner anyway," I attempted to close my case.

"I'll go with you!" she <u>led</u> me toward the car. I felt a little bit braver when she was with me, and I knew she wouldn't stop persuading me until I said yes.

With trembling <u>fingers,</u> I buckled myself into the seat of the car.

"I don't want to do this," I stated with a grimace.

"It'll be fun!" Rachel attempted to encourage me.

All of a sudden, the cars started slowly moving forward. My whole body was shaking, my heart was racing, and my nerves were escalating. "No, no no!" I thought. I was terrified, but it was too late to turn back now. We slowly rounded a corner; <u>my anticipation was building</u>. My hands were sweaty and I held tight to Rachel's hand. My **grasp** was like iron.

Blast off! As the cars rounded the corner, we suddenly felt a boost of momentum. The speed had gone from 0 to 50 mph in three seconds. I screamed like I had never screamed before. We zoomed toward the incline of what looked like 90 degrees! Shooting up the sky-scraping height, my sense of gravity had gone haywire. In just a few seconds, the cars slowed down and I opened my eyes. That was a mistake. We were at the top of a very tall precipice. As I opened them, I saw how high I was. I heaved difficult breaths of air. I looked at Rachel expecting her to be as terrified as I was, but she was laughing! I didn't get to ask her what was so funny, because all of the sudden, we dropped.

Down the enormous, vertical hill, we plummeted toward the ground. I let out a long-winded scream. Suddenly I felt the ride twist and turn through big loops. Spiraling upside down, I wondered if I would ever be on solid ground again.

At last the end of the track came into sight. I was beginning to recover from the shock and terror that had enveloped me for the entirety of the ride. I laughed a little and was glad when the car came to a complete stop. Still trembling, I stepped out of the car. It felt like my stomach had completely disappeared! I attempted to walk down the stairs, and I realized that I was very dizzy!

"Wow," I said shakily.

"Did you like it?" said my sister, Rachel.

"I think so, but I'm not sure. I am definitely glad that I did it, but I'm not sure I would do it again!"

Rachel laughed.

"Oh yeah, what were you laughing at?" I asked.

"What? Oh! Well I guess I was laughing at you!"

"Me? Why?" I was surprised.

"Haha, your face was so funny! You looked absolutely **paralyzed**! And the moment it started, you screamed a lot!" she said.

"Oh! I thought you would be scared too!"

"Me too, but I guess laughing at you made it easier; it kind of distracted me from being scared!"

"Wow! I can't believe I did that!" I shuddered. "I'm glad I went on it though. If I hadn't, I probably would have wondered what it was like for a while."

With that, we walked away to the next adventure.

This rollercoaster was a great object-lesson for me. It made me realize how afraid I am to do new things. Sometimes we need that one person or thing to help us conquer a fear that we have. In my case, I was judging a book by its cover. I didn't want to try something that I really knew nothing about. If I hadn't gone on that ride, I would never have known what trying something new and scary felt like. Now I do! Next time I am unwilling to try something new or scary, I will remember this experience, and have fun!

Activities

Key Terms

Define the following key terms: editing, conventions

Comprehension

1) What are the limitations of spell checkers?
2) Why should you use a thesaurus as you edit?

Practice

1) Answer the questions in the sidebar for Student Example #1.

Application

1) Edit a paper that you have taken through the revision process.
2) Find a paper that you have already completed—even from a year or two ago. Read through it again for editing mistakes. Change any words using a thesaurus to make it sound like you.

More activities and student examples available at **www.writefromtheheart.org/resourceguide**.

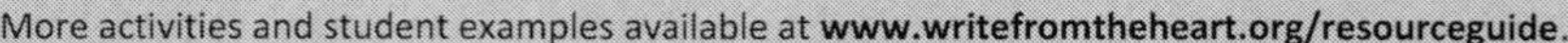

Section 7: Research

Research is a type of writing that every student has to do at some point in their secondary school career—most of you will have to do it more than once! It's something that a lot of students dread, but it doesn't have to be a painful process. In fact, it can become something exciting and interesting if you pick the right topic and take the time to pace yourself throughout the project.

Research writing is either expository or persuasive. Both of those have been explained in **Section 5: Academic Writing Styles**. Many projects in middle school and high school are expository writing: we are writing to inform others about a person or event that we have researched. Sometimes the project can be persuasive: we try to persuade the readers to view an issue or idea a certain way, and we back it up with expert opinions and statistics.

Whether it is expository or persuasive, what research writing adds in is sources. Instead of telling/persuading the reader from our own knowledge, we are looking at what others have said or discovered and using it as support for our perspective. This section explains how to find these sources, evaluate them for usefulness, and how to insert them properly into papers.

Chapter 25: Finding and Organizing Sources

There are many different types of sources that you can use in your research. Depending on the kind of paper you are writing, you may need a specific kind of source. For example, if you are doing a historic research paper, you will likely be looking at primary sources and biographies - the kinds of sources that you might find in a library, an online newspaper archive, or in a local historic archive. A lot of these sources could have been published long ago, and many will be in book form. If you are doing a scientific research paper, on the other hand, you will be looking at scientific articles and books, some of which you will find in hard copy, but many of which you will need to find online. If you are writing a paper to persuade readers to believe a certain way about a current issue, you will be looking at recent news articles, video commentaries by experts, statistical surveys, and other types of recent materials. A lot of these will be found on the internet and online library databases; you will likely use less books or materials published long ago.

In general, though, there are two categories of sources you will use in a research paper:

Primary Sources: Sources that were written/created by someone directly connected to the topic. Examples: Diary entries, historic newspaper articles, scientific studies, autobiographies, memoirs, letters, photographs. These sources were written by the person who actually experienced the event or did the experiment.

Secondary Sources: Sources that are not written or created by someone directly connected to the topic but still utilize primary source information. Most non-fiction books are secondary sources. Examples: Biographies, non-fiction books on a war or event, articles and essays about an event, news articles and videos, and reviews.

You also need to consider whether your source is a scholarly or a popular source. A **scholarly source** is one that is written by experts or knowledgeable authors and investigates their topics in depth. Usually they appear in professional journals, university presses, or professional academic organizations. A **popular source** is one written for a more general audience by a reporter or a professional author. This does not mean that they are less well researched or informative; often, a popular source is more readable and quotable. But it does mean that you will need to do a little more investigation to make sure that they are reputable and that you understand the bias that they might include. See **Chapter 26** for more information on evaluating sources.

Types of Sources

- Non-fiction books
- Essays/articles in books
- News/magazine articles
- Scholarly journal articles
- Documentaries
- Websites
- Online news articles
- Interviews

Determining Sources Needed

The first step in doing research is figuring out what sources you need and how many you will need to include in your paper. In order to do this, look at your topic an ask yourself the following questions:

- What background information do I need?
- What am I trying to prove or show?
- Where would I most likely find information about my topic?
- What facts do I need to make sure I have a source for?

Sometimes the project assignment will give you a minimum number of sources to use. It's a good idea during your preliminary research to find at least twice the number required for the final draft. Sometimes sources end up not being as helpful as you first thought, or two of them repeat the same information. Even if you end up using all of them, that's okay! A "minimum of xx number of sources" means that this is the least number of sources you are *required* to have; you are always welcome to find more than that!

A helpful practice for focusing your search is to ask a research question. A **research question** is the overarching question you have for your project.

This is what your thesis will eventually answer. It should be a "how" or a "why" question, addressing the reason you are starting out on this search. Think about why you picked this topic: why does it matter to you, and why should it matter to others? Put this in question form. Your research question should be something that you have to do research to fully answer.

Examples:

Why is social media popular and is it harmful?

How is the Kyoto Protocol affecting national policies on climate change laws?

How can we reduce childhood obesity?

Why was the Battle of the Bulge important in World War II?

How did Abraham Lincoln affect the United States with his presidency?

Why is Mozart considered a great composer?

Then, begin thinking through sub questions that you will need to answer or statistics/facts you will need. A good system is the **note card system**. Use 4x6 note cards to list as many questions as you can think of that you would like to get answered during your research. Just list one question per card so that as you research, you can record the answer on the note card. You can also write down the source you used to answer this question on the card, so you can keep track of where you found your information.

Once you have completed all of your research and begin planning a draft, your thesis statement should be the answer to your research question, and your supporting points will be the information you will use to show your readers how you came to this conclusion. Your sources will help develop these points. For information on how to plan this draft, **see Section 2**.

Using the Library

If you don't already have a membership to your local library, this is the perfect time to join! Libraries are wonderful starting points for your research.

Search the **library catalog** for books on your topic that are at your library—or at other libraries. Most libraries today allow you to borrow from a larger system through an **interlibrary loan**. Often, you can search catalogs in larger city libraries and have the books sent to your local library for your use free of charge. Your librarian can help with this.

Search **library subscription services** for essays, journal articles, newspaper articles, documentaries, and more. A library subscription service is a service that pays journals, newspapers, and magazines all around the world for access to the full text of the articles published in those periodicals. Libraries and colleges then subscribe to this service, and all their patrons are free to search through all of the information available. This means that instead of a library having to subscribe to thousands of magazines and you having to look through them individually for what you want, it is all available online in one single search. Some popular subscription services are: Academic Search Premier, InfoTrac, Lexis-Nexus, ERIC, and GaleNet Group. Your librarian can direct you to the best database for your particular project.

Ask a librarian if they can help! Librarians love to help students with research. They are experts at helping you to use the online catalog and know about all the services available to you. In addition, the librarians can help you to learn how to effectively use online databases when searching for articles.

Using Internet Searches Effectively

There are a few strategies for how to most effectively use Google and other internet search engines:

1. Try to use short, simple phrases rather than complex questions or search terms. For example: "How old was Anne Frank when she went to a concentration camp?" is a very long phrase to search. Instead, keep your search phrase simple, and focus on keywords: "Anne Frank concentration camp" will result in more articles and webpages on the topic you're interested in.
2. If you are searching a topic that's longer than one word, try searching that topic in quotes. For example, if you are researching Anne Frank, put Anne's name in quotes: "Anne Frank." In this case, if you didn't put Anne Frank inside quotation marks, you might get a few results that are relevant, but you will also see some search results that are related to other people named Anne or even Frank! For that reason, if you search your topic in quotes, you will find so many more sources relevant to your topic.
3. If you want to search multiple words or phrases at once, you can use the words "and" and "or" to your advantage. For example, if you want to learn about Anne Frank's experience of the Holocaust, do this search: "Anne Frank" AND "the Holocaust." If you want to learn about Anne Frank or the Holocaust, do this search: "Anne Frank" OR "the Holocaust."

Remember, just because a search result comes up first, that doesn't make it the most reliable source. Use websites from reputable sources, which we will discuss in **Chapter 26**.

Wikipedia is not a reliable source and should never be cited in a paper because users can change the information. However, a lot of Wikipedia articles have footnotes that direct you to good sources. For example, if you go to the article on Anne Frank and click on footnote 3, it redirects you to the Anne Frank House website, which would have reputable information you can use in a paper. Think of Wikipedia as a good way to locate *other* sources, but not an actual source you should quote in your paper.

Keeping Track of Sources

After you gather your sources and write your outline, make sure you keep your sources organized so you can cite them later. You will learn how to properly use citations in **Section 8**. Keep in mind that you will need a citation for direct quotes and also any place where you summarized material from your sources that isn't general knowledge. You may have more than one source in a paragraph, so if you can keep your research material organized from the beginning, you will find it much easier to create citations at the end.

A few good ways to stay organized:

- As you write notes on notecards, make sure to also record the author's name and the title of the work, as well as a page number if there is one.
- If you are doing an internet search, it's a good idea to bookmark sites that you are going to use. You might want to even create a bookmark folder for the project so that everything is in one place.
- Print out or copy important pages that you might use and highlight the parts that have important information. Keep everything in a folder or binder. Be sure to write down the source information on the printed pages!

Keeping good notes might seem tedious as you research, but it will save you time in the long run. You don't want to read through all your research material again as you are writing your paper in order to find the quote again to cite it correctly!

Activities

Key Terms

Define the following key terms: Primary source, secondary source, scholarly source, popular source, research question, note card system, library catalog, interlibrary loan, library subscription services

Comprehension

1) What is the difference between a primary and a secondary source?
2) How does a research question help you do research? How does it help you write the outline of your paper?
3) What are some ways to make sure you know which source you used to get information?

Practice

1) Write a possible research question for the following topics: drunk driving, video gaming, texting, hunting
2) Find out what library subscription services your local library subscribes to and how to access them.

Application

1) Write a paragraph explaining a current event that is happening, and quote from at least one source.
2) Research your favorite author using at least three sources and write a paper about them.

More activities and student examples available at **www.writefromtheheart.org/resourceguide**.

Chapter 26: Evaluating Sources

As you gather sources for your research, you need to consider whether the source is a good one to use or not. Sometimes a source should be eliminated because it is too short or doesn't tell you any additional information beyond what you already found somewhere else. But other times, you need to eliminate a source because it has problems within the article or book itself—maybe it is not trustworthy, or it is biased in a way that would not give accurate information.

There are times, though, where you might *want* to use a biased or unreliable source. For example, you might be writing a paper on the Holocaust, and you want to explain what Adolf Hitler's philosophy was. You could certainly quote from his book *Mein Kampf*, but you would want to make sure that you made it clear that those views were *his* views, not yours!

In a less extreme example, perhaps you are writing a paper about a current issue that has two sides. In order to write a good persuasive paper, you need to have a counterargument, where you state what the opposing view is on the issue and create a rebuttal. In that case, you *want* to find a source that is biased to a specific side of an issue so that you can quote that opinion and say why it is incorrect.

Evaluating sources does not mean "throwing out" sources that have a bias or are unreliable. Everyone has biases and perspectives—if you threw out every source that had an opinion, you would have no sources left. Instead, it means making sure you know what biases or problems exist in the source so that you can note them in your paper—sometimes this even becomes part of your argument! Don't be afraid of sources that are skewed; just make sure you know what they are presenting.

So what do we need to consider when we are evaluating a source to understand its perspective?

Consider Purpose

Why is the author writing? Why does the site exist? Asking questions about the purpose of the source will help you decide if you can trust all the information. There are many different types of sources, so focusing on the purpose can help you evaluate the bias or reliability of the information. Here are the main types of publications/sites:

- **Mainstream news sources.** These sources are generally there to inform readers (but please see the bias section for more information).
- **Religious or special interest publications.** These sources come from a particular perspective and have a code of beliefs that it is trying to assert in all of its articles. This could be anything from The Gospel Coalition to The Jehovah's Witness Watchtower to PinkNews to mom blogs. Regular readers generally agree with the sentiments presented, but often when articles are shared with people outside of that perspective, it can cause controversy or arguments.
- **Corporate public relations.** These are sources created by businesses to sell a product or provide information to consumers about products. They are often reliable about their products, but obviously are trying to put their items in the best light.
- **Scientific or academic publications**. These sources publish research findings.
- **Entertainment magazines/websites**. These are sources interested in celebrity gossip, satire of current events, or entertaining the public. Some are more reliable than others, but they are not held to exactly the same standards as a mainstream news source.

Note that it is not wrong to read or share any of these sources, but it is good to remember that the purpose can affect accuracy and are not always applicable in all situations or for all readers, nor will everyone be persuaded by the same information.

Consider Reliability

Any time we look at a source, we will often run up against the question, "Is this reliable?" In some senses, every source has reliability issues (what if the writer was biased? What if the article was written before key information was discovered? What if someone didn't fact check before the story was reported?). But we don't want to base our paper on a bad source. A good example of this problem is when Dan Rather reported on *60 Minutes* in 2004 about George W. Bush's military record. The story was based on what turned out to be forged documents that were completely inaccurate. It appears that the sources were not carefully checked by staff and producers. Several people lost their jobs, and Dan Rather himself had to step down from his position.

This becomes even more complicated when we add in the internet element—any Joe Schmo from Palooka, Tennessee, can post his thoughts on anything and the world can read it. If he's wrong, and then you quote him as if what he says is truth, you're wrong too! These problems are essentially what the term "Fake News" has come to mean—we can't always know if a source we are reading, especially on the internet, is true or accurate.

Note: just because something is reliable—there are no factual errors—does not mean it is unbiased.

In general, the information found within books and magazines are checked and rechecked by experts and editors, so aside from an errant *opinion* of the author, the INFORMATION is accurate and can be trusted for use in an essay.

Here are some tips for checking reliability:

- **Read more than one source!** If one is in error, you will catch it by finding mismatching information in another source. Thankfully, the truth is reprinted many times, but mistakes are usually only printed once. If you can find two or more sources that say the same thing, you can usually trust the information (unless one source is quoting the other—be careful of this on the internet!).
- **Some sources are better than others.** You can usually trust print sources. It costs a LOT of money to print a book, newspaper, or magazine. The people who publish these things do NOT want to risk their reputations and, often more importantly, their money, on printing errors or untruths!! These sources (and their digital counterparts) are generally more reliable than an internet-only publication.
- **Evaluate your internet sources**.
    - Internet versions of printed newspapers or television news are reliable for information.
    - If it ends in **.edu** it is extremely high on the accuracy scale. Only universities and colleges are allowed to use these endings. These sources and databases are accurate.
    - If it ends in **.gov** it is extremely high on the accuracy scale. Only government sites are allowed to use this ending. The

government doesn't like to be wrong and therefore checks its sources carefully. It might be biased, though!

- If it ends in **.org** it is average to high on the accuracy scale. Usually only organizations and serious groups use this ending. However, .org site endings can be bought by anyone and some have special interests or very low standards for their contributors (Wikipedia would be an example of an unreliable site for this reason).
- If it ends in **.com, .net** or **.us** it is anywhere from low to extremely high on the accuracy scale. Anyone can purchase these sites, so you need to ask additional questions before proceeding. You should look in the "about us" portion of the website to determine what qualifications the site has for sharing the information. Confirming information from another website is a good idea.
- Watch out for "website spoofing" or phony sites: sometimes malicious or unscrupulous people will buy sites that appear to be legitimate sites, but are trying to defraud people, or generate money through clicks. An example would be www.nbc.com.co instead of www.nbc.com (note the additional ending—the first site is fake!).

Consider Bias

While the media often talks about being "unbiased" or "balanced," that is harder to do than it seems. We all come from our own worldview that has been influenced by our experiences, our values, and our beliefs. A New Yorker, for instance, could discuss farm practices, but a cattle farmer from Texas would know things that the New Yorker wouldn't, and they could sound very opinionated to each other, even when they themselves think they are being fair and impartial. That's human nature—we all do it.

So yes, that media is often biased. But remember that you are biased, too!

The goal isn't to find something completely unbiased; it's to be able to reflect on bias while we are reading. However, with that said, there are definitely sources that are MORE biased than others! Here are some helpful ideas for evaluating sources:

- **Try to get your major news from mainstream news sources**. Even the mainstream media is biased, but generally it is less skewed because of its large audience. Looking at very biased sites means you have to make a lot of effort to find facts in between the biased reporting.

- **Remember your own "confirmation bias."** A **confirmation bias** happens when we read something that supports an idea that we already believe—we read it and think "see? I KNEW this was true!" But if we only read sources that agree with us, our ideas won't become more nuanced and we will often misunderstand all the factors surrounding an issue.
- **Try to read one source that skews AGAINST what you believe.** Reading the other side's opinion is never a bad thing—it can help you understand others, as well as solidify your own thoughts and beliefs when countering those arguments. At the very least, you will be more well-rounded and educated on an issue!
- **Avoid calling someone you disagree with "fake news."** Just because someone doesn't agree with you doesn't make their opinion false. It's their opinion, and you can disagree and think they are wrong, but that doesn't make it "fake." A better choice would be to say "I don't agree with..." or "that doesn't line up with what I find important on this issue." Reserve the words "fake news" for news that is deliberately trying to lead you astray, or is so biased that it doesn't really include facts.
- **Choose sources that do not deliberately use bias as a manipulative tactic.** While everyone has bias, some people choose to use their bias to incite others to anger and outrage. They take a few facts and then spend so much time on opinion that the facts get lost. These are not good places to get information.

Consider Word Choice and Pictures

Along with bias, sources can sound "factual" but use words and pictures to influence your opinion. When looking at words and pictures in a source, ask the following questions and analyze whether that source is worth continuing to use as a place to get your information:

- **Is the picture showing the person/event from a specific perspective?** Ask what the picture is trying to get you to feel, and if that matches the facts.
- **Does the picture alter reality in any way?** That is not necessarily "wrong" if it is being done in a satirical, comical, or commentary way. But it is wrong if it is done in a way that will mislead people.

- **Does the headline place a certain perspective in a better light?** English allows us to write sentences several ways. We could write "Johnny beat up Billy" or we could write "Billy was beaten up by Johnny." The first one focuses on the aggressor, while the second focuses on the victim. Read a headline and ask who is doing the action or who is being highlighted.
- **Does the article include "hot button words"?** In writing and in speech, **hot button words** are words that could automatically incite people to an argument. This could be saying something like "he always..." or "she never..." or using historically loaded terms, like calling someone a "Nazi" or a "terrorist." Articles that talk in extremes and with loaded terms are less reliable, even if the facts might be correct: the bias is getting in the way!
- **Does the source directly insult those who disagree?** These sources share their biased opinion by using disparaging adjectives and manipulative terms. For example, they might choose to say "the lying senator" or "the racist words she spouted." These terms are a way to sneak an opinion into an otherwise factual piece.

Finding sources can often seem overwhelming, not because you can't find anything on your topic, but because there is so much information out there! Learning to weed out the sources that don't meet your standards can save you time and give you more sources with usable material and good quotes. By employing the information in this section, you can research smarter. And remember, the librarian really doesn't mind answering your questions. Don't hesitate to ask if you need help!

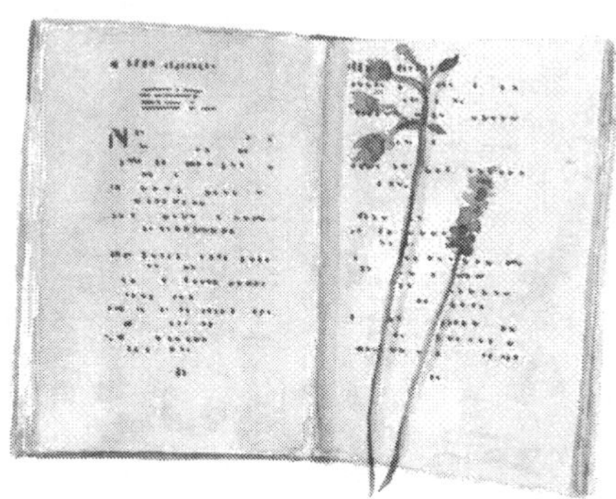

Activities

Key Terms

Define the following key terms: evaluating sources, bias, confirmation bias, hot button words

Comprehension

1) Explain how we can evaluate a source.
2) Should we use a source we disagree with in our paper? Why or why not?
3) What sources should we never use?

Practice

1) Pick a current issue or recent event that happened and find two articles with opposite opinions about it.
2) Evaluate your own favorite website for reading articles. What is its purpose? Who is its audience? What beliefs does it share with its readers? What biases does it confirm? What type of language does it use, and how is it specific for its audience? Who would disagree with it, and why?

Application

1) Write a paragraph about an issue or idea that you feel strongly about. Then imagine you were a person with the opposite opinion and write a paragraph from that perspective.
2) Using the articles you found for Practice activity #1, write an essay about that current issue or recent event. Be sure to choose a thesis you can show or prove. Use both articles in your essay. Find additional sources as necessary.

More activities and student examples available at **www.writefromtheheart.org/resourceguide**.

Chapter 27: Using Your Sources

As you start to write your research paper, keep this in mind: YOU are writing this paper. Your voice and your words should make up the majority of the paper. You should be utilizing your sources to support your work, but most of the words should be your thoughts, summaries, and conclusions.

Another way to think about it is that you are entering a conversation about your topic. Other people have said things about it, and you should reference them and let them "speak" for themselves in quotations, but don't forget to use your own voice! This can come in the form of creating factual descriptions, drawing conclusions and meaning from a summary, and playing with time to choose what details you focus on and what you leave out. For more ideas on using your voice in factual writing, **see Section 3**.

Avoiding Plagiarism

Whenever you use the ideas or words of someone else, you need to give them credit. If you don't, it is called **plagiarism**. A lot of times, students don't do it on purpose—they read something and they think it sounds good, so they type it into their paper. But that is not the right way to do it. If you take any words or ideas from someone else, you need to give them credit by putting a **citation** in your paper.

A good way to avoid accidental plagiarism is to take notes! If you write the information on a notecard and then use those as your reference when you type, they are more likely to be in your own words. If you do read a source while you are typing your paper, read it, then CLOSE it and type what you remember from reading it. You can open it back up to double check dates or other facts, but you are far less likely to copy long phrases exactly if the book is closed!

Citing Your Sources

Whether you are directly quoting a source, or you are summing up what they said, you need to have a citation. A citation is like a little hand waving from your information. It tells your reader, "Hey! This isn't my idea. It was ______'s idea!" Not only do sources add credibility to your writing, but they are also the most effective way to avoid plagiarism. You MUST cite any information that you found from another source, whether you quote it or not. Another way to say this is that you need to cite anything that is not common knowledge.

But, how do you know if your information is considered common knowledge enough to not need a citation? Things that *most* people would know don't require a citation. For instance, a sentence in your essay saying that many students attend public school, but some are homeschooled is considered common knowledge. The fact that vegetarians don't eat meat or the concept that brothers and sisters have the same parents are also common knowledge.

However, if you're pulling ideas from another source, not from your brain, and using it to supplement your main points, you will need an **in-text citation**, or a citation that is marked within the text immediately after the borrowed information, to show where your information came from.

There are three ways to borrow information in this way: direct quotes, paraphrasing, and summarizing.

Direct Quotes

Sometimes, an author says something so effectively, so succinctly, and just so perfectly that you really want to use that in your own writing. But you can't just steal it. That's plagiarizing. Instead, you use a **direct quote**. Using quotation marks, you surround the direct quotes to indicate which words you borrowed.

Examples:

Marcus Tullius Cicero once explained, "A room without books is like a body without a soul."

Eleanor Roosevelt persisted that people are unable to "make you feel inferior without your consent."

Notice the difference in capitalization in these quotes. The first quote contains a complete sentence, so the first letter is capitalized. However, the second starts mid-sentence, so it begins with a lowercase.

Also, it's important to avoid hanging quotes. A **hanging quote** occurs when a direct quotation is its own sentence without any other explanation. You should always work to include the quotation with some of your own words.

Examples:

Hanging Quote: Music is an important part of life. "Without music, life would be a mistake." Friedrich Nietzsche's quote is relevant, even today.

Correct Quoting Format: Music is an important part of life. Even today, Friedrich Nietzsche reminds us that "Without music, like would be a mistake."

You want to make sure that is clear somewhere around the quote how it connects to your paper.

Paraphrased Information

When you paraphrase information, you're essentially changing it into your own words. Replacing a few words of the sentence with synonyms is not enough. You must completely revise the word choice and sentence structure to properly paraphrase something. Otherwise, you run the risk of plagiarizing.

Example:

Let's take a look at this sentence that came from a source:

> People everywhere are moving away from their hometown, claiming that they believe there are greater opportunities for career growth and better living options.

To paraphrase this sentence, we need to completely reword and restructure the sentence. We might write something like this:

> In a search for more job advancement potential and a better place to live, many across the country are planning to leave their hometowns.

Keep in mind that, even though you have completely re-worded the information, it is still a borrowed idea and, as such, needs to include an in-text citation.

Summaries

A **summary** is a condensed version of large amounts of information. Often, it touches only on the main points of the original text. In writing a summary, be sure to avoid adding any opinion or bias. Your goal in summarizing is not to analyze; you simply want to restate the information in a more succinct way.

To summarize a text, use the following steps:

1. Read the text.
2. Read the text one more time to ensure you understand it well.
3. Put the text aside so you can't see it.
4. Write what you remember. Try to avoid using phrasing that is too similar to the original.
5. Re-read what you wrote and compare it to the original text. Ensure that you have not written anything verbatim, and make sure the details are accurate. Note where you have missed any important points and add that information to your summary.

This is a good way to cover a lot of information from a source. A historical figure's childhood might be three chapters long in a book, but it could be one paragraph in your paper.

Again, even though you have completely re-written the information from a source into your summary, it has not become *your* idea. You must include a citation.

Formatting Your Citations

In order to show your reader where a quote, paraphrase, or summary came from, you need to put a citation. At the end of your research paper, you will also need to include a page listing all your sources—called a **works cited page**. There are standardized rules for how to format citations in every field of study from history to science to business. But not every subject follows the same rules. In most of your high school and college classes, you will be expected to use MLA (Modern Language Association) format. Once you learn this format, it becomes a little easier to switch to the specialized rules of other styles. The instructions about how to create citations in your paper and your works cited paper are in **Section 8**.

Student Example #1

Chernobyl

By Spencer D., 14

"Chernobyl is like the war of all wars. There's nowhere to hide. Not underground, not underwater, not in the air." (Alexievich 45)

"Why did that Chernobyl break down? Some people say it was the scientists' fault. They grabbed God by the beard, and now he's laughing. But we're the ones who pay for it." (Alexievich 49)

"He started to change—-every day I met a brand new person. The burns started to come to the surface. In his mouth, on his tongue, his cheeks—-at first there were little lesions,and then they grew. It came off in layers—-as white film... the color of his face... his body...blue...red...gray-brown. It's impossible to describe! It's impossible to write down! And even to get over." (Alexievich 11-12)

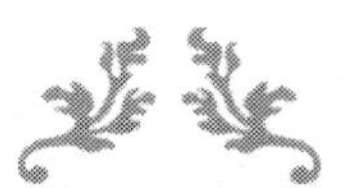

Questions as you read:

- How many sources does this paper use?
- Mark an example of something that was summarized from a source with a star.
- Underline an example of common knowledge information that did not need a citation.
- Circle or mark a place where the author used their own voice to explain information.
- Underline the thesis, and double underline where their opinion of the topic is in the thesis. What was the research question this student possibly used for this project?

The quotes above are from survivors of the accident at Chernobyl, the worst nuclear disaster of all time. It released about 100x more radiation than the atomic bombs dropped on Hiroshima and Nagasaki combined. Chernobyl was a seven on the International Nuclear Event Scale (INES) scale which is the worst rating on the scale. The only other nuclear event with an INES rating of seven occurred at Fukushima. Fukashima and Chernobyl are both a seven but Chernobyl released much more radiation which is why it is the worst nuclear disaster in history. (International Nuclear and Radiologic Event Scale). Even worse is the fact that it could have been easily avoided. Low quality materials, untrained workforce, and poor construction resulted in a nuclear disaster which profoundly impacted many people in the surrounding area for 50 years.

After the Cold War, the Union of Soviet Socialist Republics (U.S.S.R.) made a very aggressive nuclear power plant scheme. An area near the city of Chernobyl in northern Ukraine was chosen as a good location to build a nuclear power plant because of its proximity to the Pripyat River and the larger city of Kiev. Construction was started on the Chernobyl Nuclear Power Plant in 1977 and the fourth reactor was finished by 1983. The new plant employed so many workers that a town was needed close to the power plant. And so the town of Pripyat was born. The town was intentionally designed to house the workers but eventually became a very nice place to live. It became so successful that a hospital, parks, pools, and other nice things were built there. Relative to the rest of the U.S.S.R. Pripyat was a safe haven from the communist government (Higginbotham 16-18).

Surprisingly, the plant was very successful despite many corners being cut. The plant successfully produced the expected 4000 megawatts of electricity providing 10% of Ukraine's energy at the time. Although the plant was very successful, it had some underlying problems from the start. One of those problems was a very restrictive budget because the Soviet government was quickly running out of money. The U.S.S.R was low on funds for this plant because of their aggressive nuclear power expansion plan. This ambitious plan was required because the average household was using much more energy than ever before, and the U.S.S.R wanted to be ahead of America. Due to the government's aggressive approach to expand nuclear power the work had to be very rushed. The plant was built from poor quality materials. Not only was the quality of the materials lousy but the parts used to build the plant were very poorly manufactured. In fact, the workers had to disassemble the parts and then reassemble them correctly before the parts could be used to build the plant. Because of the time limits there was a lot of lying through the chain of command. If something was not finished, for example, the builder could easily lie and say that they did finish it. Lying in this manner could easily cause problems. The U.S.S.R.

was also running out of nuclear physicists very quickly because it was a newer technology and there was a short supply of educated professionals. Electricians were given some very basic knowledge and then left to run the plant. They told electricians that running a nuclear power plant would be easier than being an electrician, but it obviously wasn't. So pretty much nobody really knew what they were doing (Higginbotham 19-20).

The plant was very successful for quite some time. It was so successful that two more reactors were actually planned to be built. But on Saturday, April 26th, 1986, something went drastically wrong. Before a routine shutdown, the scientists were running a test on one of the two turbogenerators. They were trying to determine how much electricity would be produced while the generators were slowing down to a stop. During the test they turned one generator off. An hour later they ignored proper procedures and turned off the emergency cooling system. Once the test started one of the staff members forgot to add some vital information into the computer that ran the reactor. This caused the reactor power to drop too low too quickly. The rapid decline in power caused the reactor to become uncontrollable and overheat. To counteract this, the workers removed many safety rods in an effort to get the power to go back up. They removed too many rods causing the warning alarms to go off. The managers ignored the alarms because they thought they could handle the problem and complete the test. With the safety systems being shut off and the core overheating, the workers tried to cool it down but unfortunately it was too late. The explosion that ensued let off more radiation than both of the nukes dropped on Hiroshima and Nagasaki combined (Nardo 24).

Shuddering, shaking, rumbling. Dust falls from the ceiling as emergency sirens blare loudly. The temperature in the reactor rapidly became 100 times hotter than normal. As the protective casing got hotter and hotter, the metals inside melted, steam pressure built up, and suddenly the whole building exploded with a huge shake. The protective ceiling covering the top of the reactor got tossed in the air like a flipped coin. Over 30 tons of uranium, chunks of radioactive materials, control rods, and other debris flew through the air starting fires everywhere they landed on the ground. The explosion created a massive radiation cloud shaped like a mushroom. Minutes after the explosion, some witnesses describe a strange blue glow coming from the plant (Nardo 28; Higginbotham 87-96).

Immediately after the explosion the Soviets scrambled to contain the radiation. They tried to stop the spread of radiation by first using helicopters to drop boron and sand on the reactor to bury the radiation. They also sprayed molasses on the radiation which caused it to clump up and then the radioactive materials could be buried. The liquidators would use bulldozers to build a trench then bulldoze an entire house into it and bury it with dirt. Many places were destroyed and buried like this (Nardo 28-30).

The effects of the explosion were severe. While only one person died immediately due to his proximity to the explosion, the radiation near the plant was so bad that nearly 50 deaths were directly attributed to the disaster in the weeks and months following the event. Many other people who got close to the site suffered from radiation burns on their bare skin. But the effects of radiation did not stop there. The town of Pripyat was completely evacuated because of the high radiation levels. The town was abandoned and danger warning signs were put up in a 30km zone around the reactor. Inside this exclusion zone, the amount of radiation is too high for humans to live in. Over 2 million people were affected by the radiation and those people will have a higher chance of cancer for at least 50 years (Nardo 26-28).

The radiation was carried so far in the wind that radiation levels were noticeably higher across the entirety of Europe. In fact, shortly after the explosion, radiation was detected by workers doing a routine test at a nuclear plant in Sweden. The workers were measuring radiation levels outside of the plant as an extra precaution so they would know if the reactor was leaking. Suddenly, the level of radiation shot way up. The plant was immediately shut down but the radiation was still much higher than normal levels. Eventually, the Swedish scientists figured out that the radiation was coming from the Ukraine area. It didn't look

good when Sweden discovered the radiation disaster before the soviets made a public announcement (Nardo 20-23).

Historically, the U.S.S.R. was very secretive about many things. But the leader of the U.S.S.R during the Chernobyl crisis, Mikhail Gorbachev was much more transparent than previous leaders. Mikhail Gorbachev was honest and acknowledged the disaster. Due to his openness some of the older leaders weren't very fond of him. However, in the long run being open and honest was very good because it brought help and sympathy from foreign countries. Some specialist doctors were sent from America to help with patients that had high exposure to radiation (Nardo 40-42).

Fear of another massive nuclear meltdown similar to what happened at Chernobyl has caused many people to oppose nuclear energy. However, despite the risk, overall nuclear energy is better for the planet. The main benefit is the use of the earth's abundant resources of uranium instead of fossil fuels to produce electricity. Nuclear power plants are safer now than ever, especially in America. The disaster at Chernobyl was a result of the use of low quality building materials, poor construction, and human error by a poorly trained workforce. With the right precautions, an accident like the one that happened at Chernobyl should never happen again.

Student Example #2

Mia Hamm

By Grace F., 13

The ever present and distracting cameras were the only downside to playing professional soccer. Mia tried to ignore the cameras as she ran around the field. She darted around, trying to get open so that one of her teammates could pass to her. Unfortunately, the other team had at least two defenders on her at all times. This was not an uncommon situation for Mia to be in. She was a feared offender and would often have more than one defender preventing her from getting the ball. Mia waited for her chance, and then broke free of the defenders at the same time her teammate passed the ball right in front of her. Several seconds later, the ball had hit the corner netting of the goal. Mia had many moments like this in her professional career. Through her career Mia Hamm inspired many people, especially young girls, to start playing soccer, and started a soccer revolution to the U.S.

Questions as you read:

- How many sources does this paper use?
- Mark an example of something that was summarized from a source with a star.
- Underline an example of common knowledge information that did not need a citation.
- Circle or mark a place where the author used their own voice to explain information.
- Underline the thesis, and double underline where their opinion of the topic is in the thesis. What was the research question this student possibly used for this project?

Mariel Margret "Mia" Hamm was born on March 17, 1972, in Selma, Alabama, to Bill and Stephanie Hamm. Mia was born with partial club foot, and had to wear casts and orthotic shoes for the first few years of her life. Once the casts came off she was able to run around like all the other kids. Mia's father was an Air Force pilot she would spend a lot of her life moving around. In 1973, Bill Hamm was stationed in Florence, Italy, so he moved his family with him. As a sports fanatic, Bill was slightly disappointed when soccer was the only sport to watch, which was very popular in Italy at the time. This is when Mia saw her first soccer game, although she did not start playing until she was back in the U.S (Axelrod- Contrada 5-8).

After two years, the Hamm family moved to California for a short period of time, before settling down in Wichita, Texas. Lucky for Mia, soccer was becoming more popular in the U.S. Unfortunately; she

was too young to play on the youth league in Wichita alongside her older sisters. Around this time the Hamm's decided that they were going to adopt a boy, but they actually adopted two boys. Garrett was eight and Martin was an infant. Four-year-old Mia was thrilled to have a brother to play with. Mia and Garrett were instantly inseparable. When the kids played pickup games of soccer everyone would avoid picking Mia because she was so tiny. However, Garrett knew that while Mia was very fast and could score a lot of goals, despite her tininess. For thus reason Garrett would call Mia his secret weapon. After Mia turned five, she was able to play on the team with her sisters. Pretty soon she had excelled and was playing other sports as well (Axelrod-Contrada 9-10) .

While Mia liked other sports, none of them compared to her love for soccer. She joined a soccer "school" when she was 14. Soccer school was an Olympic developmental team that taught girls how to improve their game. This would later help them in their chances of becoming an Olympian. Her first day consisted of a bruising that reminded her that she was not playing at a middle school level any more. While Mia might have been happy with having soccer as her only subject she still had to go to real school. Mia attended Lake Braddock High School on top of the Olympic developmental team (Schnakenberg 25-26).

At this point soccer was becoming more popular in the U.S. The most recent addition to national sports teams was the women's soccer team. This team would play at the international level, against other countries. Anson Dorrance was the coach of the U.S. women's national team, as well as the University of North Carolina (UNC) Tar Heels soccer team. As the coach he was constantly looking for new talent for the national team. He had seen a lot of good players, but none of them could compare to Mia, especially at the age of 14. Dorrance first saw Mia in an under-nineteen soccer tournament. One of the first things that Dorrance noticed about Mia was her speed. "I watched her take a seven yard run on the ball," Dorrance later recalled. "... I had never seen speed like that in a women's game" (Schnakenberg 26-28).

At age fifteen Mia was asked to play on the U.S. Women's National soccer team. The National team consisted of young girls most of which were still teenagers. "I didn't even know that there was a [women's National soccer] team until I got there" (Dare to Dream. HBO. 2007). At the time Mia was trying to play on the national team and attend school. Eventually she arranged with her school to graduate at sixteen, so that she could go to UNC. This made it easier for her to train since Dorrance coached there, and some of the players on the National team went there. Once she was in college, she played for both UNC's team and the National team (Schnakenberg 30).

Mia might have been the youngest player in the women's national team, but she fit right in. Since she was sixteen she had youthful qualities in her playing that her teammates did not. Her speed helped her blast past defenders, her quick thinking helped her outsmart the goalie, and her stamina helped her last through the whole game. Her presence on the field was not to be ignored. Mia soon became one of the most feared women offenders in the game. Dorrance was confident in her, so she quickly became the star player of the team. However, Mia always gave credit to her teammates and actually preferred staying out of the limelight. She would often say, "There is no ME in MIA" (Hamm 3). This is basically Mia's version of the quote, "There is no I in TEAM". Mia always considered it an honor to be able to be on the team representing women's soccer for her country, especially at her young age of 15 (Dare to Dream. HBO. 2007).

In 1991 FIFA(Federation International Football Association) decided to hold the first ever Women's World Cup. However, since they were not sure how if it would be successful so they called it the M&M's cup after the sponsor. When Mia was asked to play in the world cup she struggled with the choice of staying at UNC and playing in the championships, or going to the World cup. She was unable to do both, as the world cup was in China. She was very torn. If she stayed at UNC she would most likely be a star offender. However, if she went to the World Cup she would be able to up her defensive game. She chose to play on the World Cup so that she could become the best all-around player that she could be. Later she was glad she made this choice. After beating four of the other six teams, only Norway stood between the U.S.

and winning the world cup. After a hard game the U.S. finally beat Norway 2-1! The U.S. had won the first women's World Cup! The team thought that when they got home they would finally be noticed, since everyone was caught up in other sports. They headed home with the hopes that they had changed soccer for the U.S. forever. However, when they got home there were only three people waiting to greet them when they got to the airport. This was big disappointment, as they had just worked so hard to win. Four years later they were heading to the 1995 World Cup, with hopes of winning. Unfortunately, they did not do as well and lost to their rivals the Norwegians in the semi-finals (Schnakenberg 40-43; 50-51).

Just one year later the summer Olympics were being held in Atlanta, Georgia, and they had added women's soccer to the sports that would be played. Mia and the rest of the national team were pumped and anxious to gain redemption form the previous year's loss. The atmosphere in the stadiums that they played at was much different from what they were used to. Sometimes they were lucky to have a dozen people in the stands, and that would only be immediate family. Now they had fans from all over the U.S. filling up the stadium. They made it to the finals and went up against China. This game was the first time that they had ever sold out a stadium. It was a critical game, as the whole U.S. was watching. Mia had recently sprained her ankle and was having trouble playing to the full extent of her ability. In the last sixty seconds of the game she was pulled off as her ankle was causing her so much trouble. The next minute was the longest minute of Mia's life. She had no reason to worry as the U.S. held onto their 2-1 lead. This was a moment Mia and the rest of the team would remember forever. They had won the first Olympics that allowed Women's soccer in front of their friends, family, and country (Schnakenberg 56-58).

However, Mia's excitement was about to come to an end. In 1997 Mia's brother Garrett passed away. Garrett was the reason why in 1999 Mia founded the Mia Hamm Foundation. The Mia Hamm Foundation is dedicated to raising funds and awareness for bone marrow/cord blood transplants. Garrett passed away due to complications related to aplastic anemia, which is a rare bone marrow disease. It also helps increase opportunities for young women in sports. Mia gave all of her success to the efforts of other female pioneers that had worked hard to provide opportunities for women to play sports (Mia Hamm Foundation).

Mia continued to play soccer for the National team, until she retired in 2004, at the age of 32. "I feel good about my contribution. I think my body needs a rest, and this is just the right time," Mia said when asked about her retirement. (Dare to Dream. HBO. 2007) She set many records and won many awards during her career. She is even featured in the soccer hall of fame. One of her greatest achievements was winning the first women's world cup. Another was becoming the first U.S. soccer player to reach 100 goals in their career. Mia inspired many girls to start playing soccer. She left behind a legacy in women's soccer that would last forever (Axelrod-Contrada 104-106).

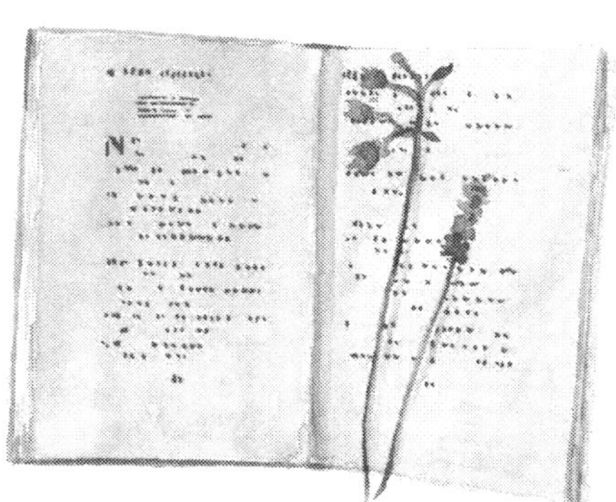

NOTE: Student examples appear in original format and may contain slight grammar errors.

Activities

Key Terms

Define the following key terms: plagiarism, citation, in-text citation, direct quote, hanging quote, works cited page

Comprehension

1) Explain how to avoid plagiarism.
2) What are the three ways we can use sources in our papers?

Practice

1) Answer the question in the sidebar next to Student Example #1.
2) Answer the questions in the sidebar next to Student Example #2.

Application

1) Write a paragraph that summarizes an entire article of two or more pages. Be sure to cite the article.
2) Write an essay about a historical figure or event. Be sure to choose a thesis that focuses your research. Use at least four sources and proper citations.

More activities and student examples available at **www.writefromtheheart.org/resourceguide**.

Section 8: MLA Citations

When you are completing a research project, citations are extremely important. It tells the reader where you got the information (and if it was reliable), as well as giving credit to others' work that you are quoting.

There are many different ways to cite sources. The MLA (Modern Language Association) style is used in humanities courses. The APA (American Psychological Association) is used in psychology and the sciences. Chicago/Turabian style is used in business and history. Every one of them have different rules: some use parenthetical references, and others use footnotes. But they all focus on making sure that we are giving credit to the works that helped us in our research.

This section focuses on the MLA style of citation. This is used most often by students in high school and college. Although you might have some classes in your college career that use one of the other styles, learning MLA now will help you easily transfer your learning into the other specialized styles for a specific class.

Chapter 28: How Citations Work

It might seem like some of these rules are picky and frustrating. But standardizing the way we give credit to others helps legitimize our own work. It shows that we care about giving credit to the hard work of other authors.

Citations are necessary for two reasons: to give credit to the original authors, and to avoid plagiarism. Plagiarism is when a student knowingly or unknowingly copies another person's work and claims it as their own creation. As you learned in **Section 7**, citing reliable sources is the primary way to make your research paper effective.

When we talk about citations we are talking about two parts: the works cited page, and in-text citations. Let's look at each to see how they work together.

Works Cited Page

A **works cited page** lists everything that you used in your research. You cannot have anything in the works cited page that isn't used in your paper. Everything in your paper must be listed in the works cited page.

A works cited is NOT the same thing as a bibliography. A **bibliography** includes every source that you accessed when you researched your paper. You may have quoted, paraphrased, or summarized *some* of these sources in your paper, but you may not have used other sources at all. Perhaps they were just helpful to you as you learned more about the topic, or you had multiple sources with similar information, but you only used one of them in your paper. For example, if you were to write a biographical paper about the author Laura Ingalls Wilder, you will probably cite several biographical books about Wilder in your essay. You probably will not, however, cite one of Wilder's fictional books as a source in your paper. That said, reading Wilder's fictional books may have contributed to your understanding of her as a person and may also allow your readers to further understand her. For that reason, you might want to include *Little House in the Big Woods* or another one of Wilder's books as a resource that some readers might appreciate. In a bibliography, you could do that!

Unlike a bibliography, a works cited page at the end of your paper ***only*** includes the sources that you cite within the body of your paper. In the Laura Ingalls Wilder example above, you would *not* cite the fictional book *Little House in the Big Woods* if you did not cite the book in your paper.

Bibliographies are not used often in student papers. They are reserved for large research papers, professional projects, and published works. However, you might be asked to start your project with a bibliography and then later only include the sources you used in a works cited page. Teachers often do this to help students keep track of their sources, and to practice formatting skills. A teacher might say "make a list of all the sources you gathered from the library and put them in correct MLA format." This is a bibliography. Then later in the project, they would say "select the works in your bibliography that you used within your research paper and include them at the end of the paper." This is a works cited page.

In-text Citations

When you are completing research, there are three ways to borrow information from another source: direct quotes, paraphrasing, and summarizing. For more information on how to include these in your research paper, see **Chapter 27**.

An in-text citation is simply a notation within your paper that the sentence or paragraph came from another source. In MLA format, we do that by putting a parenthetical at the end of the sentence. A **parenthetical** includes all the information to help the reader know where you got all your information. In this format, we use the first word of the works cited entry and the page number, if there is one. We will talk more about how to properly format these in **Chapter 29**.

The Connection between Works Cited and In-text Citations

Think of a works cited page as the "index" that helps your reader find more information. For example, let's say your paper has a sentence like this:

> New parents shouldn't worry too much about allergies after mealtime. According to one expert, most allergic reactions happen "within an hour of the food being eaten" (Kulp 62).

I know that the quote or paraphrase or summary came from a source by a person named Kulp and it was from page 62. But I know nothing else about this "Kulp" person or the source. So I go to your works cited page and look through the list of sources until I find Kulp. And I would see this:

Kulp, Adrian. We're Parents! The New Dad's Guide to Baby's First Year. Emeryville, Rockridge Press, 2019.

Now I know that this quote came from Adrian Kulp's book, and it was published in 2019. It is really easy for me to verify which source you meant because the name in the in-text citation matches the first word in the works cited entry—they both say Kulp. Now I can go and read the book myself!

A common error that students make, particularly with websites, is to use the url as the citation. This is incorrect. The url is never the first word in a citation. Take this example:

Stern, Liz. "Blast from the Past: Newsboy Strike of 1899." New York Historical Society, 2012. Accessed 10 June 2020. http://historydetectives.nyhistory.org/2012/07/blast-from-the-past-newsboy-strike-of-1899/

If you were going to cite this in your paper, you would still use the first word (Stern) rather than the web site address. Besides making your paper look incredibly messy to have such a long address in your paragraph, it makes it difficult for me to find the reference in your works cited—the url is never the first thing in a works cited entry!

In the next two chapters, we will be talking about the rules for formatting the works cited page and in-text citations. But don't forget the connection between the two—your works cited page directs the reader to the source with all the information they need, and the in-text citation tells you which source to look at to get the additional information.

Chapter 29: Formatting a Works Cited Page

As mentioned in **Chapter 28**, creating your works cited or bibliography page should be one of the first steps of your research process. Once you identify the sources that you think you may use to write your paper, it is important to create your sources list. Remember that when you list all the sources you referenced, this is a bibliography, and only including the sources you used in the paper is a works cited page.

Many students wait until their final draft to create their works cited, but waiting for such a long period of time makes it more likely that you will forget to list a source - which would be considered a form of plagiarism. In addition, properly creating in-text citations is much easier when you are able to reference your works cited for the information you need. It is good practice to create a preliminary bibliography before writing your paper, and then whittling down your list to a works cited page during the final edits.

There are nine main components that you need to know in order to create *any* kind of works cited entry (a book, a webpage, an article, television show, etc.). If you use these items as a kind of template, you will be able to accurately create most citations in the MLA format!

Here are those nine components—the only components that ever appear in a works cited entry. Each of the nine components is in its correct order, and it is followed by the punctuation (comma or period) that you would need to use when you include that component.

1. Author(s) listed by last name, first name.
2. Title of Your Source.
3. Title of the container where your source can be found,
4. Other contributors (editors, translators, etc.),
5. Version (volume number, ebook, etc),
6. Number (issue, episode, etc),

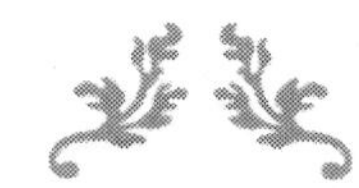

7. Publisher,
8. Date of publication,
9. Location (page number, web address).

If you are creating a works cited entry for a source, and you cannot find a component for your entry, skip that component!

These nine elements represent the possibilities of what an entry includes, no matter if it's a book, article, webpage, or movie. Not all these items will be in each works cited/bibliography entry. Some entries will contain only three or four of these nine components. Not every book has an author *and* an editor, and not every webpage will include an author.

Sample Works Cited Entry: Book

Format:

Last Name, First Name. *Title of Book*. City of Publication, Publisher, Publication Date.

Example:

Nichols, Wallace J. *Blue Mind: The Surprising Science that Shows How Being Near, In, On, or Under Water Can Make You Happier, Healthier, More Connected, and Better at What You Do*. New York, Back Bay Books, 2015.

Sample Works Cited Entry: E-Book

Format:

Last name, First Name. *Title.* E-Book, Publisher, Publication Date.

Example:

Wooden, John and Steve Jamison. *The Essential Wooden: A Lifetime of Lessons on Leaders and Leadership*. E-Book, McGraw-Hill, 2007.

Sample Works Cited Entry: Webpage

Format:

Last Name, First Name. "Title of webpage." Name of Publisher, *Name of Website*, Date of Creation, www.websitename.com/samplewebpage. Accessed x Month 20xx.

NOTE: If the publisher and the website name are the same, you only need to give the name of the website.

Example:

Mayo, Edith. "African American Women Leaders in the Suffrage Movement." *Turning Point Suffragist Memorial*, 2020, suffragistmemorial.org/african-american-women-leaders-in-the-suffrage-movement. Accessed 26 April 2020.

Sample Works Cited Entry: Online News Article

Format:

Last name, First name. "Article name." Name of Publisher, *Name of Website*, Date of Creation, www.websitename.com/samplewebpage. Accessed x Month 20xx.

NOTE: If the publisher and the website name are the same, you only need to give the name of the website.

Example:

Garvey, Ellen Gruber. "How a New Exhibit Corrects Our Skewed Understanding of Women's Suffrage: Addressing Racism in the Suffrage Movement." *The Washington Post*, 29 March 2019, https://www.washingtonpost.com/outlook/2019/03/29/how-new-exhibit-corrects-our-skewed-understanding-womens-suffrage/. Accessed 26 April 2020.

Sample Works Cited Entry: Interview

Format:

Last Name (of interviewee), First Name (of interviewee). Personal interview. Date.

Example:

Gardner, Joyce. Personal Interview. 25 November 2010.

Sample Works Cited Entry: Film

Format:

Title. Directed by John Doe. Film studio/distributor, year.

Example:

Ocean's Eleven. Directed by Steven Soderbergh. Warner Brothers, 2001.

With these general principles and examples in mind, creating a works cited entry for each type of source will be much easier. This list of sample citations is far from exhaustive. For many more examples and explanations for specific situations like what to do when listing two books by the same author, you can check out several great resources:

Purdue Online Writing Lab:

owl.purdue.edu/owl/research_and_citation/mla_style

The MLA Style Center: style.mla.org/mla-format/

Zotero: https://www.zotero.org/

In addition, understanding the guiding principles of MLA format will be very helpful if you choose to use the citation function in your Word processing program, or if you choose to use online software such as EasyBib, RefWorks, Zotero, or Noodle Tools. Note that these citation tools work for creating works cited and bibliography entries, but they do not help you to create in-text citations. In order to create in-text citations, you will need to understand the rules and principles of MLA format!

Adding Your Works Cited to Your Paper

When adding your bibliography or works cited to your paper, there are a few rules to follow:

1. Your works cited or bibliography MUST begin on a fresh page.
2. At the top of the page, center the phrase Works Cited OR Bibliography. Do not italicize, underline, or embolden the title.
3. After the title, all your cited entries should be aligned to the left margin of the page.
4. The first line of each entry should be aligned with the left margin on the page. The second line - and any additional lines of each entry - should be indented 0.5 inches. You can create this kind of "hanging indent" with the ruler at the top of your word processing software.
5. Alphabetize your list by the first word of each entry (in most cases the author name, but sometimes the title if no author is listed).
6. Double-space all entries.
7. Make sure that there is no additional space between your entries. This is usually a feature underneath the "Line Spacing" button in your word processing software - make sure that "Remove space before paragraph" and "Remove space after paragraph" are both checked!

Chapter 30: Formatting In-Text Citations

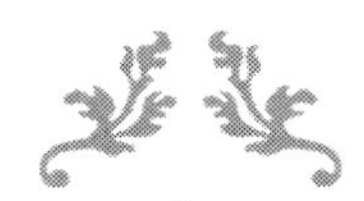

Remember: your in-text citation is an "index" reference to send the reader to your works cited page for more information.

Recall that when you are completing research, there are three ways to borrow information in this way: direct quotes, paraphrasing, and summarizing. For more information on how to include these in your research paper, see **Section 7**. Here, we are going to discuss how to place and punctuate your citations properly.

MLA style requires very little information in an in-text citation since it's designed to send the reader to the full reference at the end. To cite using this format, your citation is the same, regardless of whether you're quoting, paraphrasing, or summarizing.

The ONLY thing you need to include in your reference is:

The first word of your works cited entry for the source

The page number (if there is one)

Most of the time, the first word of the works cited entry is the author's last name. We will discuss what to do if there is no author below.

Citing and Punctuating a Simple Quotation

Citations for a quotation must go immediately after you have stated the information from the source. You need to put the citation information in

parentheses and include the final punctuation for the sentence *after* the citation.

Example:

Researchers have discovered that several cultures in which "left-handedness is considered a curse" (Higgins 290).

Let's dissect the punctuation of this type of in-text citation.

- The quote ends with a closing quotation mark followed by a space.
- The opening parentheses is followed by the author's last name.
- There is no comma or any kind of punctuation between the author's last name and the page number.
- There is no "p." before the page number. The page number is followed directly by a closing parenthesis, with no space between.
- The period to end the sentence comes *after* the closing parenthesis, with no space between.

If you're using a source that does not have page numbers, you simply leave it out, offering only the author's last name in parentheses.

Citing and Punctuating a Longer Quotation

Sometimes, you find a really good quote that is several sentences long. You can absolutely use that in your paper! There are just a few different rules for how to punctuate this to make it easy for your reader to understand. Any quotation of more than 3 lines needs to be set off from the rest of the text. Introduce the quote with a colon, then indent the quote itself two tabs. The citation goes after the final period of the quote. Do NOT put quotation marks around the quote.

Example:

The play *A Doll's House* shows what marriage is not supposed to be, helping the audience see why the characters are never really honest with each other:

> We have been married for eight years. Doesn't it occur to you that this is the first time you and I, husband and wife, are having a serious talk? I've been your doll-wife, just as I used to be papa's doll-child. (Ibsen 415)

This shows that the two never communicated the way a husband and wife should.

Let's dissect the punctuation of this type of in-text citation.

- The quote is set off in its own section—it is indented 0.5 inches in from the margin
- The parentheses include the author's last name and page number with no punctuation in between.
- The period to end the sentence comes *before* the closing parenthesis.
- A sentence (or more) of the writer's own words must come after the quotation to summarize or explain it. A longer quotation should NEVER end a paragraph.

If you're using a source that does not have page numbers, you simply leave it out, offering only the author's last name in parentheses.

Citing and Punctuating a Paraphrase or Summary

Imagine that you've been writing this really long research paper. For one of your essay's main points, you've written a rather long paragraph. Almost every sentence in that paragraph contains either paraphrased or summarized information from sources. It would be so repetitive to add a citation again... and again... and again... and...

Well, you get the picture.

There is a kind of shortcut for these instances. The principle is the same for all of them—you just need to adjust your citation for each situation.

All Paraphrased/Summarized Information from One Source

If you pulled information for each detail sentence of your paragraph all from the same source, and no information came from a *separate* source, you can create one single in-text citation at the end of the paragraph to indicate this.

Example:

> During the Medieval period, the inclusion of singing and music within one's worship became commonplace. However, those in the monasteries took this practice and elevated the practice to something more akin to art. These monasteries were religious communities where people would devote their lives to the greater good of their communities, while also practicing a quite difficult lifestyle. Often, many of these individuals would begin their day at 2 or 3 o'clock in the morning, focusing on their

singing as a way to worship, followed by a day full of hard labor to support the monastery. Some also took a great interest in preserving knowledge for future generations. Hildegard of Bingen was one of these individuals, and her use of vivid imagery and creative word painting culminated in some of the most beautiful musical pieces of her time and beyond. Hildegard's skill in weaving text with music is most apparent in her song, Alleluia, O virga mediatrix. (Forney 73-87)

Notice that the entire paragraph is written fluidly. There are no citations between sentences, though it's clear that some research has been done due to the fact that this information is not common knowledge. You are allowed to put a range of pages in the citation if the information from the source was spread across them.

All Paraphrased/Summarized Information from Multiple Sources

If you found information for each sentence of your paragraph from a few different sources, and you do not quote any of it, you can create one single in-text citation at the end of the paragraph to indicate this. All of your citations go in the same parentheses and are separated by semicolons.

Example:

James Joyce was disappointed in the reception of his last book. He didn't start working on any future projects; his writing career was over. Shortly after finishing the book, World War II shattered his spirit and caused him great sadness. Then, after surviving numerous surgeries during his life, Joyce died in 1940 of a complication during a surgery to fix an intestinal affliction. He was with his family in Zürich. His wife, two children, Helen Joyce and Giorgio Joyce, and some grandchildren survived him. (Atherton; Gorman 350-351)

—Gavin N., 17

This paragraph used two sources: Atherton (an online source with no page numbers), and Gorman (with the information spanning two pages). The citation includes both sources and are separated by a semicolon.

Paraphrased/Summarized Information in a Paragraph with a Direct Quote

Sometimes, your paragraphs will include paraphrased or summarized information AND a direct quote. You need to handle each of them according to their rules: a quote must have a citation immediately after it, but paraphrased/summarized information can be cited at the end of the paragraph.

Example:

> A sailing ship steering the Atlantic waves in 1644, carried Klaes Martensen van Roosevelt to New Amsterdam . "From that time for the next seven generations from father to son every one of us was born on Manhattan Island," wrote Teddy Roosevelt in his autobiography (Roosevelt 1). On the 27th, of October, 1858, Theodore was born into this world with a restless spirit for adventure. Theodore had the same "settler" spirit that reached across his ancestry. With direct Dutch blood, Theodore Roosevelt's family religion was the Dutch Reformed faith (Ruddy 3-7).
>
> —Savannah M., 14

This paragraph includes a direct quote from Teddy Roosevelt, with the citation directly after it. It also includes facts that came from another source: Ruddy, on pages 3-7. The summarized information is cited at the end of the paragraph.

Alternate Citation Options

Not all of your information *always* has to go into the citation. For example, perhaps you want to mention the author's name or the other important information in the text of your sentence. If so, you simply withhold that detail from the in-text citation at the end of the sentence.

Example:

> Professor Higgins of Harvard University recently discovered that several cultures in which "left-handedness is considered a curse" (290).

Notice that the citation information wasn't just added for no reason. It created more value within the sentence. In this example, it gives the author more

credibility to mention his name and where he works because the added information shows how much of an expert they are on the matter.

Missing Information

Research isn't perfect. In fact, many times during your educational career, you'll come across a wonderful, reliable source that will add a lot of value to your paper. But, when you look a little more closely, you'll notice that something needed for a citation is missing. Perhaps it's an online article that doesn't have an author, or maybe the magazine doesn't show which year it was published. Don't panic! There are still a variety of ways to compensate for missing information.

Missing Author

If there is no specific author you can find for a source, you move to the next identifying element: the title of the work. Remember: if the title is a magazine, website article, encyclopedia entry, or other short piece of writing, use quotation marks around the title. If it's a book or other major work, you will *italicize* the title.

Example:

> Many students report feeling nervous about using in-text citations ("Citing the Source" 3).

Missing Page Number

MLA format suggests that you should simply omit a number in the citation if no page numbers are available.

Example:

> Studies show that students who attend a technical college are still working towards a viable career path (Jones).

Concluding Thoughts

In-text citations can be a quite intimidating process, especially if you are unfamiliar with structure, style, and formatting. However, as you practice and gain familiarity with how to create these within your writing, you'll feel much more confident whenever you're challenged to write a research paper.

Section 9: Grammar

Proper grammar is an important part of writing. It is the way that we make sure our ideas are coming across clearly and one of the tools we use to express our voice. Some writers love to use semicolons; others think they are pretentious and prefer a period. Sometimes an ellipsis is called for... other times a hyphen would be the right choice—knowing which one is best is part of understanding grammar. Yes, grammar is "rules" but it's also a way to expand your options as a writer.

This section should be viewed as a reference while writing. It's a good place to come to review rules and make sure your work is free from errors. There are no exercises here in this section because grammar is best used in a larger context. If you are taking a class, you will read these chapters and then apply them in class in practical ways. If you are working through this book on your own, there is a companion grammar workbook to offer you practice.

Chapter 31: Parts of Speech

Humans naturally love organization. We love to see things neatly lined on a shelf, placed thoughtfully on walls and tables, and fitting perfectly into just the right slot. We also love to categorize things. Everything from music, to books, to types of food can be broken into categories. It makes sense that we'd categorize our words, as well. We call these categories **parts of speech**.

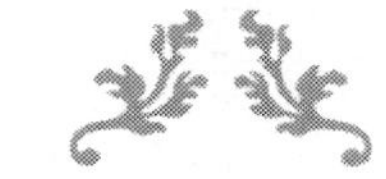

Nouns • Pronouns
Verbs
Adjectives • Adverbs • Prepositions
Conjunctions• Interjections • Appositives

Any word you can think of falls into one of these categories:

Each category contains specific words and follows rules for how to identify what fits there.

Nouns

A **noun** is any word that names a person, place, thing, or idea. Because this is such a huge group of words, we break them down into subcategories according to their kind, number, and use.

Kinds of Nouns

A **common noun** is any generic word that names a person, place, thing, or idea.

Examples: boy, school, kitchen, stairs, independence

If it refers to a specific noun, like a person's name or the name of a city or event, it's considered a **proper noun**, meaning it requires a capital letter.

Examples: Tokyo, Christmas, Mrs. Johnson, Friday, January

Concrete nouns are things that exist in the real world and that can be seen, touched, smelled, heard, or tasted.

Examples: house, chicken, box, carpet, street, flavor

In contrast, **abstract** nouns include all nouns that cannot be seen or touched. They exist in the real world only as a concept.

Examples: truth, safety, anger, joy, friendship, loyalty

Finally, **collective** nouns are words that name a group of things. It's a single word to represent several of the same kind of noun. Collective nouns can become plural, as well.

Examples: family, staff, community, team

Number of Nouns

Nouns can represent one thing or many things.

A **singular noun** is only one person, place, thing, or idea.

Examples: family, vacation, teacher, woman

Plural nouns are nouns that indicate there are more than one of the noun.

Examples: families, vacations, teachers, women

Note: there are rules for how to change singular nouns into plurals. Most words end in -s or -es, but some nouns are considered irregular nouns and their spelling changes completely.

In this world, you can either count nouns, or you just plain can't count them. **Count nouns** are those that are countable. You can point to them as you count, 1... 2... 3...

Examples: cars, dollars, pieces, oranges, children

Mass nouns differ in that you can't count them. When we talk about them, we can't figure out a plural form of the word, either.

Examp*le:* money, happiness, time

Uses of Nouns

Nouns can be used several different ways in a sentence.

Subject nouns are the subject of the sentence—the person, place, thing, or idea that is doing something or being talked about.

Examples:

The boy went to the store.

My mom said I need to be home by dark.

Predicate nouns are nouns that follow a "to be" verb (is, are, was, were, been) and rename or replace the subject noun. The "to be" verb functions as an equals sign for the two words.

Examples:

The school is a place to learn. (school=place)

Sam Ricardo has been a senator for eight years. (Sam Ricardo=senator)

An **object noun** occurs when a noun is used as the object in a sentence.

Examples:

You will enjoy the movie.

I went to the market yesterday.

Possessive nouns show ownership, and can be singular or plural. They end in an apostrophe along with an 's,' indicating that the singular noun owns something. If the apostrophe comes *after* the 's,' it means that the item in question belongs to more than one of the noun.

Examples: family's, vacation's, teachers'

Notice that the example, *teachers'*, ends with the apostrophe after the 's.' That is considered a **plural possessive** noun because it shows that more than one teacher (plural) owns something (possessive).

Pronouns

A **pronoun** is a word that takes the place of a noun. They're very important in making sure that writing and speaking doesn't become overly repetitive. For example, take a look at this sentence:

Elizabeth has her backpack with her, so she doesn't need her mom to bring it.

Imagine that we didn't have pronouns. Our sentence would be something like this:

Elizabeth has Elizabeth's backpack with Elizabeth, so Elizabeth doesn't need Elizabeth's mom to bring the backpack.

- She/He
- It
- You
- Me
- I
- They
- We
- Who
- Him/Her
- Them
- Anyone
- Somebody/Something

When you look at it that way, it becomes clear why pronouns are so important to the English language.

When you include a pronoun in your writing, it's important to look at its **antecedent**, which is the noun that it represents. You must include an antecedent somewhere before the pronoun to help the reader understand who or what the pronoun is referring to.

Examples: Josie found her shoes under the bed. [Josie is the antecedent]

Pronouns, just like nouns can be singular or plural, and can be used as the subject, object, or possessive in a sentence. However, pronouns also have **person**.

A **first-person pronoun** refers to the speaker (I, me, we).

A **second-person pronoun** refers to the person being spoken to (you).

A **third-person pronoun** refers to a person or thing being spoken about (he, she, they)

Special Types of Pronouns

Some pronouns don't refer to a person or thing, but function in the sentence in specialized ways.

A **relative pronoun** is a word that connects a dependent clause to the main or independent clause. The most common are who, whom, whose, which, whose, and that.

Example:

The Americans, <u>who</u> got lost yesterday, finally found the Eiffel Tower.

An **interrogative pronoun** is used in a question. The most common are who, what, which, whom, and whose.

Examples:

Who wants to go with me?

Which shoes are yours?

A **demonstrative pronoun** identifies something, almost as if you were pointing, or demonstrating, which ones (this, that, these, those).

Example: This is my lunch, and that one is yours.

Intensive pronouns are "extra" pronouns that emphasize a noun. These end in -self (himself, itself, themselves). They are never necessary in the sentence, but make the noun stronger.

Example:

My mom herself finally marched down to the creek to see why I wasn't home.

Reflexive pronouns are pronouns used when a subject noun is doing an action to itself. These end in -self (himself, itself, themselves). They are necessary in the sentence, which is how you tell the difference from an intensive pronoun.

Example:

My mom looked at herself in the mirror and fixed her lipstick.

An **indefinite pronoun** is one that has an implied antecedent, but it is not named. They include words like all, some, many, most, other, and several. Using this pronoun incorrectly can lead to a sentence error, which is discussed in **Chapter 33**.

Examples:

Does anybody know where I put my glasses?

Somebody will discover the cure for cancer, I hope.

Verbs

A **verb** is a word that represents an action or a state of being. It says what a noun does or is. In general, verbs can express four things:

Verbs can express a physical action (**action verb**):

The doctor examined the patient.

Ally jumped on the bed.

Tyler ran after the ball.

Verbs can also express a mental action (**action verb**):

The librarian considered a new filing system.

The quarterback chose a certain play.

Jason guessed the correct answer.

Verbs can express a state of being (**linking verb**):

She is excited about the party.

Mr. Williams was my old neighbor.

I am really sleepy right now.

Verbs can help other verbs make sense in tense and voice (**helping verb**):

He would be mad if he knew I broke his toy.

Susan may have come to the party, but I don't remember.

I should go, but I don't want to.

Verbs are not singular or plural. Instead, they change the ending depending on the noun they are with. See **Chapter 33** for how to avoid errors in noun-verb agreement. Instead, when we talk about verbs, we talk about type, voice, and tense.

Types of Verbs

An action verb can transfer action (or act on) another noun or pronoun, called the object of the sentence. Depending on their action, we call them different things.

Transitive verbs act on something and transfer their action to something else, meaning they have a **direct object**.

Example: The teacher explained the rules.

In the example, the verb is *explained*. The teacher is the one doing the explaining, but does the verb act on another noun? Yes! The verb acts on "the rules," which is our direct object in this example.

Example: Max ate the pizza.

This example also contains a direct object. Max, the subject, performs the verb, "ate." What did he eat? The pizza. That means "the pizza" is our direct object, and "ate" is a transitive verb.

If a verb does NOT have a direct object, it's considered **intransitive**. It completes the action without transferring it to something else.

Examples:

- My throat hurt.
- The dog sneezed.
- Macy slept.

Voice of Verbs

The voice of the verb tells whether the subject is doing the action or is receiving the action.

Active voice is used when the subject is doing the action.

Examples:

Sarah jumped on the bed.

Ben answered the phone.

Passive voice is used when the subject is receiving the action.

Examples:

The bed was jumped on by Sarah.

The phone was answered by Ben.

Generally, it is advised that you write in active voice. Look at how much clunkier the passive voice sentences sound. They require a "by —" phrase. Most teachers will recommend that you change passive to active voice.

However, there are times when passive voice is effective. Use it when you want the focus to be on the thing receiving the action. Sometimes it works because you can imply the "by —" when the person is ambiguous: "The doorbell was rung ten times. It was so annoying!" You could change that to active by saying "Someone rang the doorbell ten times." But if you want to focus on the doorbell, use passive voice.

Another place passive voice is important is when two people are doing an action. Take this active sentence:

Matthew punched Simon in the face.

In this sentence, the focus is on Matthew doing the action. But what happens if we put it in passive voice?

Simon was punched in the face by Matthew.

Now the focus is on Simon. He's the victim, and the action feels a little bit different, doesn't it? Simon wasn't doing anything...he just got punched! This is an interesting technique that persuasive writers employ to subtly shift your loyalties in an argument.

But these are special cases. Usually you should use active voice.

Tense of Verbs

The tense of verbs refers to whether the action is happening in the past, present, or future. In English, we change the endings of our verbs to indicate the "when" of an action.

Present tense refers to an action that is happening right now, or that happens regularly or continually.

Examples:

Planet Earth **is** made up of mostly water.

I **love** you!

Past tense is used when an action happened at a particular time in the past.

Examples:

My baby **took** a nap this morning.

George Washington **was** the first President of the United States.

Future tense is used when an action will take place at some point in the future.

Examples:

I **will go** to the store tomorrow.

Izaak **will take** classes at the high school next year.

But what happens if something crosses over times, or lasts for a long period of time? How do we express something that is happening for a *period* of time? This is where we use the **perfect tense**. Perfect tense uses a version of has, had, or have to show action continuing over time.

The **present perfect tense** is for an action that started in the past but continues into the present. It adds *has* or *have* to a past tense verb

Examples:

More planets **have been discovered** as our technology gets better.

I **have wondered** what it will be like to have children.

The **past perfect tense** is for an action that started and ended in the past, but went on for a period of time. It adds *had* to a past tense verb.

Examples:

I **had hoped** to see a lion at the zoo.

She **had grown** vegetables but doesn't anymore.

The **future perfect tense** is for an action that will start and keep going in the future. It adds *will have* to the future tense verb.

Examples:

> In the next twenty years, we **will have found** the cure for many diseases.
>
> By the time she is two she **will have** long hair.

There is one other tense that is specialized in writing. Any time you are discussing literature, you use what is called the **literary present tense**. All verbs in a sentence describing a work of literature MUST be present tense verbs. This would include stories, plays, poems, essays, films, and television shows.

Why is this? The idea comes from the continuous nature of art. Every time you read a story, you start at the beginning right? The characters aren't married in the first chapter, and the crisis hasn't occurred yet. A story is always happening at the moment that you read it. It always IS. It can never be a WAS because it is new every time you open the book.

Example:

> At the beginning of Pride and Prejudice, Elizabeth hates Darcy because she thinks he wronged Wickham.

Elizabeth can't "hated" Darcy because when you open the book to that part, she is still hating him for all eternity just the same. It never becomes the past.

Adjectives

Adjectives are words that describe. In particular, they describe nouns and pronouns.

For example, *friendly, fluffy,* and *five-year-old* are all considered adjectives. We might use them to describe something like a dog:

- The friendly dog
- The fluffy dog
- The five-year-old dog

Anytime you are describing a noun or pronoun, you're using an adjective. These words can describe, compare, or tell how much or how old. There are a few special types of adjectives, too.

Possessive Adjectives

A **possessive** adjective is a word used to describe a noun or pronoun that shows ownership. There are seven in all: My, his, her, their, its, your, our.

Examples:

- My birthday
- His backpack
- Its tongue
- Your generosity
- Our anniversary

In each of these instances, the possessive word works as an adjective, or describing word.

Articles

In the English language, there are three **articles**, which are considered a subgroup of adjectives. **Indefinite** articles refer to non-specific nouns. There are two indefinite articles: **a** and **an**.

- A teacup
- An invitation
- A student
- An achievement

There is one **definite** article: **the**. It indicates a specific noun.

- The teacup
- The invitation
- The student
- The achievement

Notice how the change in article makes the nouns more specific, as though you are pointing directly to each one.

Adverbs

Adverbs are also describing words. However, they describe verbs, adjectives, and other adverbs. Often, adverbs are recognizable thanks to the -ly ending, but there are many that don't use that suffix. They often answer the question of **how**, **when**, **where**, **to what extent**, and **why**.

Modifying Verbs

Example: She slowly crept out the door.

In this example, our verb is "crept." The -ly suffix helps us identify "slowly," as our adverb, which expresses how she crept out the door.

Modifying Adjectives

Example: Blake was surprisingly tall.

In this sentence, our adjective, "tall," describes the noun of the sentence. How tall was he? He was "surprisingly" tall. That is our adverb.

Modifying other Adverbs

Example: The dog barked very loudly.

This sentence actually has two adverbs because one describes the other. "Loudly" is an adverb that describes the verb, "barked." Then, "very" expresses to what extent the dog barked loudly.

Prepositions and Prepositional Phrases

Prepositions are words that show relationships between a noun or pronoun and some other word in the sentence. Think of them like little fishing hooks that reach out, catch nouns, and real them into the structure of the sentence.

Others like to think of a tree trunk and a rabbit. If the word can be used to describe how the rabbit can relate to the tree trunk, like being above, below, around, or made of the wood, then it is a preposition.

Example Sentences:

- The water poured **into** the tub.
- Megan walked **through** the maze.
- The book is **on** the shelf.
- Marissa is **with** her friend.
- Travis stood **behind** the tree.

Some of the most common prepositions include:

About • After • Among
Behind • Between • Down
From • Of • Underneath
With • Against • Below
During • In • Off • Since
Until • Within • At
Beside • By • Except
Into • On
Through • Without
Across • Before • For • Like

Conjunctions

A **conjunction** is like sentence glue. We use them to connect words, phrases, and clauses. Conjunctions can be divided into three categories.

Coordinating Conjunctions

There are only seven coordinating conjunctions in the English language. You can use the acronym **FANBOYS** to help you remember them:

F—For **A**—And **N**—Nor **B**—But **O**—Or **Y**—Yet **S**—So

Coordinating conjunctions are used to tie together elements of sentences that have equal importance.

Examples:

- Two words—juice **or** milk
- Two phrases: over the hill **and** far away
- Two clauses: We wanted to take the same class, **but** our schedules didn't coordinate.

Subordinating Conjunctions

A subordinating conjunction is a word used to connect a subordinate clause (one that CAN'T stand alone as its own sentence) to a dependent clause (one that CAN stand alone as its own sentence).

Some commonly used subordinating conjunctions include: *unless, whenever, since, because, although, as,* and *when.*

> Example: **After** the concert was over, we decided to get something to eat.

In this example, we have two clauses: "after the concert was over" and "we decided to get something to eat." Notice that the second clause can stand alone as its own sentence, but the first clause cannot. "After" is our subordinating clause that ties the two together.

- She failed the class **because** she didn't complete her homework.
- **Unless** it rains, the picnic should be a fun trip.
- We'll skip class that day **since** it's a holiday anyway.

Correlative Conjunctions

A **correlative conjunction** is used to indicate pairs in a sentence. And, like the pairs they express, correlative conjunctions also come in pairs. This category includes:

1. Both/and 2. Either/or 3. Not only/but also

Examples:

- **Both** students **and** teachers are invited to the meeting.

- You should bring **either** a laptop **or** a tablet.
- Apples are **not only** nutritious **but also** delicious.

Interjections

It's not often that you'll see interjections in academic or formal types of writing, but they are all over the place in other styles. An interjection is a word that works to convey an emotion or feeling. They can appear almost anywhere in a sentence, and they can even be a complete sentence all on their own.

Examples:

- **Sheesh**, that test was hard.
- **Oh**, I didn't know that!
- You're already busy this weekend, **huh**?
- Holy cow!
- She pulled off the lid, and, **yuck**, the contents were disgusting.
- **Goodness**, I didn't realize how late it was getting!
- Oh, no!
- Ouch!
- **Ugh**, I don't want to do my chores.

Appositives

An **appositive** is an interesting kind of phrase. It's actually a noun or a noun phrase that renames the noun or pronoun of a sentence. This may sound repetitive, but appositives actually help writers provide important information in a way that doesn't require them to write two sentences, which *would* be repetitive.

Examples:

Mason, <u>the next-door neighbor</u>, is coming over for dinner tonight.

"The next-door neighbor" is a noun phrase used to describe Mason, who is the subject of the sentence. It helps clarify who he is.

Ally, <u>the messiest eater at the table</u>, sprayed everyone with bits of macaroni and cheese when she began laughing.

"The messiest eater at the table" is the appositive that describes Ally. It helps the reader understand why it's pretty plausible that she was a not-so-wonderful dinner guest that evening.

Appositives are, perhaps, the simplest of the phrases to identify because they are simply a renaming of the noun, and they are always right next to the noun they describe. Be sure to always use commas to separate an appositive from the rest of the sentence.

If you would like to have practice identifying and using these parts of speech, we offer a companion Writing with Heart Grammar Workbook!

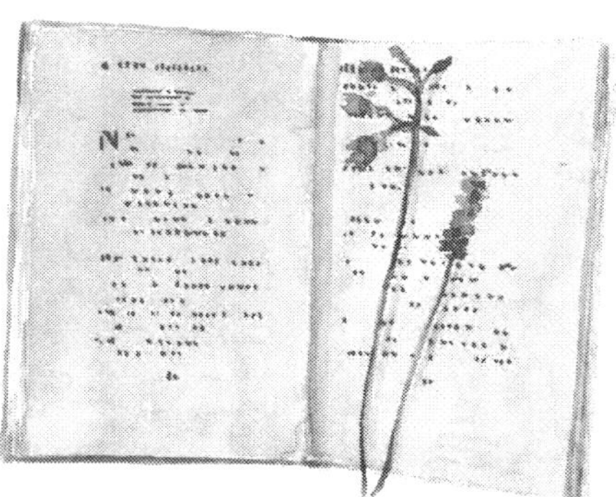

Chapter 32: Sentences

A sentence is a unit of words that includes a subject and a predicate that together make a complete thought. It begins with a capital letter and ends with punctuation—a period, question mark, or exclamation point. Sometimes, we might see a group of words together with a capital letter and end punctuation, but we always need to check if it has a subject, a predicate, and a complete thought. If we are missing one of these pieces, it becomes a fragment. If we have more than one complete phrase without correct connecting words or punctuation, it becomes a run on. We will talk more about these in **Chapter 33**.

Parts of the Sentence

The **subject** of the sentence is the part of the sentence doing something, or who the sentence is about. A **complete subjec**t is the subject and all the words that modify it (any adjectives or additional words). For example, "The tall, freckle-faced girl" would be the complete subject, but "girl" is the **simple subject**.

Sometimes, a complete subject can have two or more simple subjects together—this is called a **compound subject:** "long daisies, pansies, and bellflowers" would be a compound subject.

The **predicate** of the sentence is what is being said about the subject. It always includes a verb. A **simple predicate**, like a simple subject, is just one word—for the predicate, that is the verb. A **complete predicate** is the verb and any additional words or phrases that modify it. For example, "was very excited" is a complete predicate, but "was excited" is the simple predicate (verb).

A **compound predicate** can also happen when there is more than one verb and words modifying them: "was excited but scared."

It is possible to have a compound subject and a compound predicate:

Example: Jackie and Ryan danced and sang together.

It is also possible to have a two-word sentence from a simple subject and a simple predicate: I laughed. He cried.

The **direct object** is a noun or pronoun that receives the action of the verb.

Example: Francis held a book.

An **indirect object** is a noun or pronoun that for whom the object is done.

Example: Francis gave Ben the book.

Note that if the indirect object is in a prepositional phrase, it is no longer an indirect object because you can't separate it out of the phrase.

Clauses and Phrases

When we group words together, they are no longer just words; they become phrases and clauses—key components of sentences. It's important to understand that a phrase and a clause are *not* the same thing, even though both define a group of two or more words.

A **phrase** is a group of words that do *not* have a subject or a verb. They are usually named for the main word in the collection of words—prepositional phrase, verb phrase, adverb phrase, adjective phrase.

Examples:

to the game (prepositional phrase)

protecting her children (verb phrase)

quite quickly (adverb phrase)

In contrast, a **clause** *does* have both a subject and a verb. A clause can sometimes be considered a sentence, if it also has a complete thought. But some clauses don't have a complete thought, so they would not be considered sentences. In fact, the large majority of fragments are clauses that aren't complete sentences because they don't have a complete thought in them.

Independent Clause

An **independent clause** is any group of words that contains both a subject and a verb and that expresses a complete thought. That is, it CAN stand alone as its own complete sentence. A good way to remember this is that it is *independent*; it doesn't need anything else to help it be a complete sentence.

Examples:

I love dancing.

This sentence has a subject (I) and a verb (dancing), and it expresses a complete thought. It can be its own complete sentence.

The crowd applauded for the performer.

This sentence is also an independent clause. "The crowd" is the subject, and the verb is "applauded." This also expresses a complete thought, meaning it's a complete sentence.

To help yourself identify independent clauses, ask yourself three questions:

- Can I identify who/what the clause is about?
- Does the subject perform an action or is there a linking verb?
- Does this express a complete thought?

If you can answer "yes" to all three questions, then you are looking at an independent clause.

Dependent Clause

A **dependent clause** is very similar to an independent clause because it also contains both a subject and a verb. However, it *does not* express a complete thought. When you read it, it's a fragment or an incomplete sentence. To help you remember, you could say that it *depends* on another clause to become a complete sentence.

Examples:

When school is over.

This clause has a subject (school) and a verb (is), but notice that it's not a complete thought (what will happen when school is over??). It's a fragment. That means it's a dependent clause.

Even though there are a number of opportunities we might consider.

Again, there is a subject (there) and a verb (are), but the clause doesn't make a complete thought (it is saying "even though"...even though what?). It's a dependent clause.

When you look for dependent clauses, focus on whether or not there is a subject *and* a verb. If both are present, but you still don't have a complete thought, know that you are looking at a dependent clause.

Relative Clauses

A **relative clause** is also called an "adjective clause" because it's a group of words that describe a noun or pronoun. It is also a kind of dependent clause, meaning it has a subject and a verb, but it doesn't express a complete thought.

You can usually identify relative clauses based on signal words, including relative pronouns and relative adverbs.

Relative pronouns include: Who, whose, whom, which, that.

Relative adverbs, on the other hand, are clauses that answer the questions of **when, where,** and **why**.

Examples:

> That he dripped water from one end of the kitchen to the other.

Notice that this clause starts with a signal word: that. Then, it has a subject (he) and a verb (dripped). It also describes the situation of *where* the water dripped: all over the kitchen. But adding the "That" at the beginning of the clause makes it a relative clause.

> Where they were playing video games.

This clause begins with a relative adverb, "where." Then, the subject is "they," and the verb is "were playing." Notice that it's a description of the place where they'd play. It's definitely a relative clause!

If you're on the hunt for more relative clauses, just be sure to keep an eye out for those relative pronouns and adverbs! They're the best clue that you're looking at a relative clause.

Types of Sentences

Simple Sentences

A **simple sentence** is one that contains a single independent clause.

Examples:

> The dog wandered down the road.
>
> James loves to play basketball.
>
> The class made Valentines for one another.

However, simple sentences don't always have to have just one subject and one predicate. Sometimes, there can be more.

Recall that a sentence can have a compound subject or a compound predicate, or both.

Examples:

> A woman and her dog took a jog through the park.
>
> My mom and I are going shopping.

Midge finished her homework and completed her chores.

The cookies and the pie were burned pretty badly but still tasted okay.

Freshmen and sophomores can take advanced courses or participate in an internship.

Notice that, regardless of the type of simple sentence created, no comma or extra punctuation is required to form the sentence correctly.

Compound Sentences

A **compound sentence** is one that contains two or more independent clauses, and it needs additional punctuation.

There are two ways to properly format a compound sentence. The first is to use a comma and a coordinating conjunction. Recall from **Chapter 31** that our coordinating conjunctions include the FANBOYS: for, and, nor, but, or, yet, so.

The second way to format a compound sentence is to use a semicolon (;) to separate the two clauses. No capital letter is required after the semicolon since it's technically not the start of a new sentence.

Examples: *We went to the movies, and we ate a bunch of popcorn.*

This sentence has two independent clauses:

1. We went to the movies.

2. We ate a bunch of popcorn.

These two independent clauses are separated by a comma and a coordinating conjunction (and).

The movie was supposed to be really scary; it wasn't.

This sentence also has two independent clauses:

1. The movie was supposed to be really scary.

2. It wasn't.

Notice that there are no extra words, like conjunctions, to separate the clauses. The semi-colon is all that is needed.

Complex Sentences

A **complex sentence** is one that includes an independent clause, along with one *or more* dependent clauses. If the dependent clause comes *before* the independent clause, you need a comma. If the dependent clause comes *after* the independent clause, you do NOT need a comma.

Examples:

Before I went for a run, I put on my favorite shoes.

This sentence has one independent clause (I put on my favorite shoes) and one dependent clause (before I went for a run). Because the dependent clause comes first, the sentence needs a comma.

I put on my favorite shoes before I went for a run.

This sentence uses the same clauses but in a different order. The independent clause (I put on my favorite shoes) comes before the dependent clause (before I went for a run), so no comma is needed to complete the sentence correctly.

While I was reading, I heard a noise outside.

I heard a noise outside while I was reading.

These sentences are similar because they have the same independent clause (I heard a noise outside) and the same dependent clause (while I was reading). However, the first sentence has the dependent clause first, so it needs a comma. The second clause has the independent clause first, so it doesn't need that comma.

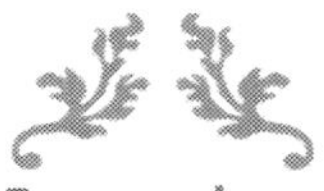

Remember:

Dependent clause first = add a comma

Dependent clause second = no comma needed

Compound-Complex Sentences

Compound-complex sentences have an interesting structure. That is, they include two independent clauses and at least one dependent clause.

Examples:

Although I confirmed the appointment, the office was closed when I arrived, and no one was answering the phone.

This sentence has two independent clauses:

1. The office was closed when I arrived.

2. No one was answering the phone.

Notice that they are combined using a comma and coordinating conjunction (and), which is the correct form for a compound sentence.

This example also has a dependent clause:

1. Although I confirmed the appointment.

This dependent clause came before the independent clauses, so it still needed that comma to separate it.

> I was so excited about the party, but I didn't have anything to wear because I don't normally buy fancy clothes.

The two independent clauses include:

1. I was so excited about the party.
2. I didn't have anything to wear.

They are combined using a comma and coordinating conjunction (but). These two clauses are followed by the dependent clause (because I don't normally buy fancy clothes), so no comma was necessary to separate that final dependent clause from the rest of the sentence.

Compound-complex sentences will always contain at least three clauses, and two of them must be independent, meaning they can be complete sentences on their own. Keep that in mind as you include this sentence structure in your own writing!

Kinds of Sentences

In writing, there are four kinds of sentences. Each type of sentence has its own end punctuation.

Declarative Sentences

A **declarative sentence** is one that makes a statement of some kind. This is the most common type of sentence within the English language. They will always end with a period.

Examples:

> The librarian was wearing an interesting lime green bowler hat today.
>
> Our vacation went well, but I'm glad to be home now.
>
> The dog had buried his bone in the backyard.
>
> Students everywhere are applying for this scholarship.

Interrogative Sentences

An **interrogative sentence** is one that asks a question, meaning we end it with a question mark.

Examples:

Would you like a cookie to go with your juice?

Are there any volunteers available next weekend?

What consequences will likely follow if we continue on this path?

Is there anything more relaxing than a good book and a hot cup of tea?

Imperative Sentences

An **imperative sentenc**e involves telling someone to do something. The subject of these sentences is the implied "you," which means the sentence doesn't actually say "you," but you know that's who the speaker is talking to. Like declarative sentences, these also end with a period.

Examples:

Go check the mail.

Add his name to our list of recipients.

Offer the guests something to drink.

Hand me that book, please.

Exclamatory Sentences

Exclamatory sentences are ones that indicate a strong emotion. This can be positive or negative, like excitement or anger. We use an exclamation point to end these types of sentences.

Examples:

The elephant was huge!

Leave me alone!

I just can't wait to get started!

I am not one bit sorry!

If you would like to have practice identifying and using these parts of speech, we offer a companion Writing with Heart Grammar Workbook!

Chapter 33: Sentence Errors

With all these sentence structures available to us, it's no wonder that there are a variety of ways in which we might go wrong in our own writing. All of the most common sentence errors come from a violation of one of the rules discussed in **Chapter 32**.

As you edit your writing, you want to eliminate these errors in your essays.

Fragments

Fragment errors occur because the writer has left out one of the elements of a complete sentence: either the subject, the predicate, or the complete thought.

What if you completely forget to include a subject or a predicate? These occur when writers try to use a phrase as a stand-alone sentence.

Examples:

The woman from the bank.

All that sugar in those donuts.

Expressed a deep concern for her.

To fix this error, you need to add the missing parts!

Examples corrected:

The woman from the bank <u>is a nice lady.</u> (predicate added)

All that sugar in those donuts <u>is not healthy</u>. (predicate added)

<u>He </u>expressed a deep concern for her. (subject added)

Perhaps there is a subject and a predicate, but the clause doesn't express a complete thought. This happens when writers try to use dependent or relative clauses as a sentence. But remember, these types of clauses can't stand alone because the complete thought is not there!

Examples:

Although we were looking forward to the trip.

Because there are so many opportunities.

While we wandered around the museum.

To fix this, you either need to write the missing part of the sentence, or attach it correctly to the sentence before or after the error. Often, there is an independent clause next to it and changing the period to a comma to connect them will solve the problem.

Examples corrected:

Although we were looking forward to the trip, the cost was too high and we had to cancel.

I really like my new job because there are so many opportunities.

While we wandered around the museum, we saw sculptures and paintings from the Renaissance.

Remember, a dependent clause at the beginning of the sentence needs a comma after it, but a dependent clause at the end of the sentence does not.

Run-Ons and Comma Splices

Another common error is the **run-on sentence**, where there is more than one independent clause included in a sentence, but it doesn't contain the proper parts of speech or punctuation.

Example:

People visit the aquarium every day the most popular attraction is the penguin exhibit.

This sentence has two independent clauses:

1. People visit the aquarium every day.

2. The most popular attraction is the penguin exhibit.

However, these clauses are just thrown together in a single sentence, making it a run-on.

One specific type of run-on sentence is the **comma splice**. This is a common error, because the writer knows that the two independent clauses don't belong jammed together, but instead of having the correct punctuation, they put a comma.

Example:

He baked the cupcakes, I frosted them.

Commas are not a strong enough punctuation to separate two independent clauses. That's like putting a yield sign where a traffic light is needed!

To fix run-ons and comma splices, we can choose one of four options.

1. Add a coordinating conjunction after the comma:
   He baked the cupcakes, but I frosted them.

2. Change the comma into a semicolon:
   He baked the cupcakes; I frosted them.

3. Put a period between the two sentences.
   He baked the cupcakes. I frosted them.

4. Make one of the clauses a dependent clause. If the dependent clause comes first, use a comma!
   After he baked the cupcakes, I frosted them.

   He baked the cupcakes before I frosted them.

Rambling/Wordy Sentences

Rambling sentences are sentences that are too long. Unlike run-on sentences, rambling sentences join together clauses with the appropriate conjunctions and punctuation, but the sentences go on too long.

> *Example:* While I frosted the cupcakes, he took out the garbage, and Chloe practiced piano, but she couldn't play the song very well.

Notice that these clauses are joined together with the appropriate conjunctions and punctuation, but the sentence joins together too many independent clauses. The sentence is difficult to follow.

To fix this error, the easiest solution would be to split the sentence in two: While I frosted the cupcakes, he took out the garbage. Meanwhile, Chloe practiced piano, but she couldn't play the song very well.

Another solution would be to recraft the sentence to emphasize the simultaneous actions of each individual: I frosted the cupcakes, he took out the garbage, and Chloe practiced piano. Unfortunately, she couldn't play the song very well.

Wordy sentences are those that use too many words to deliver their message.

Example:

> I frosted the cupcakes, which were chocolate flavored and also looked delicious and tasty.

Notice that this sentence contains some redundant words (*delicious* and *tasty*), and it also contains some unnecessarily long phrases that could be condensed (*which were chocolate flavored*). Here is one way of streamlining this wordy sentence to make it more concise: *I frosted the delicious-looking chocolate cupcakes.*

Often, wordy sentences are also rambling sentences. Making your language more concise can also help to tighten up your sentence structure.

Unclear Pronoun References

Recall that any time you use a pronoun, there needs to be an antecedent. But sometimes, when you write sentences with more than one noun, it isn't clear which noun is the antecedent. There are three common pronoun problems that crop up in writing. All of them are considered to be **unclear pronoun references**.

Example 1 (multiple antecedent possibilities):

> Michael Jordan and Scottie Pippen enjoyed playing basketball together, but he felt that he was underpaid.

Notice how, in this example, the "he" could refer to either Michael Jordan OR Scottie Pippen.

To resolve this error, you could restructure the sentence: Michael Jordan and Scottie Pippen enjoyed playing basketball together, but Scottie felt that he was underpaid.

Notice that the second "he" is kept, because the antecedent has been clarified by replacing the first pronoun.

Example 2 (indefinite pronoun):

> Scottie Pippen was ranked in the top ten in the NBA by most statistical measures. This was not reflected by his contract with the Bulls.

In this example, notice that the "this" is unclear. What exactly does it reference? There isn't an antecedent, because the idea it is referring to is implied (or indefinite) in the first sentence.

To resolve this error, you need to define the idea that your pronoun is referring to: *This level of achievement was not reflected by his contract with the Bulls.*

Example 3 (pronoun not in agreement):

> The government announced that they will be requiring all individuals to wear masks in public spaces.

In this example, *they* is an incorrect pronoun. The antecedent of *they* is *government*, which is a singular noun. *They* is a plural pronoun.

To fix this error, you could instead say, The government has announced that it will be requiring all individuals to wear masks in public spaces.

Example 4 (pronoun person shift):

> Because new parents are busy and have a lot of responsibilities, you should remember to take time for self-care.

In this example, using *you* is an incorrect pronoun. The antecedent of *you* is *parents*, which is a third person subject. *You* is a second person pronoun.

To fix this error, you could instead say, Because new parents are busy and have a lot of responsibilities, they should remember to take time for self-care.

Subject-Verb Agreement

In the English language, it's important that each sentence has something called **subject/verb agreement**. For example, when we have a singular noun for a subject, meaning it's just one, we must use the proper verb ending for singular nouns.

> Examples: The list ___ (is/are) on the table.

In this sentence, we have just one list. We would say the list IS, not the list ARE, because "is" is a singular verb.

Sometimes there are more than one noun in the complete subject, and one is singular and one is plural. It's important to identify which noun is the simple subject to match the verb with that word.

> A bouquet of flowers ______ (is/are) a lovely gift.

What is the subject of this sentence? It's a bouquet, which means just one. We'd use a singular verb: is. "Flowers" is part of a prepositional phrase, so it can't be the subject.

You also need to be careful with mass nouns that are groups of people counted as one (like team, group, household):

> The crowd ______ (flock, flocks) to the stadium.

Because we only have one crowd in this sentence, we use "flocks" to match the verb and subject.

If we are using a plural noun, meaning we have more than one, we have to use a verb to match, as well.

> Examples: The lists are on the table.

We have more than one list, so the verb that matches would be "are."

> Bouquets of flowers are lovely gifts.

Again, we have more than one bouquet, so we would use "are" to match the subject.

> The crowds flock to the stadium.

If the subject is plural, we have to match the verb! "Flock" matches the "crowds" of this sentence.

Misplaced and Dangling Modifiers

A **modifier** is a group of words that gives more information about another element in the sentence. They can be prepositional phrases, clauses, or even a limiting word (such as *only, almost, hardly, nearly,* or *just*).

Limiting words must always be immediately in front of the word(s) they modify. It is a **misplaced modifier** if it is in front of the wrong word.

> Example: Juanita almost ate the whole pizza.

The word "almost" goes with pizza—she didn't "almost eat" because that would mean she put a slice up to her mouth and didn't bite it! The correct way to write it would be: *Juanita ate almost the whole pizza.*

A misplaced modifier can also be a phrase that describes the wrong element because it is placed incorrectly.

> Example: Tom saw the Empire State Building flying over New York City

Tom was flying, not the Empire State Building! The correct way to write it would be: *Flying over New York City, Tom saw the Empire State Building.*

A **dangling modifier** is called that because it appears to be "dangling" or hanging at the beginning of the sentence with nothing to modify. The word that the writer is attempting to modify is implied, but is not actually in the sentence.

> Example: Writing down the groceries, the pen ran out of ink.

My pen wasn't writing down anything, I was! The correct way to write it would be: Writing down the groceries, I ran out of ink in my pen. OR While I was writing down groceries, my pen ran out of ink.

Parallelism

Parallelism refers to the structure of a sentence. Similar parts of a sentence need to have similar structure. Parallelism is needed in pairs and lists, in comparisons, and with correlating conjunctions.

Any time you present two or more items in a series separated by the words *and* or *or*, the items must be in similar form.

> Example: At the party, we danced, were listening to music, and told stories.

The verb phrases in the list are in different tenses—make sure they are all the same. The correct way to write it would be: At the party, we danced, listened to music, and told stories.

When comparing two things (using words like than or as), both things in the comparison must be parallel. Sometimes you might need to add or drop a word to make the sentence parallel.

> Example: I enjoy movies more than playing soccer.

The first choice is a noun, and the second choice is a verb phrase, so they are not parallel. You would need to change one of them. The correct way to write it would be: *I enjoy movies more than soccer.* OR *I enjoy watching movies more than playing soccer.*

Correlating conjunctions are a set of conjunctions that link two equal elements and show a relationship between them (such as *neither...nor, both...and, rather...than*) The items on either side need to be parallel.

> Example: Being in marching band is both fun and it will be a good learning experience.

In this case, there are two phrases but the second one has an added "it will be." The correct way to write it would be: *Being in marching band is both fun and a good learning experience.*

If you would like to have practice identifying and using these parts of speech, we offer a companion Writing with Heart Grammar Workbook!

Chapter 34: Comma Punctuation

Commas are perhaps one of the most difficult elements of punctuation to master for the simple fact that there are just so many rules. However, once you get a good handle on how commas work and where they belong within writing, you'll feel more comfortable adding those little pauses throughout your work.

Lists

Whenever you have a list of three or more items in a sentence, you should separate them with commas. Some believe that the final comma between the last two items in the list isn't necessary. This is known as the **oxford comma**. However, leaving that comma out may actually decrease your writing's clarity, so you should aim to include it in your lists.

Examples:

She'd been reading books, magazines, and poetry all weekend long.

I enjoy playing basketball, football, and soccer.

My mom reminded me to clean my room, finish my homework, and brush my teeth before heading to bed.

Compound Sentences

We've already talked about compound sentences in **Chapter 32**. Recall that it contains two independent clauses put together. They must have punctuation between them. One option is to connect them with a coordinating conjunction (for, and, nor, but, or, yet so). If you do this, you also need a comma to help separate the clauses correctly.

Examples:

We went to the movies, and we bought a huge bucket of popcorn.

I turned in my assignment almost a week late, but my teacher still gave me full credit.

She wanted to buy a new computer, so she went to the store that afternoon.

Note: You can NEVER connect two independent clauses with only a comma. This is a sentence error called a comma splice (**see Chapter 33**). You must include both the comma and the coordinating conjunction for it to be punctuated correctly.

Dependent Clauses

Recall from **Chapter 32**, a dependent clause is a group of words that contains a subject and a predicate, but it doesn't not express a complete thought. When you begin a sentence with a dependent clause, you must follow it with a comma to separate it from the independent clause of the sentence.

Examples:

<u>Before you leave for work</u>, would you mind taking out the trash?

<u>Although she was excited about her trip</u>, she wasn't looking forward to packing.

<u>Unlike the presidents before her</u>, she truly cared about the citizens of the country.

Notice that the underlined portion of each sentence contains a subject and a predicate, but when you read it on its own, it doesn't make a complete sentence. That's why those are considered dependent clauses.

Interjections

An interjection is a word that works to convey an emotion or feeling. They can appear almost anywhere in a sentence, and they can even be a complete sentence all on their own. Anytime you use an interjection within a sentence, you should always surround it with commas.

Examples:

Man, it's hot outside!

Hey, don't forget your coat.

Green is your favorite color, right?

The dog rolled in something, and, whoa, she stinks.

Yikes, that car almost hit us.

Melissa, you're next in line for karaoke.

Note: a person's name can be an interjection, and always needs to follow the rules here.

Appositives

An appositive is a renaming phrase and can be inserted into a sentence for emphasis.

Similar to interjections, these phrases should always be surrounded by commas.

Examples:

Michael, my husband, is working outside all day today.

I went to the picnic and took baked beans, the ones my mom always makes.

Sometimes, instead of renaming the noun, you'll include a negative that gives the opposite of something that you're explaining. It's important to treat these similar to appositives and surround them by commas.

Examples:

She opened the blue bag, not the red one, earlier today.

He agreed to a week, not a month, of extra chores.

There were 20 geese, not swans, floating in the pond.

Transition Phrases

When you begin a sentence with a transition word or phrase, you should always follow it with a comma.

Examples:

In conclusion, reading a book will always be superior to watching a movie.

However, I wasn't sure if I wanted to follow through with the plan.

First, you should preheat the oven to 350 degrees.

Elements of an Address

When you use a location's address within a sentence, it actually needs quite a few commas. First, you need the commas you would use normally when addressing an envelope, like the one that falls between the city and the state.

Then, you also need one where you would normally put a line break on an envelope.

Example:

Let's work with the following address through this example:

158 State Street

Wilmington, South Carolina 28326

To add this to a sentence, we would write the following:

Please send the package to 158 State Street, Wilmington, South Carolina 28326.

Or, if more information follows, we add another comma after the address:

The package was sent to 158 State Street, Wilmington, South Carolina 28326, but wasn't received.

Dates

A date within a sentence will always require the following a comma between the day and year, as well as after the year if there is more information after it in a sentence.

Examples:

Her birthday falls on July 8th, 1990.

July 4, 1776, is the day our country signed its Declaration of Independence.

Even if it doesn't feel natural, you should always follow a year with a comma.

Exception: if you only list the month and the year, you do not need any commas at all.

Examples:

I am expecting my baby in July 2019 and we know it's another girl!

If you would like to have practice identifying and using these parts of speech, we offer a companion Writing with Heart Grammar Workbook!

Chapter 35: Other Punctuation

In addition to end punctuation, sentences often need punctuation within them so that the clauses and modifiers all make sense. Most internal punctuation functions as a "pause" in your reading (as opposed to end punctuation, which is a "stop" marker). Other times, it is used as a divider—you can more easily see the separate but connected ideas within a sentence.

If you look at that previous paragraph, I used several internal pauses and dividers: commas, parentheses, quotation marks, a dash, and even a colon in this sentence! Knowing options for pauses and dividers will help you create more complicated sentences that allow you to have variety within your paper.

Capitalization

Capitalization is an important part of correctly following the conventions of writing. There are a few clear-cut rules of capitalization:

- Capitalize the first letter of a new sentence.
- Capitalize names and proper nouns.
- Capitalize days (ex: Wednesday), months (ex: June), and holidays (ex: Christmas).
- Do not capitalize seasons (ex: winter, spring).
- Capitalize individual's titles (ex: the President, the Governor).
- Capitalize family titles of a specific person (Ex: Mom, Grandpa).
- Do not capitalize familial references (Ex: my mom, my grandpa).
- Capitalize geographic regions of the country or world (Ex: the Middle East, the South).
- Do not capitalize geographic directions (Ex: north, south).

Titles

When recording the title of a work, you should capitalize almost every word. Read the five rules below for specifics on when to capitalize and not capitalize.

1. The first word of a title is always capitalized.
2. Never capitalize articles (a, an, the), conjunctions (and, but, or) or prepositions (with, because, for, etc.) unless it is the first word.
3. All other words are always capitalized.

Different kinds of works need to be punctuated differently. Long works (books, plays, films, TV shows) should be italicized. Short works (short stories, songs, poems, articles) should be put into quotation marks.

Examples:

Little Women (novel)

Romeo and Juliet (play)

Frozen (movie)

"And Still I Rise" (poem)

"The Tell-Tale Heart" (short story)

"Here Comes the Sun" (song)

Note: Long works are sometimes underlined instead of italicized. This is considered acceptable. Before computers, underlining was used in handwritten and typeset pieces because that was all that was available. If you are handwriting a long works title, you should underline it, but use italics when it is available on computers.

Hyphens and Dashes

The **hyphen** is a little line that connects words that are related. This appears on typical QWERTY keyboards between the 0 and the "+/=" buttons on the top row and is the shortest line. We use a hyphen to connect compound adjectives before a noun. Remember that adjectives are describing words. When two or more words connect to create a single adjective, we call them a compound adjective and use hyphens to connect the words.

Examples:

She wore a yellow-colored dress that day.

The 5-year-old boy loved going to the park.

The hotel was very dog-friendly, which made our trip easier.

An **en dash** is the same size as a hyphen and uses the same key on the keyboard, but it has a very different purpose. We use en dashes to connect numbers to show ranges.

Examples:

The Great Depression lasted from 1929–1939.

The movie lasted from 3:00–4:30 pm.

We plan to take a break for 10–15 minute before we start the next chapter.

An **em dash** is one of the most versatile pieces of punctuation we might use in our writing. This is a dash double the size of a hyphen, and you create it by typing the hyphen button twice (a lot of word processors then automatically connect them to make a longer line).

Unlike hyphens and en dashes which connect words and numbers, an em dash is a form of a long pause in writing. It can take the place of a comma, a colon, or even parentheses. However, use them carefully. They indicate slightly longer pauses in your writing that are stronger than a comma, but weaker than the full stop of a period.

We use em dashes to add information to a complete sentence that helps clarify or adds an aside.

Examples:

The teacher marked every error—all 187 of them—in his essay.

Can you bring me that book—the one with the red cover—from the shelf?

After the jury debated for more than 3 weeks, they came to a verdict—guilty.

She felt frustrated by her boss's instructions—or lack of instructions—for this week's project.

When using an em dash, you do not need spaces between the words and the punctuation. They all touch.

Parentheses and Brackets

Parentheses are a kind of punctuation used to offer asides or to clarify information in your writing. To refer to just one, you would say a parenthesis, but two are parentheses ( ). These are *not* interchangeable with brackets, which are squared, like this: [ ].

Examples:

He gave her the money ($100) that he owed her.

She wanted to offer some advice (which really was good advice), but she held her tongue.

The teacher brought Mr. Sniffles (his dog) into class today.

She could weave baskets with her toes (amazing, right?).

Notice that, even if the parentheses end a sentence, the period still goes on the outside of the second parenthesis. Even more, there are no spaces between the parentheses and the words that start and end the information within.

Brackets are the squared marks next to the p key on your keyboard. These are only used in specialized situations, and are not the same as parentheses. You only use brackets when you are quoting someone else in an academic paper and need to clarify something within the quote. Usually this is to give the antecedent to a pronoun or to explain what an abbreviation means. It indicates to the reader that the words within the brackets were not in the original quote, but that you added them in for clarity.

Examples:

"He [James K. Polk] was the only President who kept all his campaign promises."

"John McCain was a POW [prisoner of war] for five and a half years."

Colons

A **colon** is a symbol made up of two dots, one stacked on top of the other. This is NOT interchangeable with a semicolon because it has a very different job. A colon appears in a sentence as sort of a "here's what I mean" or "here comes some information" kind of symbol.

Examples:

The farm sold three kinds of fruit: apples, oranges, and strawberries.

There was only one explanation for the missing jewels: a thief.

I finally saw what was behind the curtain: nothing.

Please send in the following items: canned goods, boxed dinners, and non-perishable snacks.

Note: If you use "including" to introduce information, you do not need a colon.

Semicolons

The **Semicolon** is an interesting symbol. They consist of a comma with a dot directly above it. In general, there are two ways to use semicolon. The first is to separate two related sentences. The sentences must be complete thoughts, meaning they are independent clauses, and there should be no coordinating conjunction (for, and, nor, but, or, yet, so) between them.

Examples:

Incorrect: We baked so many cookies this afternoon; and it took forever to frost them.

Correct: We baked so many cookies this afternoon; it took forever to frost them.

The incorrect sentence uses a coordinating conjunction (and) to separate the clauses, so a semicolon is the wrong punctuation for that sentence—when you use a coordinating conjunction, you need a comma not a semicolon. The correct semicolon version does not have a conjunction.

The clauses on both sides of the semicolon need to be complete sentences in order to be correct.

Incorrect: After visiting the zoo that afternoon; we went into town for lunch.

Correct: We visited the zoo this afternoon; we went into town for lunch.

The incorrect sentence has an issue because the first clause is a dependent clause. The revision includes a complete sentence on either side of the semicolon to make it correct.

Another use for a semicolon is to separate elements of a list. However, we only use a semicolon in a list where one or more of the list elements contain commas already.

Examples:

We visited Paris, France; Venice, Italy; and Berlin, Germany.

After school, I need to feed and water my cows; sweep, mop, and wipe the counters in the kitchen; and finish up my homework.

Ellipses

An **ellipsis** is probably something you use all the time, but you just don't know the proper term for it. Ellipses are those "dot dot dot" trails used to show that your train of thought is not quite finished, like you're trailing off.

Examples:

I wasn't quite sure...so I asked my mom what she thought.

Could you...

I was just looking for something...I still can't find it!

What do you think will happen if...?

If the sentence is an interrogative, meaning it asks a question, you should include a question mark after the final dot in the ellipsis.

Ellipses are also used to show that words in a quote or citation have been omitted or taken out.

Example:

If a quote says, "There were a number of sources, all of whom wish to remain anonymous, that all gave the same story," a writer might want to use this in their own writing, but they might not want the entire sentence.

They would revise to: "There were a number of sources... that all gave the same story."

When using an ellipsis, remember that you only use THREE dots, no more and no less. Also, there should be a single space after the final dot and before the next word to be considered punctuated correctly.

Apostrophes

An **apostrophe** can be used in two ways: to show ownership and to indicate a contraction. When we show ownership, there are three rules that go along with apostrophes.

1. If the noun is singular, we show ownership with an apostrophe and an 's'.
2. If the noun is plural and ends with an 's', the apostrophe goes *after* the 's'.
3. If the noun is plural and *doesn't* end with an 's', we add an apostrophe and an 's'.

Examples:

1. Bob's dog was such a cutie!
2. The journalists' editor was very proud of the team he had assembled.
3. The women's group encouraged newcomers to join.

Apostrophes are also used to indicate a contraction, which are two words that have been combined into a single word.

See below for a chart containing some common contractions.

Original	Contraction
would not	wouldn't
have not	haven't
will not	won't
they are	they're
it is	it's
he would	he'd
do not	don't
you are	you're
she is	she's

If you would like to have practice identifying and using these parts of speech, we offer a companion Writing with Heart Grammar Workbook!

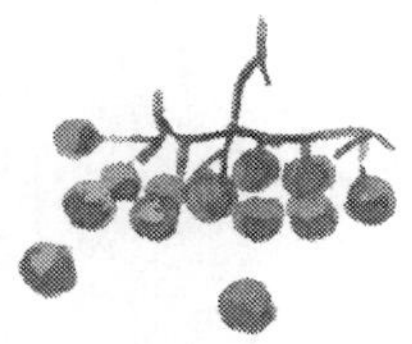

Section 10: Additional Resources

Links

Write from the Heart—We offer online classes for middle and high school students. Included are full credit classes that apply all of the techniques that are discussed in this book, as well as 4-week skill workshops focusing on things like grammar, poetry, creative writing, and essay tests. www.writefromtheheart.org

Purdue OWL— The online writing lab at Purdue University has created an online resource that can answer almost any grammar question you can possibly think of. It also has a section for help with research and citations as well as general writing questions. owl.purdue.edu/owl/

Dictionary.com—Define any word and learn new ones. It also offers word games, crossword puzzles, and help with slang and emojis. www.dictionary.com

Rhyming Dictionary—Helps you find any kind of rhyme you would like: internal, external, and even last-syllable rhymes. www.rhymer.com

Word Hippo—A great online thesaurus. www.wordhippo.com

Thesaurus.com—Another excellent thesaurus. www.thesaurus.com

Goodreads— This is the ultimate social media platform for book nerds. It allows members to keep track of books they've read, books they want to read, books they're reading, etc., as well as leave reviews and interact with their fellow readers. www.goodreads.com

Citation Help

Want help creating a perfect works cited page? These resources can help:

Citation Machine

EasyBib

Cite This for Me

Made in the USA
Columbia, SC
16 September 2020